Joseph Spence

A CRITICAL BIOGRAPHY

Joseph Spence

A CRITICAL BIOGRAPHY

By

AUSTIN WRIGHT

THE UNIVERSITY OF CHICAGO PRESS

CHICAGO · ILLINOIS

THE UNIVERSITY OF CHICAGO PRESS, CHICAGO 37
Cambridge University Press, London, N.W. 1, England
W. J. Gage & Co., Limited, Toronto 2B, Canada

Copyright 1950 by The University of Chicago. All rights reserved
Published 1950. Composed and printed by THE UNIVERSITY OF
CHICAGO PRESS, *Chicago, Illinois, U.S.A.*

TO MY MOTHER
and the
MEMORY OF MY FATHER

Preface

THE studies leading to the preparation of this volume have occupied me intermittently for an embarrassingly large number of years. The decision to investigate the life and works of Joseph Spence grew out of conversations with my colleague Professor Lester M. Beattie, and the resulting doctoral dissertation at Harvard University was written under the guidance of the late Professor Chester Noyes Greenough. Meanwhile, materials for the study of Spence were immeasurably increased when a rich hoard of his papers among the Clumber manuscripts in the library of the Dukes of Newcastle was deposited in the British Museum for the use of scholars. I am grateful to His Grace the Duke of Newcastle for the opportunity to study this material during the summer of 1936 and for permission to have some of it photographed. The Spence papers among the Clumber manuscripts were sold at auction at Sotheby's in 1938, when they became the property of Mr. James Marshall Osborn, of Yale University. Along with a few additional manuscripts acquired separately, they are now known as the "Spence Papers" and are referred to as such throughout this book. I wish to express particular gratitude to Mr. Osborn for generously granting me access to them and permission to quote extensively from them.

Other persons who have assisted me in various ways are so numerous that they cannot all be listed here. I must, however, acknowledge special indebtedness to Professor George Sherburn, who has given richly of his time and knowledge to eliminate difficulties from my path; to Mr. T. Doran Cox, of London, who was of significant assistance during my sojourn in England in 1936 and has been an interested and helpful follower of my studies ever since; to Mr. L. R. Stevens, formerly of Byfleet, Surrey, and now of London, who was one of the first to encourage my investigations and has provided valuable information; and to Major P. C. D. Mundy, of Ickleton, Cambridgeshire, through whose kind offices I obtained possession of letters from Spence and from Edward Rolle that have contributed importantly to this volume. Many other persons who were of assistance in specific matters receive acknowledgment in notes. To all these and to unnamed friends who helped in other ways I express sincere appreciation.

For countless courtesies I thank the officers and personnel of the Harvard University Library, the British Museum, the Bodleian Library, the library of New College, Oxford, the Public Records Office, the Yale University Library, the Columbia University Library, the Folger Shakespeare Library, the New York Public Library, the Carnegie Library of Pittsburgh, and the libraries of Carnegie Institute of Technology and the University of Pittsburgh. I thank the British Museum, the Huntington Library, and the University of Chicago Library for permission to photograph and quote from manuscripts in their possession, and the Historical Society of Pennsylvania for permission to quote from a letter in the Gratz Collection.

Professor Sherburn and Mr. Osborn were so good as to read the work in manuscript and to make valuable suggestions concerning it. But I am, of course, solely responsible for all judgments expressed and for any errors that may remain.

It is impossible to express adequately my gratitude to Mr. Leon Falk, Jr., whose generous grant to Carnegie Institute of Technology made possible the publication of this book.

My wife, who has known Joseph Spence almost as long as she has known me, has been a patient listener and a faithful helper.

AUSTIN WRIGHT

CARNEGIE INSTITUTE OF TECHNOLOGY

Contents

CHAPTER I

Family and Early Life

THOUGH Joseph Spence was regarded in his own time as a man of letters of some stature, the position which he occupies today in the history of English literature is not a lofty one. Nevertheless, that position, though humble, is honorable and secure. Students of the literature of the seventeenth and eighteenth centuries owe to Spence no small debt of gratitude; for had he never lived, our knowledge of the literary history of those centuries would be considerably less than it is. Scholar, traveler, divine, philanthropist, intimate friend of authors and aristocrats, he lived a full and varied life which brought him into association with many of the leading figures of his time, and he is in some respects peculiarly representative of the spirit of the age. It is true that the books on which his literary reputation rested among his contemporaries have sunk into oblivion, though some of them—notably the critical *Essay on Pope's Odyssey*, the little treatise on aesthetics entitled *Crito*, and the learned *Polymetis*—deserve respectful attention as ranking among the best works of their sort to appear in the eighteenth century. But the significance of the posthumously printed *Anecdotes* is universally recognized, and the man who produced them has earned, like Enobarbus, "a place i' th' story."

Spence met Alexander Pope in 1728, and though he had already begun the habit of jotting down remarks of friends and acquaintances concerning literary and other topics, it was his association with the poet that prompted him to

I

undertake that keeping of extensive records of the conversation of Pope and his eminent friends which led to the compilation of the *Anecdotes*. Spence lived for sixteen years on terms of intimacy with Pope and should have written his biography. He almost certainly planned to do so but was thwarted in his design by William Warburton's preemption of the field—and perhaps partly by his own diffidence. Nevertheless, Warburton and the hack who wrote the more or less official biography, Owen Ruffhead, drew heavily from Spence's records, and these were also available to Joseph Warton, who incorporated considerable material from them into his *Essay on the Genius and Writings of Pope* and in his edition of the poet, and to Samuel Johnson when he was engaged in writing the *Lives of the English Poets*. Upon the eventual publication of the *Anecdotes* in 1820, more than half a century after the death of Spence, they became at once a significant part of the materials of English literary history, and subsequent dependence upon them by countless writers has established Spence's claim to permanent recognition.

Joseph Spence, the anecdotist, was the son of another Joseph Spence, a clergyman almost certainly to be identified with the man of his name who received the degree of Bachelor of Arts from Cambridge in 1681/2 and that of Master of Arts in 1685.[1] The elder Spence is several times described as "A.M.," and the Cambridge Spence is the only man of that name to receive a degree from either university until the graduation of the anecdotist himself.

The elder Spence, son of a still earlier Joseph,[2] was born at Cambridge, probably in 1661,[3] attended St. Paul's School in London under Dr. Thomas Gale, and was admitted to St. John's College as a sizar on July 14, 1677. On April 8, 1685, the year in which he was made a Master of Arts, he was admitted to a fellowship at St. John's,[4] and on September 15, 1687, was installed as rector of Winnall, near Winchester.[5] Five days later he took the oaths of supremacy and of obedience to the statutes of the cathedral church of Winchester and was admitted to the office of minor canon.[6] In 1693 he was appointed precentor, appearing as such on the records for the first time on November 25.[7] By March 27, 1694, he had resigned his fellowship at St. John's, for on that date his place was filled by another.[8] On June 23, 1701, he was appointed curate of Crewkerne (or Crookhorne) in Somerset by the Dean and Chapter of Winchester Cathedral, the rectors thereof, at a stipend of £80 a year,[9] and on August 3, 1703, he resigned his living at Winnall in favor of the rectorship at Alverstoke, near Gosport, Hampshire.[10] Meanwhile, at least from 1699, he apparently maintained a residence at Kingsclere in the same county.

The elder Spence continued his duties at the cathedral until 1712, when on June 28 he wrote from Kingsclere to Vaughan Richardson, organist and master of the choristers at Winchester, "My sickness rendring me uncapable of performing my Duty in the Choir; I am willing to resign the place I have there, if the Dean & Chapter will give me leave to keep Crewkern during life."[11] This request was granted, and Spence accordingly yielded his post as precentor and also the office of minor canon. On March 15, 1714/5, he vacated the living at Alverstoke,[12] and a successor was appointed to Crewkerne on June 23, 1715.[13] These facts would seem to establish his death early in 1715, but the matter is clouded by the additional fact that his will, written October 19, 1698, when he was still rector of Winnall,[14] was not proved until October 7, 1721.[15]

Whereas Joseph Spence the younger was descended on his father's side, it seems reasonably certain,[16] from humble ancestry, he could lay claim on the maternal side to more distinguished antecedents. Mrs. Spence had been Mirabella Collier, or Collyer, daughter of "Thomas Collyer, Brewer, of Shoe-Lane, London," and Maria Lunsford, who were married at Lawrence Waltham, Berkshire, on November 30, 1665.[17] Maria was the youngest daughter of the notorious Sir Thomas Lunsford,[18] who had a spectacular career during the Civil Wars. She was born in the Tower of London in 1647 while her father was lieutenant there.[19] Lunsford fled to Virginia in 1649, taking with him his three young and motherless daughters. His second wife and the mother of his children had been Katherine Neville, who had died at Deal on the eve of the voyage to America. She was the daughter of Sir Henry Neville or Nevill of Billingbear, Berkshire, and of Elizabeth, daughter of Sir John Smith and later the wife of Sir John Thorowgood.[20] After Lunsford's death in Virginia his young daughters were sent back to England, and by an order of the Middlesex Quarter Sessions dated January 11, 1653/4, Sir John Thorowgood was required to support them.[21] Through the Nevilles, Spence was descended from Queen Elizabeth's ambassador to France and was related to Colonel Henry Neville, the political lampooner of the seventeenth century.[22]

Mrs. Spence, who was apparently born in 1670,[23] long survived her husband and was the object of tender devotion from her son, a devotion which reminded observers of Pope's love for his mother.[24] Even during Spence's most active years the two were often together, and she spent the latter part of her life as a member of his household. When abroad, he wrote her frequent letters which show mother and son in a close and loving relationship. On one occasion he writes: "But I shall have, I hope, a much greater Tye to England than any I have mention'd: I mean, your Ladyship. When we are once fixt in a way of living together, I shall look upon it as my Duty, as well as my Inclination, to stay with you in old England; & shall not think of stirring a step out of our Island, unless you shou'd turn Traveller. . . ."[25] And again: "As much as I long to see Rome, I long more to be with you; & to be settling our little affairs, in order to live together in a comfortable ma[nner] the rest of our time, that we have to be in this wicked world."[26] A friend writing in 1764 said of Spence: ". . . with a fond generous Affection, he made the Life of his dear honored Mother smile in Age, and happy in Affliction; when the chief Glories of his youthful Soul, were to please her that gave him Birth; when, like the Stork, he made the Nest of Comfort for his Parent, and bore her into Light and Life on his industrious Wings; then, pleased alone with all Mankind, when they were pleased with her. . . ."[27]

Prior to her son's settlement in London about 1742, Mrs. Spence seems to have lived chiefly at a Mr. Morecroft's in Colebrook Street, Winchester, though she also passed some time with Spence at his living at Birchanger in Essex and with her son Richard in London. From 1742 until her death she probably lived with Joseph, first in London and later at Byfleet in Surrey. She was still living on December 19, 1755,[28] but she may have died later in that month, for on January 1, 1756, Spence made some notes which seem to refer to the settlement of her estate.[28a]

Spence was not an only child. The baptism of his brother John was recorded at Kingsclere on March 24, 1699/1700, and that of his brother Richard on March 16, 1700/1701.[29] Nothing more is known of John except that he was still living in 1731,[29a] but Spence occasionally wrote to "Dick" at the African House in Leadenhall Street, London, where he was living as late as 1757. There was also a sister, of whom almost nothing is known.[30] Spence mentioned no near relations in his will, and it is almost certain that if he ever had nephews or nieces, he survived them. The daughter of his father's sister, a Mrs. Mary Lawman of Cambridge, seems to have been his nearest relation at the time of his death.[31]

Joseph Spence was baptized at Kingsclere on May 28, 1699. According to his own statement,[32] he was born on the preceding April 28, which is the date given also in an account of his life probably prepared by his close friend and executor, Edward Rolle.[33] The writer adds that Spence "came into the world several weeks before the usual time, & was kept alive by art & contrivance during that imperfect state, & until what might be termed his second Birth." In later life Spence was thin and slight in stature, and never enjoyed robust health. He spoke of his own "spindleshanks,"[34] a friend observed that he was thin and "trama figurae,"[35] and Horace Walpole was to refer to him as "little Spence."[36] Rolle wrote to Massingberd on October 30, 1741, that on Spence's impending return from abroad his Oxford friends were "like to have but little of him, all of whom is yet so very little, here." In reply to the queries of various correspondents Spence referred frequently in his letters to attacks of illness, and his notebooks are full of suggested remedies for different ailments. For the most part he led the careful life of a valetudinarian, and Rolle says that he early set fifty years as the ultimate limit which a man of his physical disadvantages could hope to reach.[37]

After passing his early childhood at Kingsclere, Spence was sent in 1709 to a school at near-by Mortimer in Berkshire. His early education was supervised and financed by a Mrs. Fawkener of Kingsclere, of whom Rolle writes: "Mrs. Fawkener was his relation, & what was a nearer connection still, his great Friend & Benefactress; since it was by her means, that he w^d have succeeded to an estate of 600£ p^r an. but for some delay or neglect of the person who was concerned to execut [sic] this. This however he used afterwards to look upon as an escape, since he was wont to say, it would at that age have certainly made him Idle & good for little." Spence says that he lived chiefly at Mortimer until 1714, and thereafter at Winchester;[38] but Rolle asserts that after the Mortimer period he was at Eton for a short time, leaving that school "upon some little school-boys disgust."[39] Since there are no lists of Eton students extant for the years 1708–17,[40] Spence's attendance cannot be established or disproved, but there is no reason to doubt Rolle's statement. At any rate, he removed to Winchester in 1714.

At Winchester application was made for Spence's admission to the College, and the College records are almost the sole source of information concerning his next few years. In the election indenture of 1715 he was given a place on the "Roll ad Winton" which entitled him to be the fifteenth boy to be admitted as Scholar of the College if enough vacancies occurred before the election of 1716.[41] At this time occurred the first of a series of apparent errors in the reckoning of Spence's age in the Winchester records. He is described on the roll as "annorum 15 vicesimo nono die Maii ultimo preterito"—that is, the Electors deemed ᵗhim to be fifteen years old on May 29, 1715, whereas on that date he was really sixteen. On September 22, 1716, just a few days before the election of that year, he was admitted as a scholar, but in the Register of Scholars an even greater blunder was made concerning his age: in the entry of his admission he is described as "annorum 14 vicesimo nono die Maii 1716." Such confusion continues throughout the records, and nowhere is his age given correctly.

At Winchester Spence made the acquaintance of three of his most intimate friends of later years—Christopher Pitt, Edward Rolle, and Gloster Ridley. His name appears on the list of members of "Quinta Classis" for 1716 and of "Sexta Classis" for 1717. In the latter year he apparently contemplated leaving Winchester for Oxford, for he matriculated at Magdalen Hall on April 17, 1717, his age being entered on the Matriculation Register as sixteen.[42] For some reason he abandoned the plan and remained at Winchester. There in the election held on or about August 31 he obtained fifteenth place on the "Roll ad Oxon," which entitled him to a scholarship at New College if so many as fifteen vacancies occurred there during the following year.[43] That not being the case, he remained at Winchester and the next year was again placed upon the "Roll ad Oxon," this time twelfth on the list.[44] Once again insufficient vacancies occurred, and he remained at Winchester to be listed as head of the school on the records for 1719. At the election of that year[45] he obtained the fifth place on the "Roll ad Oxon." This time the requisite vacancy occurred, and Spence was admitted as Scholar (or Probationary Fellow) of New College on April 30, 1720.[46]

Oxford was to be Spence's chief place of residence for twenty years. On April 30, 1722, he was advanced to a fellowship at New College.[47] On March 9, 1723/4, he was awarded the degree of A.B.[48] His declamations were delivered on March 21 and 23, the subjects being respectively "Scipio a fano Dianae pecunias tolli, ut iis in tuendam Patriae suae libertatem uteretur, recte jussit," and "Athenis affectus movere per Praeconem non recte prohibebatur orator."[49]

7

Singer states,[50] without citing his authority, that in 1724 Spence published "a Defence of Mr. Woolaston's Notion of a Rule of Our Actions." This was probably the little book published anonymously not in 1724 but in June, 1725, by Joel Stephens in Fleet Street and entitled *A Defence of Mr. Wollaston's Notion of Moral Good and Evil; In Answer to a Letter, in which It is said to be Considered and Refuted*.[51] One cannot be certain that this work is by Spence, but the assumption has some justification. It can be shown from different sources that Spence was interested in Wollaston's ideas and was in sympathy with them. For instance, in some notes on conversation set down in 1726 he reported a speaker to the effect that Wollaston was "far from a Deist: had he liv^d he w^d probably have wrote on his third question,"[52] and in 1727 Spence wrote that Wollaston, "a late excellent Philosopher," had endeavored to prove "that no Action which disagrees with the truth can be good."[53] And if one accepts Singer's statement that Spence did publish a "Defence" of Wollaston, there is reason for attributing the 1725 "Defence" to him.

The little work is not notable in any way and does not demand study here. Apparently Spence—if he was the author—had little desire to continue the controversy; for, in concluding, he says: "I have but one thing more to observe, which is this: What I here answer, is the Letter, in which Mr. Wollaston's Notion is said to be refuted. As to what has been advanc'd against any thing there said, I shall think myself obliged to defend it, or to retract it as an Error, which I shall very readily do when it is prov'd to be such; but if anything new and distinct from what is laid down in the Letter, shou'd be started, as I have not Leisure nor Inclination to run on in a growing Dispute, neither shall I think myself at all concern'd in it."

On June 5, 1726, Spence was ordained into the priesthood by John Potter, Bishop of Oxford,[54] and now the young Bachelor of Arts and Fellow of New College looked about for the preferment for which his training had been intended to qualify him.[55]

8

CHAPTER II

Friend of Pope and Professor of Poetry

EARLY in June, 1726—or possibly late in May—there appeared simultaneously at Oxford and London a small anonymous work entitled *An Essay on Pope's Odyssey: in which Some particular Beauties and Blemishes of that Work are consider'd.*[1] The time was opportune for a criticism of Pope's translation. The *Odyssey*, of which only the first three volumes had yet been published (April, 1725), had not met with the admiration which had been the meed of the *Iliad* a decade earlier. The translation was felt to be well below the level of the earlier work, and readers complained of the mean appearance of the edition and the badness of the paper.[2] Pope was harassed by a financial controversy with Lintot. Furthermore, purchasers expressed resentment that collaborators had been employed,[3] and Pope was engaged in the intrigues which resulted in his laying claim to a larger share in the translation than had actually been his. The poet was bound to be interested in a criticism of the unhappy translation, and he must have opened the new work with trepidation.

What he found surprised and delighted him. "There is a book lately published at Oxford," he wrote to Broome on June 4, "called an Essay on Pope's Odyssey, which you will have reason to be pleased with."[4] This was welcome news to Broome, who promptly commissioned Fenton to forward him a copy of the book. Fenton expressed to Broome his satisfaction at the anonymous criticism in a letter of June 10: "I have sent the Essay you wrote for, but

9

have not read it over; but, upon a transient view, it appears to be writ with so much candour that I fancy the world will say we have employed a friend to fight booty against us, or perhaps that it is one of our own productions. If, after so strict and deliberate an examination of the work, they can find no more nor greater faults than they have yet discovered, they will criticize me into a much better opinion of the translation than I should otherwise have entertained."[5]

According to both Johnson[6] and Joseph Warton,[7] Pope was so much pleased with the *Essay* that on discovering Spence to be the author he sought his acquaintance and thus began their friendship. This statement is partially confirmed and interestingly expanded by the account which Spence himself gave of his meeting with Pope. When Warburton was collecting materials for his edition and contemplated biography of the poet, Spence delivered to him extracts from the *Anecdotes* and appended the following comment: "I dont know whether it may be worth while to mention that Mr Pope's friendship for me, (wch was continu'd, without any the least interruption, for 18 years,) began on my writing a Criticism, against him. T'was not perhaps so very ill-natur'd as Criticisms had generally usd to be; but still twas blunt, & rough enough, in many places.—This was publish'd, in two parts; the First, in 1726; & the Second, in 1727.—After the publishing the First, Mr Layng of Baliol Col: in Oxf^d, was desird by M^r P to enquire of my Bookseller, (Wilmot,) who was the author of it. I did not care to be known; for I did not know w^t twould bear of [?]—M^r P in his ans^r [said he?] was sorry he c^d not know [the au-?]thor; because he s^d have been glad [to become?] acquainted with him; [?] however, that he desir'd [?] thanks to him, tho' unknown. [?] Before I publishd the Se[cond? ?]; I wrote to M^r P, & desird [lea?]ve to send the copy to him; [th?]at I might not say anything [ag?]st him in it, that might be ill-grounded. He corrected the Second: with so much fairness, that he says on the Margin, Sometimes; 'this is a very great Fault': & at others, 'This is a mistake, as you will find by considering such or such circumstance.' There was but one single fault that he desir'd me to drop, in the whole piece; & that was where he had made too free with[8] the Scripture-Language; in Calling Jupiter 'The God of Gods.' Over agst wch he wrote 'I s^d be obliged to you if you w^d drop this, & spare y^r H Servt.'—I have y^t Mss, markt with his own hand, by me...."[9]

Since the manuscript which Spence describes is still in existence,[10] one can judge for one's self the extent of Pope's alterations. His comments are numerous and often interesting. In addition to occasional minor suggestions for altered phrasing, he makes twenty-seven observations on different passages, sometimes defending the translation against attack, sometimes admitting the justice of a charge, sometimes merely offering advice concerning a point which does not involve him. Spence usually, though not invariably, followed the poet's suggestions, in a few passages obligingly softening the tone of a criticism. If one judges by this manuscript, Spence told Warburton the truth when he said that on only one occasion did Pope ask to be spared—but the passage concerned the misuse not of "Scripture-Language" but of scientific terms. Pope pleaded: "These are great faults, pray dont point 'em out, but spare y$^{r.}$ Servant." Spence obliged. On the whole, however, it can be said fairly that if the comments and suggestions made by Pope on the manuscript under discussion were the only criticism which he offered, he cannot be convicted of trying to alter the tone of the work significantly, and Spence does not seem to have been guilty of a fawning submission to the dictates of the poet.

That Pope practically edited the second part of the *Essay*, however, is charged in an anonymous poem of 1743 entitled *Mr. P—pe's Picture in Miniature, but As Like as it can stare; A Poem: With Notes*. The author expresses contempt for a poet who

> With saucy Censure other's Faults has shewn,
> Yet poorly begg'd of *Spence* to spare his own.

A footnote added at this point makes more definite charges: "This learned and ingenious Critick wrote an Essay on Mr. *P*'s Translation of the *Odyssey;* the first Volume of which answered exactly to the Design specified in the Title-Page, of remarking the Beauties and Blemishes of that Work. When this Volume was made publick, Mr. *P.* alarm'd at the many enormous Blunders pointed out by this Author, sent immediately an Invitation to him, expressing an earnest Desire of waiting on him at *Twick'nam;* where, after having used all the Art he was Master of to ingratiate himself, and make any thing he should ask the more difficult to be refused, he prevail'd upon his Guest to leave the Manuscript Copy of the second Volume in his Hands; which having obtain'd, he made such Remarks upon it as he thought might best answer to his own Purposes, and then remitting it to the Author, entreated him in almost every Page, to omit such Strokes of Criticism as he look'd upon to be the most *just*, and of consequence the most offensive to himself.

"It was no Wonder, that an humble Application from a Person of Mr. *P*'s Character as a Poet at that time, and one who had so lately, shewn the Author such Marks of Civility, had its wish'd Effect. The Author, in short, complied with his Request, and by that Means, he publishing the second Volume quite alter'd from what it was, when first deliver'd into Mr. *P.*s hands, the Work itself sunk greatly in its Reputation, and the learned World lost the Completion of a most ingenious Undertaking."[11]

Since the last two volumes of Pope's translation, containing Books xv–xxiv of the *Odyssey*, did not appear until June, 1726, the first instalment of Spence's criticism had dealt with only the first fourteen books, with the indication that the remaining ten would receive similar consideration upon publication. Accordingly, in the following summer appeared the second part of the *Essay*, dealing ostensibly with Pope's last two volumes but referring frequently to those books which had already been treated.[12] It would seem, then, that Pope and Spence became acquainted between June, 1726, and the summer of 1727. After Pope's death in May, 1744, Spence told Warburton that his friendship with the poet had "continu'd, without any the least interruption, for 18 years,"[13] and, though he was no doubt speaking in round numbers, this statement would put the time of meeting in 1726. Among the Spence Papers are notes on what *may* have been conversations with Pope dated November 12, 1726, and February 28, 1727. The poet's examination of the manuscript *Essay* before August and his efforts in the autumn to procure for Spence the Professorship of Poetry at Oxford[14] make it certain that the two had become intimate by 1727.[15]

John Underhill, unaware of the account given by Spence to Warburton, sought for a mutual acquaintance who might have been the means of bringing poet and critic together, and after a detailed discussion he concluded dogmatically: "It is clear to our minds that Christopher Pitt was the common friend who introduced the anecdotist, Spence, to his hero, Alexander Pope."[16] But Underhill overlooked a letter from Spence to Pitt, dated at New College November 12, 1728, from which it appears that subsequent to the date of the hypothetical "introduction" Pope did not even know that the two were acquainted. Spence writes: "Before this I gave you Mr. Pope's real sentiment on your first book; I dare say it was his real sentiment, because, as I told you, I took care to ask him the question before I had mentioned my being acquainted with you; and it was literally what I told you."[17] It is clear that if there was a "common friend" who brought Pope and Spence together, Pitt was not he; but it is unnecessary, in the light of Spence's own account, to surmise the intervention of a third person.[18]

Returning to the *Essay on Pope's Odyssey*, one finds from a study of the work that Pope had little reason to fear Spence as a critic, even when the "blemishes" of his translation were being revealed. The young Oxford graduate—well-read and genial of temper—was different from the dunces whose angry diatribes were wont to swarm about the sensitive ear of the poet. A young scholar eager to produce an unprejudiced and generous work of criticism was likely to prove welcome to an author who had suffered so many furious onslaughts. Though the poet must have winced as he acknowledged palpable hits, the ready and sincere praise which Spence accorded him could not but be gratifying.

The critic took himself very seriously. Adopting for a motto an appropriate verse from Pope himself,

> Each finding, like a friend,
> Something to blame, and something to commend,[19]

he determined to keep before his eyes what he considered to be the great rule of ancient criticism: "Always to keep our Hearts open to the beauties of a Poem; and never to shut our Eyes against the defects of it."[20] He believed himself well qualified for the task which he had undertaken: he held Pope's ability as poet and translator in high regard, and from his Oxford studies he was versed in Homeric lore; he was involved in no controversy and had no friends to conciliate nor enemies to chastise; he was in a position to judge with the detachment of a man apart from the world of literary squabbles and rivalries. His was to be a work of criticism which should abandon the virulent methods then in vogue, which should join candor to politeness and censure to commendation, which should bring the learning and insight of the scholar to illuminate the genius of the poet—one which, in short, should attempt to rehabilitate the name of critic and restore it to the level on which he considered it to belong.

Fired by such thoughts, Spence set to work. His first task was to determine the form which his treatise should assume, and here he felt himself beset with difficulties: he must avoid the vice of monotony and dulness to which criticism is especially liable; he must provide a plausible method of mingling praise and blame; and he must shun all semblance of that conceit which the public would be ready to attribute to a youthful author sufficiently presumptuous to pronounce judgment upon so famous a poet as Mr. Pope. He sought a solution of his problems by choosing a form of composition which he was to adopt in many of his later works—that of the dialogue. He has given an explanation of his fondness for the form in the preface to *Polymetis*, where, after expressing the desirability of presenting literary criticism in an attractive form, he writes: "And indeed this was one reason for my casting the whole work into the form of Dialogue: for the introducing a scene, and characters, helps to give life to a subject, that wants enlivening; and can do no harm to one that has no need of any such help. Beside which, I have some other reasons that make me fond of writing by way of Dialogue, in general; and particularly, in the present case.—By this means one avoids the frequent use of that most disagreeable of all monosyllables, I.—The assertions are put into the mouth of other persons; and the author, at least seems the less arrogant and assuming."[21]

In his preface to the *Essay*, a preface so modest as to forestall charges of unseemly presumption, Spence gives his reasons for embarking on the work which he is offering to the world. He draws attention to the fact that only "such persons as are got into the same paths of Fame" are likely to be jealous of the eminence of others and consequently criticize them unfairly. He continues: " 'Tis for this Reason I might almost say, that I *cannot* envy Mr. *Pope*. So far at least I am unbiass'd; I can hear the Applauses, which are given that Great Man; I can admire the Passages, which contribute to the deserving them; but I cannot be uneasy at those, or detract from these, out of any prejudices arising from this Passion. Give me leave to say farther, that in reading that Work of his, which occasion'd this Essay, no one cou'd be more delighted, than I was, in several parts of it. Many Beauties I saw in it; and I imagin'd I saw some Faults: In some particular Conversations on this Head, I have found myself indifferent in the Case: and now I have here flung the Thoughts on both together, I hope, with some degree of Impartiality. But if some things shou'd be blamed without sufficient Reason, or others commended too highly, and in a manner disproportion'd to what they deserve, I submit each to the many better judges, who may happen to meet with these sheets. I ask pardon for any Errors in them: I beg to be set right." Thus the youthful author takes precautions to deprecate the resentment of Pope and to forestall the objections of critics. He modestly ranks himself low. Further, whereas he has seen "many Beauties" in the translation, he has only "imagin'd" he saw "some Faults." Finally, he submits himself and his remarks to the correction of the "many better judges" whose existence he acknowledges. Who was there to be offended by such an author? Not Pope, when he read of Spence's concern lest any should deem it arrogant in him "to find fault at all with so distinguish'd and so noble a Poet as Mr. *Pope*." Surely not the critics, when they were assured that the "some things proposed as faulty" were "only proposed," and that "the World is to judge of them."

Though Spence was of course aware that Pope had received assistance from collaborators, he wisely decided to consider all parts of the work as though they had come from the hand of the master. Indeed, with the extent of the contributions of the anonymous collaborators veiled in mystery, he found no other course open. No doubt he hoped that no undue share of his censures would fall upon the portions translated by Pope and that he would not overpraise the work of the collaborators.[22]

The *Essay* is divided into five "Evenings," each occupied by a dialogue between two learned friends, Antiphaus and Philypsus. The first three dialogues, which compose the first part of the work, amount in bulk to somewhat less than the last two. Evidently Spence, elated by the reception accorded to his original effort, decided to expand his remarks in the sequel. One is safe in assuming that the persons who converse are fictitious, in spite of Spence's express statement that Antiphaus and Philypsus are real men whose true names, if disclosed, "would add a weight to every thing they say." It is probable, however, that some of the critical opinions stemmed from discussions concerning the merit of the translation which took place at Oxford.

Spence begins, in the manner adopted by his predecessors in the use of the dialogue form, with the introduction of the characters into whose mouths he was to put his observations. He provides a means for that plausible alternation of approbation and reproof which was part of his design, for though both of the friends are men of learning, particularly fond of poetry and equally fond of a friendly dispute on a poetical subject, they differ markedly in disposition: "The enlarged Genius of *Philypsus* always led him to dwell upon the most beautiful Parts of a Poem with the greatest Pleasure; while *Antiphaus*, who has a very clear Head, and has given much into a strict way of thinking, is taken most with just Descriptions, and plain natural Ideas: The one was so possest with the Pleasure which he felt from fine Thoughts and warm Expressions, that He did not take a full Satisfaction in low Beauty, and simple Representations of Nature; the other, on the contrary, had such an aversion to *glitterings* and *elevation*, that he was distasted at any the least appearance of either. If the latter was prejudiced for the Ancients, from the Purity and Justness, which we find in most of their Works: *Philypsus* had his *foible* too, and was sometimes caught by the Flourish and Colouring of the Moderns. In a word, if *Philypsus* wou'd sometimes contemn a Point as low and mean, tho' in reality proper enough, and naturally express'd; *Antiphaus*, in his turn, might happen now and then to blame a Passage which requir'd a good degree of Ornament, as being too glaring and artificial."[23] By means of this divergence of temper Spence was able to assign his objections and eulogies, respectively, to speakers from whose lips they would fall with pertinency. The distinction between the two characters is maintained consistently and helps to impart an air of reality to their colloquies.[24]

At the outset and throughout the work, Spence is lavish in his praise of Pope's genius as poet and translator. He makes it clear that whatever he offers in the way of criticism is spoken only of the particular lines under consideration and is not intended as a reflection upon the ability of the author or the merits of the translation as a whole. Mr. Pope is "Our present *Laureate in Genius*, and the most enliven'd Translator of the Age,"[25] and again, "I take his Translation to be as good, as any Translation of *Homer*, into *English*, and in *Rhime*, cou'd be expected to be; In all probability, we might safely add, that no other Writers of the Age cou'd, in the whole, have perform'd such a task so well. But a perfect Piece of this kind cannot be expected: If *Homer* himself is allow'd to Sleep a little, his Translator certainly may Nod sometimes."[26]

But, having thus shown his respect for the poetic rank and acknowledged genius of Pope, Spence proceeds with zest to his task of criticism. He has "imagined he saw" a great many more faults than his modest preface would lead one to expect. He is by no means sparing in his objections, and at least in the first three dialogues the passages which he cites for defects considerably outnumber those mentioned for merit. In the course of his remarks he gives voice to critical opinions which are invariably sensible, and occasionally he propounds an idea which seems to place him strangely outside of his age. His criticism is, as Johnson observed,[27] commonly just. A shrewd observer, he had studied his subject with a thoroughness which leaves no doubt as to his diligence. His opinions are sound and convincing; it is seldom that he commits a blunder in judgment. Further, his style, though neither pithy nor spirited, is lucid and pleasant. The chief objection to be leveled at his work is that his procedure grows monotonous and that his prose contains little of the life essential to a first-rate work of criticism. But though he lacks the genius of the great critic, he possesses the talents.

The opening assault—if so polite a maneuver may be styled an assault—falls upon that defect of Pope's translation which is the most obvious to the general reader and the most fatal to a true rendering of the simplicity of Homer: the tendency toward ornateness, toward the piling of beauty upon beauty, toward the sacrifice of dignity to flourish, which is a characteristic of Augustan verse. One might expect this criticism after reading the words of Boileau which appear on the title-page of the *Essay:* "Le choix des grans mots donne aux choses une espece d'ame & de vie; les beaux mots sont la lumiere propre et naturelle de nos pensées: mais un discours tout simple exprimera quelquefois mieux la chose, que toute la pompe & tout l'ornement."[28] Pope, says the critic, is too much addicted to beautifying, to employing forced and unnatural diction in the hope of heightening his lines, to loading his couplets with ornamentation. Whereas Homer is plain, ingenuous, and unadorned, some lines in the translation are swelling and unnatural. Yet Pope is not entirely to blame for this regrettable failing; if he offends, he does so simply because he is a child of the age: "But however these Passages may seem to be weaken'd by the finery and luxuriance of the Language, this certainly is not so much the fault of *Pope*, as of the Age: We give much into an airy way: If a Verse runs off smooth, 'tis no matter for depth or clearness; and as the Ancients valued Thoughts more than Sound, we seem to be taken with Sounds more than Thought. To speak out, we are got into an idle manner of Versifying; and if Mr. *Pope* sometimes falls into it, we are not so much to blame him for those Particulars, as to wonder, that he does not do it more frequently, in so general a debauch of Taste among us."[29] These are strong words, and they speak well not only for the shrewdness of Spence's judgment but also for his courage.

Illustrations of the faults of the translation in this particular, as in others, are supplied in abundance. Spence demonstrates that he has made an exhaustive study of the work and compared the translation with the original at every page. By ample references to the text he supports each objection, and he is prodigal with footnotes. The book is an admirable guide for the reader who would compare Pope with Homer. The design embraced more than simple criticism: it included a treatment of the principles of rhetoric and poetic diction, and in part the essay may be regarded as an effort to promote that reinterpretation of Homer which any translation involves. Spence laments Pope's too frequent employment of antithesis, and offers convincing evidence of the poet's addiction to that mannerism. He mourns the propensity, which Pope shares with his age, to add expressions which seem to be employed for "beauties" but which "in reality perhaps only turn the Plainness and Strength of the Original, into the *Fine* and the *Artificial*."[30] Especially odious to the critic is the contemporary persuasion that pity may best be moved by a show of startling eloquence. Worst of all, this unfortunate leaning toward elevation of style leads to frequent confusion of metaphors and a disagreement between the figurative and the proper in language.

So ends the opening dialogue. Thus far there is little, aside from a general recognition of the translator's genius, to justify Pope's belief that Broome would "have reason to be pleased with" the *Essay*, but in "Evening the Second" the case is altered. With the burden of discourse shifted from the querulous Antiphaus to the genial Philypsus, the conversation revolves for a time about the "beauties" rather than the "blemishes" of the translation. Though Pope has been led, indeed, by the brilliance of his genius into an excess of beauties and an unbecoming use of figure, "how pardonable is it, for so exalted a Genius, to run sometimes into an excess of Ornament? And how admirable for such, to excell often in the just, handsome, natural *Manner*? As Mr. *Pope*, in the former, may possibly want some favourable Allowances; He must certainly command the highest Esteem in the latter."[31] Hereupon follows a host of passages wherein Pope is said to have employed an imagery so charming and a diction so affecting and natural that he has carried sublimity of expression to its zenith. On occasion he has exceeded Homer himself, especially in strength and emphasis. The entire tenth book is asserted to be "excellently Translated" and even "generally improv'd"—a pronouncement which must have warmed the poet's heart, since that portion of the translation was largely his own work.[32] In his effective repetition of the same word in just the proper manner, in the enlivened and musical turn of his verses, in his combination of the elegance of Virgil and the highest virtues of other writers with the original majesty of Homer—in all these particulars Pope has excelled. In so glowing a manner does Philypsus sing the poet's praises that the converted Antiphaus exclaims, "how many things have you repeated to me that are extremely just, pure, close, and *emphatical?* how many perfectly true, and *natural?* how many handsomly beautified, and *enliven'd?* what *Pictures* of Things? what *Descriptions* of Actions? and what beautiful Expressions, both o the *thoughts,* and of the *passions* of the soul? in a word, what *improvements,* in some strokes, upon the greatest Genius of the World?"[33] And one may add another to the succession of rhetorical questions: What could be more pleasing to the master of Twickenham than such an outburst of astonishment at his skill?

As the first dialogue had been devoted chiefly to the revelation of the faults of the translator and the second to a consideration of his special excellences, so in "Evening the Third" the pendulum swings slightly toward the side of censure; but the aspersions are softened by a mingling of highly approbative statements. If some passages are discovered to be inferior, the reader is quickly assured that the few faults of the translation "are scarce discernible among such a superiour number of Beauties."[34] And usually when the reprimands have been the most severe, they are followed by a declaration that such passages are quite contrary to the translator's usual spirit. Whereas before, the outstanding fault that was found with Pope was his inclination "to Elevate and Flourish too much,"[35] now the attack is directed at the "few *Lownesses* in his Writings," at the passages wherein he "sinks into a Diction, which borders on the *Mean* and *Vulgar.*"[36] This type of criticism must have been more galling to Pope than the other. Further, the critic adduces abundant testimony to demonstrate the justice of his contention; the lines are not always shockingly bad, but they are obviously faulty, and the poet was probably the first to give silent corroboration to Spence's judgment. Sometimes the meanness is thought to have arisen from a straining to elevate a point—a practice which, says Spence, will succeed only in making it the more mean and ridiculous. And he makes a shrewd guess as to the cause of other weaknesses, perhaps hitting upon the chief reason why the translation of the *Odyssey* is generally inferior to that of the *Iliad*, when he says, "The Poet's being in haste to get this drudgery off his Hands, sometimes draws him into the use of Expressions, which are flat and contemptible."[37]

At this juncture, after having made scattered references to the topic, Spence launches into a discussion of a subject evidently near to his heart—the relative merits of rhyme and blank verse. For their pertinency and timeliness, for their probable influence upon the age, the dozen pages containing this discussion are perhaps the most important part of his book. The topic of course is one which had been the subject of controversy for generations, and little that was new remained to be spoken about it. But quite apart from the question of originality, the fact that Spence takes up the cudgels against rhyme and attacks it with arguments peculiarly cogent and forceful must not be overlooked. For with the *Essay* a widely known book and with Spence regarded in his own day as an example to polite criticism, the tirade against rhyme must inevitably have had an effect upon the literature of the period.

Rhyme may do very well, says Spence,[38] "in *Odes* and *Sonnets* to *Armida*," but for any very solid or pathetic work it is an ornament "too Comtemptible [*sic*], as well as too much abus'd."[39] It sounds especially wretched in tragedy, and the recantation of Dryden indicates that that great poet and critic had persisted in its use only because it was the humor of the age for which he wrote. The mention of Dryden prepares the way for a summary of that author's views upon the subject, extracted from the pref-

22

ace to his translation of Virgil's pastorals, the dedication to the *Aeneid*, and the *Essay of Dramatic Poesy*. Indeed, continues Spence, there can be but one argument brought to the defense of rhyme, and to advance it is to reason in a circle; it is the fact that poets have no other recourse than to employ rhyme, because it is all the fashion. The viciousness of such a chain of reasoning is apparent. The fact that Englishmen in 1726 laugh heartily at the French for rhyming in comedy and, for the same reason, call the tragedies of the later seventeenth century insipid and flat points inevitably toward a similar fate for their own works in future years, in so far as they depend upon mere fashion for success. Surely "where the End is to stir up the Soul, by true representations of Nature,"[40] the endeavor to gain that end by the use of rhyme is unworthy of the true poet. Dryden had objected to the employment of rhyme only in dramatic writing; Spence goes further and would exclude it from the epic as well. Let but the fashion alter, and the rhyme which now sounds so natural and agreeable in English verse will be revealed as false and absurdly strained. It does not help to elevate the passions or to rouse the soul to an esteem for virtue and a hatred for vice; and, furthermore, since much of the epic procedure is carried on by apostrophe and dialogue, rhyme sounds as unnatural in the epic as it does upon the stage. Milton emancipated the form from rhyme and has revealed the path which the future should follow.

Spence then returns to the reason for which he had originally ventured upon a discussion of rhyme—that poets are led by exigencies of versification into weaknesses and even into glaring improprieties. With all other considerations temporarily waived, the fact that rhyme is almost certain to mislead and cramp a writer, forcibly to alter and often to spoil sentiments, to distract the poet's attention at the same time that it increases his difficulties, to put a false bent upon his thoughts—this of itself is sufficient to persuade the critic to disregard the trifling benefits which rhyme confers and to long for the day when the age will wake from its agreeable stupor and rhyme will appear as ridiculous to the reader as it is inconvenient to the poet. Spence feels sorrow that such eminent writers as Dryden and Pope did not rebel against the tyranny of rhyme and emancipate the world from a taste so irrational and barbarous. Future ages will read Pope with a feeling of regret that he marred with this faulty and insignificant taste of his age the poetry which otherwise is deserving of unalloyed praise and lasting admiration. And with the following fervent wish Spence brings his complaint to a close: "I have something of an Impatience in me to see this great Reformation in Poetry set on foot: I wish it cou'd be brought about in our Time: and if not, almost envy those, who in future Ages shall be so happy, as to see Men awake from this Lethargy of Verse: when all the Poets shall conspire to restore strength to their Sentiments, and nerves and variety to their Numbers: when the Writers shall throw aside all those idle Arts and Tricks, which we now play with Sounds; and *true Harmony* shall flourish, without incroaching upon *true Sense.*"[41] It is a commonplace to remark that Spence here shows that he deserves an important place among the many critics of rhyme in England in the late seventeenth and early eighteenth centuries and puts himself in interesting relation to Howard, Dryden, Dennis, Addison, and Shaftesbury.

Throughout the brief remainder of Part I of the *Essay* Spence devotes himself largely to commendation of the translator, and concludes with a paragraph which, though partly expressing disapprobation, must have been itself sufficient to fill Pope with satisfaction and set him inquiring as to the author: "I do not know how it is, (says *Antiphaus*) but I seem to be both more pleas'd, and more displeas'd with him, than I was before this enquiry: his Excellencies, from the light in which you have set them, strike me more agreeably than ever; but then this looking so closely into his Defects has made those too the more gross and visible. However (concluded *Philypsus*) you will still acknowledge with me, *That his faults are the faults of a*

*Man, but his beauties are the beauties of an Angel.—*You
don't seem to like the word: it may sound perhaps too
high; but I mean only of a *Great and Uncommon Genius.*"[42]

Between the first and second parts of the *Essay* there are
several differences. The sequel, though purporting to comprise the discussions of but two evenings as compared with
the three of the first part, is somewhat longer than the
earlier work and more prolix. The conversation tends to
diverge frequently from the main topic and to rest upon
subjects of a more general nature, with the consequence
that the style becomes rather more spontaneous and the
procedure less methodical. Illustrations from the *Odyssey*
appear far less frequently. In the course of his observations
upon the writings of Pope other than the translations of
Homer, and upon works of other writers, Spence testifies to
a wide range of reading in Pope's works that must have
pleased the poet and to a knowledge of general literature,
past and present, that speaks well for his learning. He
deals more freely with his materials, advancing his own
critical theories at every opportunity and devoting less attention to details. And, finally, whether or not the alteration be due to Pope himself, the last two evenings contain
comparatively little adverse criticism and a larger share of
praise.

At the outset of this second part Spence handles the
loquacious friends, Antiphaus and Philypsus, with adroit-
ness. They are kept before the reader as distinct characters
in a way to make him imagine that it is they, and not
Spence, who conduct the discussion. With impatience they
await the appearance of the remaining portion of the English *Odyssey*, Philypsus even making daily pilgrimages to
Lintot's to inquire concerning the progress of the work.
When the day of publication arrives, the friends seize the
earliest opportunity of considering the new volumes together, though actually their discourse turns but little
upon these last ten books of the epic. The qualities and
achievements of the poet which the critic finds especially
admirable make an imposing list: the enrichment of the

language through a cautious introduction of antiquated and foreign words, through occasional violation of the strict precepts of grammar, through the use of common words in unusual senses; the expression of the passions—particularly that of grief—by means of rapid and interrupted utterance, by breaks and pauses where the reader is left to perceive the meaning through his own efforts, by poetical prophecy and invention, by audacious and animating metaphors; improvements in the translation over the original, through the transference of "beauties" from one fine writer to another, through the harmonizing of the allegory,[43] and through the elimination of any awkwardness or inadvertency on the part of the original author;[44] the virtues of conciseness, force, and emphasis; the shunning of the meannesses of style which arise from a disproportion or inappropriateness of thoughts, from a too near approach of poetry to prose, from the introduction of words sullied and debased by popular use, from description of the vulgar or nauseous, and from all thoughts bordering on puerility—all cold fancies, all forced antitheses, any mere turns or sporting upon words; and, finally, the apt expression of the sense by the sound of the verse. For all these virtues Spence cites examples and authority, not alone from the translation of the *Odyssey*, but from Pope's *Essay on Criticism*, *Windsor Forest*, and *Ode on St. Cecilia's Day*, as well as from the Bible, Shakespeare, Pascal, Shaftesbury, Thomson, and the Latin poets.

Into the fabric of his criticism Spence weaves a number of his own cherished theories concerning the aims of poetic composition and the function of the critic. Foremost among his tenets is the idea which later took shape in *Polymetis*—that the art of the poet and the art of the painter or sculptor are fundamentally the same, that the poet should never assemble ideas in such a manner that they would not agree and harmonize if they were depicted upon canvas, and that the descriptions of the poets and the productions of the painters and plastic artists (especially in the time of the Greeks and Romans) furnish the best commentary upon each other that we have at our command. Again, he undertakes to define the lofty goal of true criticism in a manner which does him honor. Or he enunciates the first duty of a poet and the peculiar excellence of an epic poem—the great and primary virtue of the poet is to be natural, whereas the chief and distinguishing beauty of an epic poem is a true air of greatness and a style which carries with it weight and emphasis, and avoids all trifling, vulgarity, and meanness.[45] In full accord with his age, he asserts that poetry, originally calculated for the service of religion, should teach morality, and that its chief design is "to mix the *Useful* with the *Agreeable*";[46] that a virtuous and generous soul is essential to the constitution of a great poet. And, finally, voicing again the opinion of the time in which he wrote, the critic dogmatically asserts that a poet can learn to write with distinction only after he has mastered the rules of rhetoric and can follow them instinctively; or if a man "write with Flame," he can expect his poems to win the regard of the judicious only on the condition that he "correct at Leisure."[47]

For the plan of the *Essay on Pope's Odyssey* and for many of the theories of rhetoric and versification advanced in it, Spence is indebted to others. His originality lies in the detailed application of his precepts and critical tenets to the style of Pope's translation. In his preface he acknowledges a general indebtedness to Addison and Dryden, but only for the conception of his work and not at all for its content. Addison's *Dialogues upon the Usefulness of Ancient Medals* (1721) he knew thoroughly, and from it, indeed, he might well have derived all the suggestions which were necessary for the structure and method of his book. But from Dryden's *Essay of Dramatic Poesy*, which also he had certainly read,[48] he may have derived further hints. He mentions Fontenelle, but only in a general way as one of the chief exponents of the dialogue form in recent times.[49] It has been strongly contended[50] that Spence's work shows marked indebtedness to Bouhours's *Manière de bien penser dans les ouvrages d'esprit;* but, though there are undoubtedly traces of that work visible, they indicate the influence of Bouhours's critical theories, which may well have been derived at second hand, rather than direct borrowings. Spence's entire conception of criticism, of course, is modified and colored by the ideas of the French classicists, whose dominance in English thought was then at its height.

The impression produced by the *Essay* upon Spence's contemporaries was greater than the author's present modest reputation would lead one to expect. It has been seen how favorably the work struck Pope and his collaborators; the reading public, though understandably less enthusiastic, was also hospitable in its reception of the criticism. A second edition appeared in 1737,[51] and a third was published ten years later.[52] The general opinion seemed to be that Spence was "a learned and ingenious critic," and from the *Essay* he derived at least the beginnings of the reputation for polite, candid, and judicious criticism which was his throughout life and which increased with the years. His devoted friend Christopher Pitt was among those who expressed admiration for Spence's endeavor to re-establish the dignity of criticism. His poetic epistle *To Mr. Spence on his Essay on Mr. Pope's Odyssey*[53] begins:

'Tis done—Restored by thy immortal Pen,
The Critic's noble Name revives again;
Once more that *Great*, that *Injur'd* Name we see
Shine forth alike in ADDISON and Thee.

A remark of Thomas Hearne on the occasion of Spence's elevation to the Poetry Professorship at Oxford—that the young professor had "been cryed up" for his criticism on the *Odyssey*[54]—not only indicates something as to the reputation of the work but conveys the suggestion that it was largely responsible for Spence's appointment. William Somerville, himself a Winchester and New College man, paid the young critic a flattering tribute in his epistle *To*

Allan Ramsay, upon his publishing a second volume of poems:

> In vain shall canker'd Zoilus assail,
> While Spence presides, and Candour holds the scale.
> His generous breast, nor envy sours, nor spite,
> Taught by his founder's motto how to write,
> Good-manners guides his pen. Learn'd without pride.
> In dubious points not forward to decide.
> If here and there uncommon beauties rise,
> From flower to flower he roves with glad surprise.
> In failings no malignant pleasure takes,
> Nor rudely triumphs over small mistakes.
> No nauseous praise, no biting taunts offend,
> W'expect a censor, and we find a friend.
> Poets, improv'd by his correcting care,
> Shall face their foes with more undaunted air,
> Stripp'd of their rags, shall like Ulysses shine,
> With more heroic port, and grace divine.[55]

Throughout the century the *Essay on Pope's Odyssey* retained a certain degree of popularity as an example of polite and tasteful criticism at its best.[56] Joseph Warton could write in 1797: "I speak from experience, when I say, that I know no critical treatise better calculated to form the taste of young men of genius, than this *Essay on the Odyssey*. And lest it should be thought that this opinion arise from my partiality to a friend with whom I lived so many years in the happiest intimacy; I will add, that this also was the opinion of three persons, from whose judgment there can be no appeal, Dr. Akenside, Bishop Lowth, and Mr. James Harris."[57] In 1743 Johnson had been of the opinion that "the art of poetry will be best learned from *Bossu* and *Bohours* [*sic*] in *French*, together with *Dryden's* Essays and Prefaces, the critical papers of *Addison*, *Spence* on *Pope's Odyssey*, and *Trapp's Praelectiones Poeticae*";[58] by the time he came to write his *Life of Pope* he felt small respect for Spence's intellectual capacity but remained a supporter of the *Essay*: "On the English *Odyssey* a criticism was published by Spence, at that time Prelector of Poetry at Oxford;[59] a man whose learning was not very great, and whose mind was not very powerful. His criticism, however, was commonly just; what he thought, he thought rightly, and his remarks were recommended by his coolness and candour. In him Pope had the first experience of a critic without malevolence, who thought it as much his duty to display beauties as expose faults; who censured with respect, and praised with alacrity."[60] One of the warmest friends of Spence's work was Vicesimus Knox, who, in suggesting books to be perused for the better study of the *Odyssey*, recommends "above all, Mr. Spence's very elegant and ingenious Essay." This book, he asserts, will not only exhibit the deformities of Pope's translation but will "inspire a taste for the beauties of the original; and, indeed, the general remarks, which are interspersed with the greatest judgment and elegance, will contribute to teach a just method of criticism in almost every species of poetry."[61] Malone, who did not entertain a high regard for Spence's merit as a writer, conceded only a small measure of praise to the *Essay*, saying of Spence that "in his *Essay on the Odyssey* (the only piece of his that I at present recollect to have read) he appears very fond of the familiar vulgarisms of common talk. In this respect he is the reverse of Johnson. The book however is not without merit."[62] But the only entirely unfavorable opinion which I have found within the eighteenth century is that of Gibbon, who, though he held *Polymetis* in high esteem, had little regard for the *Essay*. "Pleased Pope," he commented laconically, "and can please none else; dry and narrow!"[63]

An interesting light on the favor with which Spence's criticism was regarded at Oxford half a century after publication is cast by a letter from a student at the University to his father on July 30, 1779. The lad has just begun the study of the *Odyssey*, and he writes: "The helps proper for understanding and relishing [Homer], such as Pope and Spence, I have at hand, having procured them from the circulating Library. . . ."[64]

The years since 1800 have not been kind to Spence's reputation as a critic; almost universal neglect has been the

fate of the *Essay*. It does, indeed, occasionally receive
mention as a good example of a type of critical writing now
not much regarded, but it is little known and never read.
Saintsbury, whose words may serve to illustrate the trend
of modern opinion, has nothing to say in favor of it:
"Spence . . . has sometimes received praise as a critic himself. His *Polymetis* usefully brought together classical art
and letters, and the *Anecdotes* themselves are not without
taste. But his elaborate criticism of Pope's *Odyssey*, published in 1726, is of little value, neither praising nor blam-
ing its subject for the right things, and characterised as a
whole by a pottering and peddling kind of censorship."[65]
Lounsbury is even more severe and, in particular, attacks
Spence angrily for flattering Pope: "Never, indeed, was
more abject deference paid to a great writer under the pre-
tence of correcting his errors. The direct censure was con-
veyed in such a way as to involve the highest indirect
praise. The passages with which fault was found were, it
was implied, not really bad in themselves; they were bad
because they were so good. They were unfaithful to the
original. Where that was simple, the translator had orna-
mented it, had elevated it, had given it majesty. Even for
venturing to take mild exceptions of this complimentary
character, Spence was profuse in his apologies. He further
made up for the censure, if by any stretch of language it
can be called censure, by bespattering the man he was the-
oretically criticizing with the grossest adulation. He was
not content with pointing out place after place in the
translation where Pope had improved upon Homer. In general terms, he celebrated him as one who had shown the
noblest genius for poetry in the world. He paid the highest
tribute to the generosity of his nature and the virtue of his
soul. He characterized those who had presumed to find
fault with his writings and character as Zoiluses and animals. The only redeeming feature in all the fulsome flattery
of this treatise is that Spence said nothing more than he
honestly believed. His sincerity cannot be questioned,
whatever we may think of his sense."[66] Though there is

some basis for the strictures of both Saintsbury and Lounsbury, a reading of the *Essay* will convince anyone that
both critics are something less than fair to Spence.[67] Johnson's estimate of his work is much closer to the truth.
Spence did not, indeed, possess a powerful mind, but his
learning was equal to his task, his enthusiasm for his subject is infectious, and his censures are surprisingly and almost invariably just. As literature, the *Essay on Pope's
Odyssey* can lay no claim to distinction; but as painstaking,
honest, and accurate criticism it deserves more consideration than seems likely ever to fall to its share.

The friendship with Pope which began with the publication of the *Essay* continued without interruption, as
Spence told Warburton, until the poet's death. The testimony of the *Anecdotes* and other sources proves that the
two friends were in frequent association except during the
years when Spence was absent on the Continent. Although
it is not always possible to name exact dates on which they
were under the same roof, there is abundant evidence of
repeated meetings, meetings which led to the compilation
of Spence's best-known and most important work. At least
as early as 1726[68] he had begun the practice of jotting down
records of the conversation of his associates, and this he
continued in the company of Pope and his eminent friends.
Apparently by 1728 Spence had decided to keep his records
in an orderly fashion, and gradually they took shape in the
form in which his executors were to find them upon his
death. If he had ever written his contemplated biography
of Pope, his notes would largely have been incorporated in
that work; but one guesses that after the field was pre-
empted by Warburton[69] Spence decided simply to publish
his anecdotes in a disconnected and roughly chronological
sequence.

Though it is impossible to describe his method authori-
tatively, he apparently made rough and hasty notes at the
time of a conversation or very shortly afterward, and later
worked them up into a fuller version. From such papers he
eventually made a more or less complete transcript; but he

continued to seek confirmation or denial of individual entries from qualified authorities, and there seem to have
been at least three transcripts of varying fulness.[70] Though
he included irrelevant material from speakers far removed
from the Pope circle, there can be no doubt that in
Spence's mind the notes which later became the *Anecdotes*
were chiefly intended to preserve records of the biography
and conversation of the poet.

Three months after the publication of Part II of the *Essay*, although Pope was unaware that he had just begun
one of the "most satisfactory friendships" of his life,[71] he
was sufficiently devoted to the essayist to be busy in his
interest. Spence had received the degree of M.A. from Oxford on November 2, 1727,[72] and was seeking election to
the post of Professor of Poetry in the University. That
Pope was active in his behalf is established by letters written to Edward Harley, second Earl of Oxford and son of
Pope's old ministerial friend, by Dr. William Stratford of
Christ Church. On November 20, Stratford wrote: "The
signification of your pleasure, in all cases where I am at liberty, has the obligation with me of a lawful command. It
was always my opinion that the right of voting in all public
places is only a trust to be employed strictly for the ends
designed by the benefactor. I know no one so likely to answer that end in the case of a Poetry professor as in being
directed by Mr. Pope's judgment. I beg my service to him.
I shall be proud of an opportunity to show my respects to
him by endeavouring to serve anyone he is concerned for,
but what is Mr. Spence, Whig or Tory? It is of some moment to know that, if I am to serve him with others."[73]
Nor was Oxford the only influential man whose support
Pope solicited for Spence's candidacy. On November 23,
Stratford wrote: "I had last night a letter in behalf of Mr.
Spence from Dr. Arbuthnot at Mr. Pope's desire."[74] The
outcome was Spence's unanimous election to the Professorship of Poetry on July 11, 1728,[75] but how far Pope's influence was responsible one cannot say. Spence was a man
of amiable temper, likely to have been on good terms with

the Oxford men who chose him, and he had already earned a reputation for scholarship. Both qualities are testified to by Christopher Pitt in a letter of this same year to William Duncombe, who had requested Pitt to suggest a tutor for his nephew, about to enter Oxford. The tutor was required to be "a man of letters, without pedantry, no bigot, nor violently attached to any party, but of a catholic spirit, and not unacquainted with natural philosophy and the mathematics."[76] Exacting as these requirements were, Pitt felt that his friend could more than fill them. He writes: "You desire me to recommend a tutor to your nephew. If he is designed for a gentleman-commoner, I would recommend him to New-college, (for we take no commoners) and to Mr. Spence, a fellow of the house, for his tutor. I need not enter upon his character, which is very well known; he has a more extensive character, than you insist upon in your letter. I believe he is about my age; and he is the completest scholar, either in solid or polite learning, for his years, that I ever knew. Besides, he is the sweetest-tempered gentleman breathing."[77] Furthermore, in the words of Hearne, Spence had been greatly "cryed up" for his criticism of Pope's *Odyssey*.[78] No doubt the poet's backing was of material assistance,[79] but the election indicates that Spence was highly regarded by the University authorities.

The annual stipend of the Professorship was about £180, increased by £20 through a bequest made during Spence's incumbency,[80] and was no doubt a welcome addition to the income of the new professor.

Because twice during his term of office Spence absented himself from the University for Continental tours, the belief has been expressed that he was remiss in his duties and even that he delivered no lectures at all. Saintsbury voices the general opinion when he says, "Spence, profiting by the almost Elysian tolerance of his sensible century, and finding that neither residence nor lecturing was insisted on, seems to have resided very little, and to have lectured hardly or not at all."[81] But Spence resided chiefly at Oxford except during his trips abroad, and there is evidence that he did lecture and that he was not so casual about his obligations as is generally supposed. His friend Robert Downes, writing from Ireland on January 24, 1728/9, forwarded to Spence the following paragraph from a letter which Downes had received from an Oxford correspondent: "Your Friend Spence has read his first Lecture which was universally admir'd for its Learning & Elegance— Even Hutchinson of Hart-Hall said—it was well enough."[82] Among Singer's collections were "Mr. Spence's Lectures on the Iliad, &c., as Poetry Professor,"[83] and in the British Museum are two other Spence lectures, numbered nine and ten, on the *Aeneid* as a political poem.[84] The first of these is inscribed "Read Oct. 14, 1730."[85] Moreover, though Spence was absent from England for three of the ten years of his incumbency, he seems to have arranged matters in a way acceptable to the University by having his friend Edward Rolle serve as his deputy in the interim. In a letter to his mother from Dijon on February 17, 1731/2, Spence says, "Your being acquainted so well with my Dear deputy at Oxford (Cap: Rolle) & owning him for your Son, in my absence, is just w^t I wisht."[86] The word "deputy" occurs again in a letter of the following June 21 to Henry Rolle: "I wrote the Lord knows how long ago to know how to direct to you in London, by your Cousin of New College & my good Deputy to the University of Oxford."[87] The fact that Spence was re-elected to his post a few days before his return from abroad in 1733 demonstrates at least that the Oxford authorities considered his conduct satisfactory.[88]

On July 3, 1728, eight days prior to his appointment to the poetry professorship, Spence had been presented by the Warden and Fellows of New College to the small living of Birchanger in Essex, on the border of Hertfordshire.[89] He was inducted on August 17, and on the following day he read the services and made the customary assent to the *Book of Common Prayer* and the *Thirty-nine Articles*.[90] At Birchanger, then as now a tiny hamlet, he resided occasionally until 1742, and here he had his first opportunity to indulge the taste for landscape gardening which had probably been instilled or at least encouraged by Pope, and which remained one of his major interests throughout life. Since his plot of ground at Birchanger was small, his love for gardening could be exerted, according to Rolle, "in miniature only, & by entertaining himself with, as he used to call it, his Lizard Garden." His "improvements" were effected gradually over a period of eight or ten years, for his presence elsewhere was demanded by his Oxford duties and his trips abroad. Further, the size of his purse prevented renovation on a large scale. But from letters to his mother we learn that his thoughts kept turning to the garden at Birchanger and that he engaged in considerable pruning and planting. Writing from Oxford on December 3, 1736, he inclosed a plan of his grounds and gave a detailed description of his improvements. Instead of "an ugly orchard, choakd up wth old Appletrees; & flankd with a very bad Cowhouse, & another house that shall be nameless," his mother would now find a little garden in which everything that was "bad" was decorously hidden and everything agreeable to the sight was skilfully opened. Thus at the end of a walk the visitor would come upon a prospect "5 miles broad, & 10 miles deep." He continued: "Toward ye house is a Round of Gravel, encompasd every way with Grove-work, which may be a good place to dine in. On ye E: side is a Less Round, yet more private, which wou'd do very well to drink a glass in of a summers afternoon: & if the liquor was Sack, you might have nuts enough to it; for 'tis planted with 2 Walnut trees, 8 Chesnuts, & all ye rest Filberts. On the W: Side is a Round yet less, & yet more retird; which is design'd to read in. And on the little open Plain is a Seat to talk in, or enjoy the Prospect; which lays all out directly before it."[91] Again, on October 11, 1737, he wrote to his mother from abroad concerning his plans for retirement to Birchanger after his return, which at that time was not planned to occur for two years: "By that time my little Garden at Birchanger (which I shou'd be glad at any time to hear any news of;

if at any time the fame of its Growth & Beauty reaches your ears) will begin to make some shew. . . . Tho' the place is not very magnificent, I can promise you it has quite another air than it had: for instead of walking into an Orchard adornd with nothing but Hog-stys & Little-Houses, You'll go into a Garden that will be a little Fop, strutting & pretending to be bigger than he is; where at least we shall be private & at our Ease; & unseen ourselves when we have a mind to it, tho' from yᵉ little Green-square at yᵉ end of it, we may stand like three Statues[92] on one Pedestal, & look out on a Prospect that is no inconsiderable one . . . ."[93]

As Fellow of New College, however, and as Professor of Poetry, Spence continued to reside chiefly at Oxford. There in the spring of 1729 he apparently made the acquaintance of James Thomson, who, according to the testimony of Joseph Warton, owed much to Spence's friendship. Long after Spence's death Warton wrote: "When Thomson published his Winter, 1726, it lay a long time neglected, till Mr. Spence made honourable mention of it in his Essay on the Odyssey; which becoming a popular book, made the poem universally known. Thomson always acknowledged the use of this recommendation; and from this circumstance an intimacy commenced between the critic and the poet, which lasted till the lamented death of the latter, who was of a most amiable and benevolent temper."[94] But an examination of the facts regarding the history of *Winter* after its publication seems to contradict a part of this story. The poem had appeared in March, 1726, a second edition had been published in June, and before the end of the year there had been two more editions in London and one in Dublin.[95] Now the second part of Spence's essay did not appear until August, 1727, some months after the publication of Thomson's second effort, *Summer*.[96] So Warton was hardly justified in saying that *Winter* "lay a long time neglected" when it went through five editions during the year of its publication and when a companion piece was called for shortly afterward. Further doubt is

37

cast upon the accuracy of Warton's statement by the casualness with which Spence mentions *Winter* in his *Essay*. After praising the proper and judicious use of antiquated words in poetry, he continues: "This we see in *Philips's* pieces; not to mention the new[97] Poem we were reading the other Day: the Author of which, beside several other Beauties, is by no means unhappy in his Management of this sort of Words."[98] This reference, though favorable, seems hardly so enthusiastic as to send readers hurrying to the poetry of Thomson; Warton no doubt overestimated Spence's importance in advancing the fame of *Winter*. With allowance made for exaggeration, however, it is almost certain that Spence did render Thomson material assistance. As a consequence of his position at Oxford and his friendship with Pope and various "great" men, he was in a position to help struggling authors, and there is evidence that he exerted his best efforts in behalf of Thomson.

Evidently the two did not meet before April, 1729, when Edward Young, aware of the assistance which Spence was in a position to render, gave Thomson the following letter to present to Spence at Oxford:

DEAR S^R.

I promised my Friend Mr Tompson who is now finishing his Subscription in Oxford all ye Advantages I could give him; for wch reason I beg leave to introduce him to so valuable an acquaintance as Y^{rs}: wch freedom I hope You will pardon in

Dear S^r.

Y^r most Obedient

& faithfull S^{rt}

E. YOUNG

April ye first
1729.[99]

That Spence enthusiastically supported the subscription is indicated by the following assertion by Warton: "I have before me a letter of Spence to Pitt, earnestly begging him to subscribe to the quarto edition of Thomson's Seasons, and mentioning a design which Thomson had formed of writing a descriptive poem on Blenheim; a subject that would have shone in his hands."[100] No doubt the letter to Pitt was only one of many which Spence sent to friends on this occasion, and it is not surprising that the names of Pitt and Spence, together with those of many other friends of Spence, appear in the list of subscribers to the collected *Seasons* (1730).[101]

Though there is good reason to believe Warton's statement that Thomson and Spence lived on terms of friendship until the poet's death in 1748, few records of their intimacy have come to light. They met at Lyons in the summer of 1731, when Thomson was traveling with a Mr. Talbot and Spence with Lord Middlesex,[102] and apparently again at Venice in the autumn.[103] One (undated) remark by Thomson appears in Singer's supplement to the *Anecdotes*,[104] and Spence collected some Thomsoniana from David Mallet.[105] Among memorials of friendship planned for his gardens at Byfleet late in life, Spence included one to Thomson along with memorials to such close friends as Pope, Dodsley, Pitt, and Lowth.[106]

Meanwhile, during 1729 and 1730 Spence was associating not only with Pope but with other famous persons, chiefly within the poet's circle.[107] Bolingbroke he almost certainly met often at Twickenham, and from Bolingbroke he derived a number of the "anecdotes" preserved from these years. The fallen statesman was also frequently the topic of Pope's conversation, and Spence seems to have shared the poet's admiration for him. He said to Pope: "I really think there is something in that great man (Lord Bolingbroke) which looks as if he was placed here by mistake."[108] On the other hand, his enthusiasm for the aging statesman's brilliance did not carry him to the lengths of adulation to which Pope went. Pope ranked Bolingbroke as the greatest writer of his age;[109] not so Spence. On one occasion, speaking of the Kit-Cat Club, Pope had said: "Manwaring, whom we hear nothing of now, was the ruling man in all conversations, indeed what he wrote had very little merit in it." To this statement Spence added a note suggesting "Whether this may not be the case with

Lord Bolingbroke, when he has been gone as long?"[110] In this instance he proved to be a wiser critic and prophet than Pope.

Judging by the evidence of the *Anecdotes*, one guesses that Spence had no contact with certain other friends of the poet. For example, he records no words of Swift, Gay, or Arbuthnot. Swift was in England between March and August, 1726, and again between April and September, 1727, so that it was possible for Spence to meet him at Twickenham or elsewhere; but the fact that Swift is not quoted in the *Anecdotes* is grounds for the presumption that Spence had never heard him talk. The same logic would hold in regard to Gay, who died in 1732 while Spence was abroad, and Arbuthnot, who lived until 1735. There remains, of course, Arbuthnot's letter to Stratford in support of Spence's candidacy for the poetry professorship,[111] but without additional evidence that letter, written at Pope's request, does not definitely prove that the writer was acquainted with Spence.

Jacob Tonson and John Dennis contributed a few anecdotes during this period, and some of the most interesting entries were the result of Spence's talks with the brilliant Chevalier Andrew Ramsay, whom he may have met through Pope, and with Francis Lockier, Dean of Peterborough Cathedral.[112] He chatted also with Nathaniel Hooke, the intimate friend of Pope and oddly ranked by both Pope and Spence among the best writers of the age.[113] Of Hooke's friendship Spence later spoke with some pride,[114] and he was long a close friend of Hooke's son Thomas.

That by the close of 1730 Spence was on intimate terms with Pope is indicated by the wealth of remarks by the poet recorded in the *Anecdotes* from this period. Particular meetings may be dated, from notes in the Spence Papers, in August, 1729, and in the following year in May, on November 28-29, and on December 13. The poet is said to have been responsible for an invitation which came to Spence at this time: he was asked to accompany Charles Sackville, the young Earl of Middlesex, son of Lionel, first

Duke of Dorset, on the Grand Tour—"in quality of a Companion," Rolle comments, "& not as Governour." Joseph Warton ascribes the appointment directly to Pope's influence: "And it was upon Pope's recommendation that he travelled with Lord Middlesex, which was the foundation of his future good fortune."[115] Spence accepted the invitation, and in December began a period of his life which he was later to refer to frequently as that of his "Travels."

CHAPTER III
Years of Travel

IT IS not easy to visualize Spence and young Middlesex as traveling companions. Spence was a scholarly professor of thirty-one, delicate in health and temperate in habits. The Earl was not yet twenty at the beginning of the tour, and he had already begun to show some of the unpleasant traits which were to darken his later career. Educated at Westminster and Christ Church, Oxford, he had received the degree of M.A. on September 15, 1730, and early in the tour his companion could speak of him as excelling most people in both good sense and good nature; but on his return from abroad Lord Middlesex plunged into a career of extravagance and debauchery which at times suggested madness. He became an intimate friend of Frederick, Prince of Wales, and squandered large sums of money upon the production of operas—incurring by both courses the dislike and ridicule of Horace Walpole. He did not succeed to the dukedom of Dorset until 1765, and he outlived Spence by only one year.

Yet, in spite of the dissolute habits of Middlesex, Spence —in whose nature there was a suppressed Rabelaisian streak—remained on good terms with his noble pupil for many years. That on the part of Middlesex, at least, there was little stiffness in their friendship is indicated by a letter which the Earl wrote on the occasion of a tavern brawl on January 30, 1735.[1] Writing to clear himself of the charge of wilful mischief, young Middlesex addressed his former traveling companion as "Dear Spanco"![2] Probably at the request of the Earl, Spence was early made a member of the Society of Dilettanti,[3] and he was one of the few commoners who belonged to that aristocratic fraternity. He does not appear to have taken an active part in its proceedings—a fact which does not cause wonder if Walpole's remarks concerning the society are accepted as true. Writing on April 14, 1743, Walpole observes: "There is a new subscription formed for an Opera next year, to be carried on by the *Dilettanti*, a club, for which the nominal qualification is having been in Italy, and the real one, being drunk: the two chiefs are Lord Middlesex and Sir Francis Dashwood, who were seldom sober the whole time they were in Italy."[4]

Because a hundred and fifty letters which Spence wrote (chiefly to his mother) during this and later tours have been preserved, it is possible to follow him step by step on his Continental travels.[5] Extensive selections from these he contemplated publishing under the name of "Traveling Papers." There are extant two neat transcripts in a strange hand of selected letters copied from the originals,[6] and on some of the originals themselves is the warning "Not to be copied." On one occasion Spence remarks to his mother that when his letters are in print they will be well worth her reading.[7]

The travelers made the crossing from Dover to Calais on December 24, 1730, and set out on a leisurely tour through Belgium, crossing thence to France and through Rheims to Dijon, which they made their headquarters for four months. Spence reported that here he had a servant and a separate apartment in a house taken by Lord Middlesex, and might live, he added, "just as if I were at Oxford."[8] Since it was immediately clear that his command of French was embarrassingly inadequate, Spence applied himself diligently to the study of the language, and not only employed a French master but grasped every opportunity to improve his speech through conversation. His landlady at Dijon proved to be a willing and good-natured teacher; when the two reached an *impasse* they would fall to chuckling, and Spence reports that he would laugh till he held his sides—then begin to talk again. With a touch of self-mockery he describes his foppish attire and activities at Dijon: ". . . a black Velvet Coat lin'd with red Silk, a black silk Wastcoat lin'd with white, Black Velvet Britches, & Black-silk stockings: A Sword always trickt to my side, & a Cane never out of my hands: & to Crown all, a French Wig in a Bag, wth two large black pieces of Silk y^t come on each side under my Chin, & are lost in ye buttoning of ye Breast. Beside this, I have just begun to learn to dance; & I believe verily shall come home very much a Gentleman."[9]

Wherever the travelers went, Spence cultivated the acquaintance of local celebrities and visiting notables, and made side journeys to neighboring places of interest. Unfortunately, however, his letters do not for the most part make such interesting reading for people of our day as he apparently thought they would for his contemporaries, for they dwell more upon the curiosities he saw than upon the people he encountered or upon personal matters.

From May through September the travelers sojourned at Lyons, and thence after a visit to Geneva they made the thrilling passage over Mount Cenis to Turin. They tarried at Milan and at Verona, where for "the great part of four days" Spence delighted in the conversation of the old Marquis Scipio Maffei, author and antiquary, in whose gaiety at balls and assemblies the visitor found nearly as much pleasure as in Maffei's gallery and collection of antiquities. At Venice Spence enjoyed the carnival but shivered in the damp, cold weather. He was pleased to observe the esteem in which English authors were held by the Venetian literati, and in particular he exulted upon finding that Pope was read with even more approbation than in England. The route led to Bologna and Rimini, thence along the Adriatic to Ancona and south to Rome, where the travelers arrived in the middle of March (1732). Here and later at Florence Spence passed much time with Edward Holdsworth, the Virgilian scholar, and took the opportunity to improve his classical scholarship by making notes on

Holdsworth's remarks and even following his comments with the help of an interleaved copy of Virgil.[10] He also had the pleasure of conversing in Rome with the aged Signor Ficoroni, who had acted as guide to Addison and served Lord Middlesex in the same capacity.[11] At Naples, the southernmost point on the itinerary, Spence made a pilgrimage to the tomb of Virgil, and sent thence a leaf of laurel to Christopher Pitt, whom he extravagantly termed the Latin poet's "truest successor."[12]

Proceeding north through Leghorn and Pisa, the travelers came in July to Florence, which they found so much to their taste that they loitered until the following spring.[13] Here they again enjoyed the carnival, and fraternized with many visiting English as well as Florentine notables. Spence enjoyed especially the companionship of Antonio Cocchi, physician and man of letters, who impressed most English visitors to Florence with his friendliness and learning. Many of his remarks on art and literature went into Spence's notebooks and are preserved in the *Anecdotes*. Walpole, who met Cocchi in 1740, thought him "a good sort of man, rather than a great man,"[14] but a still later traveler described him in more flattering terms: "He is a man of most extensive learning; understands, reads, and speaks all the European languages; is studious, polite, modest, humane, and instructive. He is always to be admired and beloved by all who know him."[15]

Leaving Florence in May, Spence and Middlesex advanced through Genoa and along the coast to Marseilles, thence north to Paris in early June.[16] A few weeks later they directed their course to England, where they arrived on July 9, 1733, after an absence of more than two and a half years.[17]

During the tour there had been published in London in 1731—apparently in March[18]—a pamphlet entitled *A Full and Authentick Account of Stephen Duck, the Wiltshire Poet*, purporting to be "a letter to a Member of Parliament" written by "J—— S—— Esq.; Poetry Professor for the University of Oxford." In the preface, headed "The Publisher to the Reader," appears the following explanation of the circumstances of publication: "Tis not material to tell you very minutely how the following Letter came into my hands: As to what is necessary, I can take upon me to say, that it was really written by Mr. *Spence*, and that this is a true Copy of it. The Author, who is now Abroad, I hope will pardon me, for Endeavouring to make us able still to enjoy thus much of his Conversation here at Home.

"I own it has an unfair Look to publish any thing without the Consent of the Writer. But as a familiar Letter of this kind, would scarce injure Mr. *Spence's* Character, were it written otherwise than it is: and as this may be very entertaining to the World, I hope he will forgive this Freedom; and then I shall be entirely pleas'd, tho' it be only with being the Instrument of handing to the Publick what I think will be so agreeable to all Lovers of Poetry, and indeed to all Persons that have any curiosity to know the Truth in a Case of so particular a Nature."

When the news of this publication reached him, Spence declared himself ignorant of the whole matter. Writing to his mother from Lyons on June 16, 1731, he says: "Any bookseller is certainly a Rascal that pretends to fling out things of any kind, about my old Friend Stephen Duck, in my name. I dont know what those people that deal in spoiling of paper are doing in England but whatever 'tis I wash my hands of it. Whoever did it, if it can be of any service to honest Stephen any way, I shou'd not be sorry for the scandal that I may undergo for it."[19] This denial to his mother, to whom one would not expect to find him writing disingenuously, seems at first glance to establish a strong case against Spence's authorship; but evidence that the account really did come from his pen is even more convincing. In the first place, it was revised and published under Spence's name in five successive editions of Duck's *Poems on Several Occasions* between 1736 and 1764.[20] These of course were authorized editions, and since Spence and Duck were fast friends until the poet's death, Spence must have sanctioned the ascription. In the edition of 1738 Duck makes the following modest apology for reprinting the

46

account: "I am afraid, the Letter relating to myself, wrote by a worthy and learned Gentleman, will be thought an improper Thing in a Publication made by myself: But, as I was desired to prefix it, by Persons whom I think it an Honour to obey, I hope it will be pardon'd."[21]

There is another strong argument in support of Spence's authorship. Lowth wrote to John Nichols in 1780: "The truth is, he [Spence] left this pamphlet in the hands of a friend, to be published as soon as he had left England, with that Grub-street title, which he had drawn up merely for a disguise, not chusing to have it thought that he published it himself."[22]

Lowth's testimony seems conclusive in regard to the main point of Spence's authorship. There is reason, however, for questioning his explanation of Spence's motive in acting as he did. It is possible that the account may have fallen by accident into the hands of the bookseller, who would lose no time in turning to profit such a timely pamphlet on the subject of Stephen Duck by a man eminent in scholarly and aristocratic circles. It should be observed that in the letter to his mother Spence does not make a flat denial of authorship but simply indicates that the publication was unauthorized.[23] So long as further evidence is not forthcoming, it is necessary to assume that Spence wrote the account, though he was perhaps not responsible for its publication.

The author of the pamphlet said of Duck, "I have pass'd the greatest part of Six Days with him, and had him Four Evenings entirely to my self."[24] And in September, 1730, on 10–11 and 15–18 inclusive, Spence wrote down memoranda on Duck's life and works.[25] Apparently the two met, then, in September, probably at Winchester,[26] and Spence at once interested himself in the thresher. Letters from Dr. Alured Clarke to Lady Sundon, Queen Caroline's Mistress of the Robes, show that by early October Spence was taking an active interest in Duck's reading,[27] and by the following June he could speak of "my old Friend Stephen Duck."[28]

In spite of his original denial of the authorship of the

Account of Duck, there is nothing in the pamphlet to have caused Spence embarrassment. It reveals him as a kindly, perceptive friend and patron of the man whose cause he is attempting to advance. Probably his interest in men of Duck's type did not stem entirely from the instinctive compassion of his nature; together with many others in his age, he was intrigued by the idea of the "force of nature" coming to light in the form of original genius in men whose meager education was inadequate to explain their intellectual development. This was of course a familiar neoclassic idea, and Spence doubtless looked upon Duck, as well as upon Blacklock, Hill, and others later on, partly as subjects for scientific study, observing their reaction to certain intellectual stimuli, inquiring into the circumstances of their mental experience, analyzing their views upon carefully selected topics. He questioned Duck as to his methods of composition. He tried the effect of sundry literary masterpieces upon the untutored mind of the thresher and recorded the results: "I read over to him some of *Hamlet*, and those artful Speeches of *Antony* to the people in *Julius Caesar*. He trembled as I read the Ghost's Speech; and admir'd the Speeches and Turns in the Mob round *Caesar*'s body, more he said than ever he had done before. As I was reading to him, I observ'd that his Countenance chang'd often in the most moving Parts: His Eye was quick, and busy all the time: I never saw Applause, or the shifting of proper Passions, so strong in any Face as in his."[29] One wonders whether Duck, shrewd enough to perceive that he was being put through his paces like a precocious schoolboy, was always and entirely ingenuous.

Together with this scientific curiosity, Spence had a real regard for Duck as well as a genuine interest in his poetry and, what seems strange, an apparent admiration for it: ". . . to know how much he deserves, one shou'd Converse with him, and hear on what Reasons he omitted such a Part, and introduc'd another; why he shortens his Stile in this place, and enlarges in that; whence he has such a Word, and whence such an Idea."[30] He is lavish in praise of Duck's intellectual and social qualities, and thoroughly convinced of the poet's worthiness and of the honesty and goodness of his nature: "He is really an extraordinary Man: and upon conversing with him Several times I went away, almost constantly, with greater Admiration of him than I came."[31] And Spence pays a final tribute: "I went off with a real Friendship for the Man: and my Mind is yet warm'd with his Good Sense and his Virtues."[32]

That such feelings were genuine is proved by the fact that for the rest of Duck's life Spence remained his intimate friend. For the next twenty years the two maintained a correspondence and cemented their friendship by occasional visits, and in January, 1752, they were brought into still closer association when Duck was appointed to the living of Byfleet in Surrey.[33] To Spence, who was then residing at Byfleet, is almost universally accorded the credit for procuring this preferment for Duck, and he was without doubt instrumental in the matter. Though Singer states that Spence secured the living through the medium of the Duke of Dorset—the father of Lord Middlesex—it seems certain that the person responsible for the grant was Lord Lincoln. Duck says as much in a verse tribute to that nobleman, wherein he eulogizes an anonymous "friend" who is almost certainly Spence:

Wak'd with the pleasing sound of Lincoln's name,
I felt my bosom glow with grateful flame:
For, after many storms and tempests past,
He brought me to this quiet port at last.
My fondest wish was such a rural scene;
The sage's pray'r was such a golden mean:
Above pale Poverty's dejected state;
Below the storms which often wreck the great:
Remote from giddy crowds and noisy strife;
Yet near the few whose converse sweetens life.
Here let me live—be mindful of my end,
Adore my Maker, and enjoy my friend.
That friend to whom—officious Muse forbear,
Nor with distasteful numbers wound his ear;
His ear, too delicate to hear the lay
His virtues claim, and gratitude would pay.[34]

49

During the remaining four years of Duck's life the two friends were in close association; indeed, in the periods when both were at home in Byfleet they saw each other almost daily.[35] Duck's life ended in sudden tragedy in March, 1756, when, dejected in spirits, he threw himself into a body of water at Reading and was drowned.

It is stated in an eighteenth-century biographical account of Stephen Duck that his natural modesty underwent a change in his later days and that he was spoiled by the extravagant encomiums of Spence.[36] If the poet did indeed lose the humility and modesty for which Spence expressly honored him, the loss was due probably not so much to Spence as to the flattering attentions which the humble thresher received for a time from some of the most aristocratic circles of the age. The abrupt transition from the threshing-floor to the royal palace, from the monotony of labor in the fields to the excitement of preaching before large and distinguished audiences, would be a strain upon the modesty of the most strong-minded of men. But Spence did bestow praise upon his protégé rather too freely. Fascinated by the working of the "force of nature" in Duck and pleased by "honest Stephen's" unusual personality, Spence regarded his poetry with an enthusiasm not justified by the merits of the work. Duck in return ever warmly acknowledged his gratitude to his benefactor and spoke highly of the gifts of Spence's mind and the goodness of his heart. There is good reason to believe that Spence is the "Laelius" apostrophized in sundry poems;[37] but it is in *Caesar's Camp*, published one year before the suicide, that Duck pays to his friend his most eloquent tribute:

> Spence shall in Nature's choicest mould be cast,
> Of manners gentle, elegant of taste;
> In whom the passions shall so sweetly blend,
> He ne'er shall make a foe, or lose a friend:
> Judicious, learned, and sincere of heart;
> Skill'd in the poet's and the planter's art.
> Whose care and culture shall rejoice the soil,
> And make the gloomy marshes round him smile.
> What pleasure shall he feel to form his grove?
> To plant new beauties, and the old improve?

To open vistas to the circling hill,
Or wind about his mount the pleasing rill?
Or shape the rounding walk that gently bends,
Encompassing his field of happy friends?
Where oft he shall employ his virtuous mind,
Contriving how to serve, or mend mankind.

Upon his return from abroad in July, 1733, Spence quickly resumed his intimacy with Pope. Shortly before his arrival in England he had been re-elected Professor of Poetry for a five-year term. He continued to reside at Oxford, with occasional sojourns at Birchanger, and he seems to have conversed with the poet repeatedly during the next few years, whether at Twickenham or elsewhere. Possibly to the year of his return belongs an undated note from Pope: "If this finds you in good repair, after the concussion of the stage-coach, and before you are too strongly engaged in town, I shall be heartily glad to see you for as much as you can of this week. I shall be at home to-morrow, and so on and always, dear sir, yours."[38] Nearly all of the entries in the *Anecdotes* for the period 1734–36 came from Pope. In the Spence Papers are several sheets of notes on conversations dated 1734, and, according to the same source, in 1735 Pope and Spence were together in February, in March, and in August. That the poet paid his friend at least one visit at Oxford in this year is proved by the following letter from Spence to his mother, dated September 4: "I have not seen honest Mr Duck yet, but have had the pleasure of another Visit that was wholly unexpected to me. Monday last after dinner, according to the good sauntering custom that I use here every day, I was got lolling at a Coffee House, half asleep & half reading something about Prince Eugene & the Armies on the Rhine; when a ragged boy of an Hostler came into me, with a little scrap of paper not half an inch broad, which containd just the following words; 'Mr Pope w^d be very glad to see Mr Spence at ye Cross-Inn, just now.' You may imagine how pleasd I was; & that I hobbled thither as fast as my spindle shanks w^d carry me. There I found him quite

JOSEPH SPENCE

fatigu'd to death, with a thin face lengthen'd at least two Inches beyond its usual appearance. He had been to take his last leave of Ld Peterborough: & came away in a Chariot of his Lordships, that holds only one person, for quick travelling. When he was got within about 3 miles of Oxford, coming down a Hill in Bagly Wood, he saw a Gentlemen & a Lady setting as in distress by the way side. By them lay a chaise, overturn'd, & half broke to pieces; in the Fall of wch the poor Lady had her Arm broke. Mr Pope had the goodness to stop; & to offer her his Chariot to carry her to Oxford, for help; & so walk'd ye three mile, in ye very midst of a close sultry day, to us; & came in, the most fatigu'd you can imagine. An Inn, tho' design'd for a place of Rest, is but ill suited to a man that's really tired; so I prevail'd on him to go to my Room; where I got him a little dinner, & where he enjoy'd himself for two or three hours; & set out in ye Evening, as he was obligd to do, for Col: Dormers; in his way to Ld Cobham's: which was to be the End of his fatiguing Journey: & so I think I have giv'n you a full History of all this affair."[39] In the Spence Papers is the original record of Pope's conversation on the occasion of this visit—a paper headed "Oxf. Sepr 1; 1735" which contains several entries incorporated in the *Anecdotes*.[40]

Possibly to this same autumn should be assigned the following letter to Spence dated at "Twitenham Oct. 7th" but with no year given:

D^R S$_{IR}$

I heartily thank you for y^e very kind Letter, & kind Entertainment, which gave me a greater pleasure than I almost ever receivd in any Entertainm^t; it was so easy, & so warm an one. I left you with all regrett: pray tell Mr Hay so, & Mr Ayscough: I conclude Mr Murray is gone from you—You'l oblige me in sending those Letters, not that I'll take from you any one Testimony of my Regard & Love for you, wch you think worth ye keeping. You shall have a fair acc^t of 'em when you come this way: but y^e sooner I have y^m y^e better, by a safe hand.—My health is pretty well restored, wch I know is y^e news you'l best like from this place; & the rest is only to repeat that sincere Truth you have heard so often, & shall hear while I live, y^t I am most affectionately Yours

Mr Spence. A. P$_{OPE}$.[41]

52

This letter is significant for the light it casts upon the mystery of the absence of letters between Pope and Spence. One would expect such an intimate friendship as theirs to result in abundant correspondence, but no letters from Spence have come to light, and only a few notes from Pope. Pope's request for the return of his letters makes it seem probable that Spence delivered to him, then and subsequently, all of the poet's share of the correspondence except the one "testimony of regard and love" just quoted; but what eventually happened to Pope's letters remains a puzzle. As for Spence's letters: it seems certain that Spence, devoted admirer of Pope and indefatigable correspondent, must have written frequently, particularly from abroad; the logical assumption is that this material was destroyed either by the poet or by his executors.

During 1736 Spence was of service to Pope on two occasions. He published through Dodsley an edition of *Gorboduc*, and from his words in the preface it appears that he simply contributed a pleasant little account of Sackville, to whom alone the authorship of the tragedy was attributed, and that Pope was the prime mover in the affair: "When I came to town this winter, Mr. *Pope* told me, he had given his [Sackville's] Tragedy to be printed; and ask'd me for some Collections I had made, relating to that great Man."[42]

Malone is authority for a doubtful anecdote concerning the occasion of this publication: "When Spence carried his preface to *Gorboduck* [*sic*] . . . to Pope, he asked the poet his opinion of it. Pope said, 'It would do very well; there was nothing *pert* or *low* in it.'[43] Spence was satisfied with this praise, which however was an implied censure on his other writings, and not without foundation."[44] Even assuming, however, that this anecdote is authentic, one can by no means be sure that Malone's ill-natured interpretation of Pope's possibly ambiguous remark is the correct one.

Spence's preface is entitled "Some Account of the Lord Buckhurst, and his Writings: In a Letter to the Right

Honourable The Earl of Middlesex," to whom and whose family the publication was something of a compliment. The "collections" which Spence mentions as the basis of his sketch were no doubt part of the "Collections relating to the Lives of some of the Greek, Latin, Provincial, Italian, French, and English Poets" sold among Singer's manuscripts in 1858.[45] After a brief biographical account of Sackville he discusses that nobleman's writings, showing familiarity with the *Induction* and the story of Buckingham in the *Mirror for Magistrates*, and quoting Sidney, Rymer, and Pope on the subject of *Gorboduc*. The text followed is apparently that of the 1570–71 quarto, with the spelling and punctuation modernized, and no attempt is made to provide critical apparatus. Unpretentious as the edition was, however, it did not escape the charge of inaccuracy and unintelligent handling. In 1744 Thomas Coxeter issued proposals for printing the plays of Thomas May, adding, in words not flattering to the ears of either Spence or Dodsley, "And, as a late spurious edition of *Gorboduc* is sufficient to shew what mistakes and confusion may be expected from the Medley now advertising in ten volumes,[46] a correct edition will be added of that excellent tragedy. . . ."[47]

In another transaction of these years Spence acted as an agent for Pope. He gives the following account of it: "About this time (1736), Lord Oxford was very desirous of having the Essay on Man translated into Latin verse. Mr. Dobson had got a great deal of reputation by his translation of Pryor's Solomon.—On my mentioning something of the difficulties which would attend the translation of his essay, Mr. Pope said, 'If any man living could do it Dobson could:' And by his desire I engaged that gentleman to undertake it. Lord Oxford was to give him a hundred guineas for it. He began upon it, and I think translated all the first epistle: what I showed of it to Lord Oxford and Mr. Pope was very well approved of.—It was then that Mr. Benson offered to give the same gentleman a thousand pounds, if he would translate Milton's Paradise Lost. He told me of that offer, as inclined to close with it if he could; and on my mentioning it to Lord Oxford and Mr. Pope, they readily released him from his first engagement, and so left him at full liberty to enter upon the other."[48]

With the completion of his second term as Professor of Poetry not far distant,[49] Spence laid plans to reside permanently at Birchanger, where he was gradually "improving" his little estate. That he settle at Birchanger had been the suggestion of a friend who may have been Pope. Writing to his mother from Oxford on December 3, 1736, Spence describes his landscaping operations[50] and then continues: "Now I have describ'd my Garden to you, I must tell you my great Reason for making it. One of the best & one of the most knowing friends I have in the world has been advise'ng me for some time to come & live more at London than I have done. He thinks it may be for my Interest to preach some times there, & to be more near my friends. He has said so much on this head, that I have re-solv'd when my Offices are over here, which will be after next year, to follow his Advice. My greatest ambition has been for some time, to live mostly in Town, & to have a Country House to retire to between whiles. When I was at Birchanger this Summer, I likd the country so well, that I thought with myself, why may not I make this the thing that I desire? 'Tis an easy distance from London; well placd for Stage Coaches; & if twas made a little neat & agreable, why cou'd not I be as well here, as at any other Country-Seat? A little laid out now, & something each year, may make it a very comfortable & entertain'ng place to be at, for two or three months together. I thought this over for some time; & at last began upon it; & hope to go on by little & little, till I have made it the thing that I want. If I can now & then see you there for a Visit, twill add very much to my Scheme, & to my Happiness."[51]

Rolle states that early in 1737 the Duke of Dorset of-fered Spence, no doubt as reward for his services to Lord Middlesex, the Deanery of Clogher in Ireland, assuring him at the same time "that he might depend upon him for any Future favour, even tho he should not accept of this." Under these circumstances Spence, who, one guesses, was like his friend Lowth in having no love for Ireland,[52] declined the offer.

In the same year he accepted another invitation to make the grand tour as companion to a young gentleman, this time a Mr. Trevor. This was almost certainly John Morley Trevor, "a relation of the Pelhams," as Walpole called him,[53] and later M.P. for Lewes and Lord of the Admiralty.[54] In May the travelers embarked upon what was planned as an extensive journey through Flanders, France, and Italy, but the trip was cut short in January, 1738, when Trevor was summoned home to stand for Parliament. Meanwhile, after an extended stay at The Hague they had journeyed by way of Brussels to Paris and thence to Blois, where they had remained from August to November, 1737, and on to Tours. After a sojourn of two months in that city they had set out for home.[55]

The second edition of the *Essay on Pope's Odyssey* had been published in 1737 during Spence's absence,[56] and during the year and a half which passed between his return and his departure on his third tour there is evidence that he was frequently in Pope's company. In 1739, for example, copious records of conversation in the Spence Papers and the Huntington Library manuscripts indicate meetings in April, June, July, and August, and possibly in September. Since Spence's term as Professor of Poetry had now expired, his connection with Oxford was weakened, though he retained his Fellowship at New College, and he was now presumably dividing his time between London[57] and Birchanger.

Spence seems to have taken no active interest in politics, but the following passage from a letter of March 15, 1738/9, to Massingberd in Paris contains a shrewd comment upon the tetchy state of mind of the English nation in that disturbed period: "You know that our Ministry had made some considerable steps toward a Peace, at a time that a War is not very desireable, & on conditions I shoud imagine near as good as we cou'd have hopd for after a succesful war: but the good people of England, who are (in my humble opinion) the most Happy & the most Grumbling People in yᵉ world, have taken it into their Heads not to be pleasd with this Peace; & wou'd much rather perhaps be let blood, than cur'd without any trouble. The Heats began to run high; but seem to subside again. Our Nation looks to me like a great Fool that has got the Hip; sits sullenly in the Chimney-Corner, by a good fire: cries Pish, to any body that offers it a favour: & if they are quitting it, bawls out to 'em to come back, & give it what it at first had refusd. It starts up & wants to go a fighting: Sound but the Trumpet, it squots down again; claps its hands across; & begs you not to make that damnd noise, for it shoots quite thorough its head. If you Lullaby it, it stares with both its eyes, as wide as it can stare; & if you bid it get up & mind its business; it falls a snoring. Wᵗ can the wisest Nurse do to satisfy such a peevish Brat as this? If she's a good & a wise one, she must not mind its whimpering, but do it all the service she can in spite of its teeth."

In another letter of this period to Massingberd[58] Spence shows his attitude toward war by concluding thus an ironic comment upon his countrymen's enthusiasm for the approaching conflict: ". . . but if it shou'd turn out that we shou'd have no fighting, we shall have no wooden Legs."

From his semiretirement Spence was drawn in the autumn of 1739 to accompany Henry Fiennes Clinton, Earl of Lincoln, upon what was to be the older man's final tour abroad. The opportunity was a fortunate one. Lord Lincoln, still under twenty in 1739, proved to be a pleasant and agreeable companion, and he remained Spence's friend and benefactor throughout the remainder of his tutor's life. His career was marked by a series of fortunate events. The nephew of two powerful ministers—Thomas Pelham, Duke of Newcastle, and his brother Henry Pelham—he unexpectedly succeeded to the title of ninth Earl of Lincoln in 1730 through the death of his brother, and his importance to the Pelham family became still greater when, a few months after he and Spence began their tour, Henry Pelham lost his own two sons on successive days. Newcastle himself was childless, and, though Lincoln had won the favor of his uncles before the tragedy, he now became their particular protégé. The relationship was later strengthened when in 1744 he prudently married his cousin Catherine, daughter of Henry Pelham, and on Newcastle's supposed retirement from politics in 1756 the Duke succeeded in having special remainder in his title granted to Lincoln. Accordingly, on the Duke's death in 1768, a few months after that of Spence, Lincoln became second Duke of Newcastle-under-Lyme.

There is general tribute to Lincoln's worthiness, at least as a young man. Spence told Massingberd,[59] "He has the universal character of an extreamly good natur'd man, which bids fair for making our jaunt yᵉ more pleasant." Even Horace Walpole acknowledged him to be a pleasant companion, and Lady Mary Wortley Montagu spoke in praise of his spirit and sense.[60] And shortly after his return to England he found favor in a more important quarter. Walpole wrote to Mann on November 23, 1741: "He [Lord Lincoln] came over all alive; and not only his Uncle-Duke [of Newcastle], but even Majesty [George II] is fallen in love with him. He talked to the King at his levee, without being spoken to. That was always thought high treason; but I don't know how, the gruff gentleman liked it; and then he had been told that Lord Lincoln designed to have made the campaign, if we had gone to war; in short, he says, *Lord Lincoln is the handsomest man in England.*"[61]

Not only was Spence fortunate in the character of his young companion, but on this third tour he was to make the acquaintance of a number of notable and interesting persons and to bring nearly to completion his collections for the work which was to become *Polymetis.*

On September 14 the travelers arrived at Calais, and they proceeded without much delay to Paris and thence south over the Alps to Turin. By the time of their arrival there in October they were on the best of terms, and Lord

Lincoln wrote to his "Uncle-Duke," "I should do great injustice to Mr Spence, & debar myself of a great pleasure, if I did not acquaint your Grace, how perfectly happy I am with him, & must freely own, y^t it wont be his fault, if I dont turn out what I know you wish me to be."[62] At Turin they remained until September of the following year, and there Spence became acquainted with Horace Walpole and Thomas Gray, safe from the "uncouth rocks"[63] of the Alpine crossing which had affected the two youths so differently. The quarrel which was to send Walpole and Gray home separately had not yet occurred. At Turin Spence also met Lord Sandwich, and filled his letters home with descriptions of the marvelous adventures of that youthful nobleman, who was apparently more than willing to talk about them. He had the pleasure, too, of fraternizing again with his old friends Holdsworth and Pitt.

In the midst of his studies for *Polymetis* Spence found time to enjoy the carnival and the Italian comedy. He also attended the performance by a group of strolling players of a farcical tragedy entitled *La Rappresentazione dell' anima dannata*. This spectacle he describes to his mother with much humor in a letter containing these further comments: "All this while, in spite of the excellence of the Actors, the greatest part of the Entertainment to me was the countenances of the people in the Pitt and Boxes. When the Devils were like to carry her off, every body was in the utmost consternation; and when St. John spoke so obligingly to her, they were ready to cry out for Joy. When the Virgin appear'd on the Stage, every body looked respectfull; and on several words spoke by the Actors, they pull'd off their Hats, and cross'd themselves. What can you think of a People, where their very Farces are Religious, and where they are so Religiously receiv'd? May you be the better for reading of it, as I was for seeing it!

"There was but one thing that offended me. All the Actors, except the Devils, were Women: and the person who represented the most venerable character in the whole Play, just after the Representation, came into the Pitt;

and fell a kissing a Barber of her Acquaintance, before she had chang'd her Dress. She did me the honour to speak to me too; but I wou'd have nothing to say to her."[64]

An accident which befell Lord Lincoln when he was out of his companion's jurisdiction caused the departure from Turin to be somewhat delayed. The Earl had ridden twenty-four miles out of the city to attend a ball, and the next day Spence received word that his young charge had severely sprained his ankle in a jumping-contest.[65] Taking with him a "Master Claude," an old surgeon recommended by the English resident at Turin, Spence hurried to his pupil and was relieved to find him less seriously injured than he had supposed. Master Claude, however, provided material for one of the most interesting of Spence's letters.[66]

From Turin the travelers went to Milan and the baths at Aqui, and thence through Bologna to Florence, where they lingered from mid-October until late in November, 1740. Here they met the Countess of Pomfret and her two daughters, Lady Sophia and Lady Charlotte. Lady Pomfret was a noted bluestocking, the friend and correspondent of Lady Mary Wortley Montagu and of the Countess of Hertford.[67] According to Walpole she held "a charming conversation once a week,"[68] and it was no doubt at these gatherings, while Spence was engrossed in the talk, that Lord Lincoln fell victim to the charms of the lovely young Lady Sophia, whose beauty was a byword among English and Italians alike. The progress of this love affair makes a tragic history, which one may follow best in the letters of Walpole, an interested though cynical spectator. The lady had beauty and spirit and intelligence—but she lacked a fortune; furthermore, the Pelhams were known to have other plans for their promising nephew. The cautious Spence, aware that in spite of the lady's charm the match was certain to prove unfortunate to his pupil, made every effort to prevent it, both by personal persuasion and by warning the Pelhams of how matters stood.[69] But Lincoln was infatuated, and when he and Spence were traveling with Walpole the following summer from Venice to Genoa he talked wretchedly about his love for Lady Sophia and his determination to marry her.[70] And later in London, when he met her on his return, Walpole says, ". . . he turned pale, spoke to her several times in the evening, but not long, and sighed to me at going away."[71] Eventually, however, the struggle between passion and self-interest was decided against poor Lady Sophia, who, haughtily aware of Lincoln's altered feelings, accepted the suit of Lord Carteret, recently a widower and soon to become Earl Granville, and in March, 1744, she became his wife—and the mother of stepdaughters ten years older than herself. The town knew how matters stood, and a quatrain soon appeared in mockery:

> Her beauty, like the Scripture feast
> To which the invited never came,
> Deprived of its intended guest,
> Was given to the old and lame.[72]

A few months later Lincoln made that marriage with his cousin which no doubt insured him his dukedom, and the next year the story came to an end when Lady Sophia, after giving birth to a daughter to Lord Granville, closed her eyes in death.[73]

But in Florence in 1740 all this lay in the future, and Lord Lincoln danced happily with Lady Sophia while Spence chatted with Lady Pomfret. Often in their company was another lady, famous in her century for learning as well as for less commendable qualities. This was Lady Walpole, the estranged wife of Lord Robert Walpole, brother of Horace. Though pilloried in her brother-in-law's letters as dissolute, arrogant, and absurd, she was unquestionably intelligent and shrewd, and possessed a wide knowledge of the world. With her Spence reported that he quickly became a favorite, "as being a very great Philosopher,"[74] and some of her remarks were later incorporated into the *Anecdotes*.[75] When Horace Walpole was at Florence in 1740 he awaited there with dismay the arrival of Lady Mary Wortley Montagu to join the company of

61

Lady Pomfret and Lady Walpole: "On Wednesday we expect a third she-meteor. Those learned luminaries the Ladies Pomfret and Walpole are to be joined by the Lady Mary Wortley Montague. You have not been witness to the rhapsody of mystic nonsense which these two fair ones debate incessantly, and consequently cannot figure what must be the issue of this triple alliance: we have some idea of it. Only figure the coalition of prudery, debauchery, sentiment, history, Greek, Latin, French, Italian, and metaphysics; all, except the second, understood by halves, by quarters, or not at all." [76] Lady Mary later wrote that in Florence Lady Walpole had held weekly assemblies of a group of freethinkers whose tenets scandalized all good Christians and whose meetings Lady Mary felt bound to avoid. [77] One wonders whether the Reverend Mr. Spence attended any of these assemblies!

At Florence, Lincoln and Spence received the civilities of Horace Mann, the English resident, and renewed acquaintance with Dr. Cocchi. A few remarks found their way into Spence's notebooks from the lips of the shady Prussian virtuoso, Baron Stosch, whom Walpole considered "a man of a most infamous character in every respect." [78] The habits of English visitors to Florence at this period are amusingly chronicled by Thomas Gray: "Here you shall get up at twelve o'clock, breakfast till three, dine till five, sleep till six, drink cooling liquors till eight, go to the bridge till ten, sup till two, and so sleep till twelve again." [79]

Leaving this frivolous existence late in November, Lincoln and Spence journeyed south through Sienna to Rome, where Spence resumed the studies for *Polymetis* which he had been forced to neglect since the departure from Turin. Here, too, he at last had the pleasure of meeting a woman whose acquaintance he had long desired to make—Lady Mary Wortley Montagu. She made an impression upon both travelers. "Well! My L^d," Lincoln wrote to the Duke of Newcastle, "we have at last Lady Mary Wortly at Rome, who is as extraordinary as my imagination had

fancy'd her (which by yᵉ by is not saying a little.)"⁸⁰ And
Spence devoted three long letters to a description of her
and to records of her conversation,⁸¹ beginning thus: "One
of the greatest advantages in Travelling, for a little man
like me, is to make acquaintances with several persons of
a higher Rank than one cou'd well get at in England; &
to converse with them, more on a foot, & with greater
familiarity than one ever cou'd have done, had one staid
always at home.

"I have had an Instance of this here at Rome. I always
desired to be acquainted with Lady Mary Wortley, &
cou'd never bring it about, tho' so often together in London; soon after we came here, her Ladyship came to this
place; & in five days time I was as well acquainted with
her, as a modest man cou'd be.

"Lady Mary is one of the most extraordinary shining
characters in the world; but she shines like a Comet; she is
all irregular, & always wandring. She is the most Wise;
most Imprudent; loveliest, disagreablest [sic]; best natur'd,
cruellest; Woman in the world."

Many of the remarks of Lady Mary which later appeared in the *Anecdotes* are reported in these letters, and in
the Spence Papers is what is evidently the original record
of her conversation. Both Lady Mary and Lady Walpole
interested Spence extremely, and he made the following
comparison between them: "Lady Mary more conversation Wit & Lady W more philosophical Wit."⁸² One of Lady
Walpole's most interesting remarks concerns her sister
bluestocking: "I wonder how any body can find pleasure in
the books that are Lady Mary's chief favourites: there's
no imitation of Nature in the characters: & wᵗ that how
can anything please?"⁸³ Some of the sayings of both ladies
were not admitted into the *Anecdotes*, but Lady Mary's
story of Addison's warning to her against Pope was transcribed without softening: "Leave him as soon as you can
(says Mʳ A to Lʸ M) he'll certainly play you some Devlish
Trick else. He has appetite to satire."⁸⁴ If Spence ever
chatted at Twickenham concerning his conversations with

Lady Mary, it is not likely that this choice anecdote was served up!

Having passed the winter and early spring at Rome, Spence and Lincoln set out in May on a leisurely journey to Venice by way of Bologna, but turned aside to attend the fair and the opera at the little town of Reggio, for a brief period the Mecca of all the nobility of Lombardy. Here also had wandered, a short time before, Walpole and Gray—and here they had quarreled, Gray going on to Venice with Francis Whithed and John Chute while Walpole remained at Reggio. After the departure of his friends the young man (he was then twenty-three) was struck by a severe attack of the quinsy, and Lincoln and Spence found him very ill with a badly swollen throat which he had insisted upon doctoring himself, refusing to allow a physician to be summoned. They went from his bedside to the opera, and retired about two in the morning, but between three and four Spence was alarmed by a message that Walpole was much worse and desired to see him immediately. He hurried into Walpole's coach, which had been sent for him, and found the young man so ill that he could scarcely speak. At once Spence sent a messenger to Horace Mann at Florence, requesting that Dr. Cocchi be dispatched to the sick man's aid, and he remained by the bedside until the physician's arrival. With the proper medical care Walpole mended rapidly, and Spence, who had asked and received permission from Lord Lincoln to remain at Reggio for a few days to care for the patient, was enabled to resume his journey to Venice. "You see what luck one has sometimes in going out of ones way," he commented to his mother; "if Ld Lincoln had not wandered to Reggio, Mr. Walpole (who is one of the best natured & most sensible young Gentlemen that England affords) wou'd in all probability have been now under the cold earth."[85]

During the remainder of Spence's life, he and Walpole maintained a relationship which never increased to intimacy. A few months before the Reggio incident Walpole had written to Spence to profess a friendship and a respect which he did not continue to feel throughout life: "I will not reckon you among my modern Friends, but in the first Article of Virtu: you have given me so many new Lights into a Science that I love so much, that I shall always be proud to own you as My Master in the Antique, & will never let any Thing break in upon my Reverence for you, but a warmth & freedom that will flow from my Friendship, & which will not be contain'd within the circle of sacred Awe."[86] During the twenty years that Spence lived at Byfleet his residence was not far from Strawberry Hill, and the two men exchanged calls and courtesies. On one occasion Spence supplied his neighbor with references for the biography of Richard Cœur de Lion and with details concerning that king's literary productions, for the projected *Catalogue of the Royal and Noble Authors of England* (1758),[87] while in 1759 Walpole published at Strawberry Hill the little volume which Spence had written in praise of the indigent Robert Hill, "the learned tailor of Buckingham."[88] But before long Walpole, whom one suspects of aristocratic prejudice against Spence, began to speak of him in a manner far different from the reverent style of the letter of 1741. By 1750 his "master in the antique" had degenerated into "little Spence,"[89] and it is obvious that by 1763 he would have blushed at the enthusiasm of the early letter, for in that year he sneered at his "master" for bad judgment in painting.[90] But it was not until twelve years after his preserver's death that Walpole made his most contemptuous comment upon Spence. He wrote to Cole in 1780: "As I knew Mr. Jos. Spence, I do not think I should have been so delighted as Dr. Kippis with reading his letters. He was a good-natured, harmless little soul, but more like a silver penny than a genius. It was a neat, fiddle-faddle bit of sterling, that had read good books and kept good company, but was too trifling for use, and only fit to please a child."[91] Between the Spence of 1741 and the Spence of 1780, what a difference! Though there is just enough truth in the barb to make it sting, it is hard to forgive Walpole for the ridicule which gratitude might have led him to suppress.

In 1741, however, Walpole was grateful for the companionship of both Spence and Lord Lincoln,[92] and he rejoined them in Venice, where the three stayed for a month in apparently intimate association. In mid-July they proceeded together to Genoa, whence Walpole wrote to Mann an account of their journey: "You will laugh to hear how we shortened the tediousness of the last day; as Lord Lincoln rode, Mr. Spence and I went together in the chaise, and employed ourselves the whole day in counting the number of loaded mules &c. that we met on the road. . . . We were so intent on this diversion that we were literally sorry when ever we came within sight of the posthouse; would you believe that possible?"[93] At Genoa they again met Lady Mary Wortley Montagu. Thence they traveled by ship to Antibes, and then overland through Toulon to Marseilles and north to Paris, where they arrived early in September. Here Walpole, anxious to return to England, parted from his fellow-travelers and pushed on for Calais, while they remained for two months in the French capital. Spence, ever alert to an opportunity to converse with a literary celebrity, sought out the aged Le Sage, living in retirement and in comparative poverty in the Faubourg St. Jacques. He was charmed with the old romancer's pretty little garden, and looked with reverence at the room in which most of *Gil Blas* had been written. Apparently he had neglected to bring his notebook, for one finds notes on the conversation of Le Sage scribbled on both sides of a playing card which Spence probably chanced to have in his pocket.[94]

As he turned his thoughts toward England, Spence began to make plans for the management of his remaining years. It was still his design to spend part of his time at Birchanger and the remainder in London, and from Paris he wrote to his mother a detailed description of the home he wished to establish in the city, preferably on the south —and less expensive—side of St. James's Park.[95] In more than one letter he speaks sensibly, and without parade, of his lack of ambition, his contentment with a modest income, and his philosophical attitude toward the passing of youth. His devotion to his mother is evident throughout this correspondence, and his concern for her enters into all of his plans for his own future.[96] The completion of *Polymetis* was to occupy him for the first few years after his return,[97] and he no doubt looked forward with eagerness to the renewal of his intimate association with Pope. Further, he had reason to expect kindness from Lord Lincoln and from that youth's powerful relatives. In April Lincoln had written to the Duke of Newcastle concerning "ye friendship & love I have, & ever shall have for my dearest Mr Spence,"[98] and now from Paris in October he wrote again: "I hope y^r Grace will excuse me, (I am sure you cant in reality be angry wth me) for putting you in mind of ye promise you was so good as to give Mr Spence on his coming abroad wth me, 'tis impossible to tell you my L^d ye numberless obligations I have to him; his behaviour to me has been such, ever since we have been together y^t I shall always remember as long as I live, no father cou'd ever show more fondness for his child, or study more w^t was really for his honour & advantage y^n he has done for mine, w^n I have ye pleasure of seeing y^r Grace I shall be able to give you so many instances of his friendship & attachment to me y^t will surprise you, I wont trouble you any more at present, but I cant help assuring you y^t any favour you bestow upon Mr Spence, I shall be much more obliged y^n if it was for myself."[99]

In November the travelers landed in England, and Spence was never to leave the island again.

CHAPTER IV

Residence in London

IN SPITE of his reassurances to his mother, Spence probably found himself in none too comfortable financial circumstances when he returned from abroad, but if he was uneasy his concern was not to last long. Within nine months his future was secured by two appointments which promised him an ample income for life. The first probably came through Lord Lincoln's powerful uncles. It had been preceded, on April 28, 1728, by a conditional contract on the part of Lincoln whereby the Earl legally bound himself to pay to his touring companion the sum of one hundred guineas annually during Spence's life, "or until the s^d Joseph Spence shall be possessed for the Term of his life of or in some place or preferment of the clear yearly value of two hundred and ten pounds or upwards of the Gift or procurement of the s^d Henry Earl of Lincoln. . . ."[1] This was followed in June by an appointment which almost certainly resulted from the "procurement" of Lord Lincoln and hence canceled the earlier contract. Spence was appointed by George II to the Regius Professorship of Modern History at Oxford, with its annual stipend of nearly £400.[2] A second preferment followed swiftly when on July 2 Spence was presented by the Warden and Fellows of New College to the living of Great Horwood in Buckinghamshire.[3] This rectorship, for which he vacated the less valuable living at Birchanger, brought him probably £500 a year.[4] When one adds to the income from the history professorship and from Great Horwood the money which was soon to accrue from subscriptions to *Polymetis*, it becomes clear that he was hereafter to enjoy financial security.

Spence later gave London as his home during the years between 1741 and 1748,⁵ and Rolle, too, says that from 1741 he "for some years lived chiefly in London."⁶ The house at Birchanger was, of course, his no longer, and it must have cost him a pang to give up forever the beloved garden upon which he had lavished so much care. He seems never to have resided at Great Horwood—nor, after 1738, at Oxford. His working hours he devoted to the preparation of *Polymetis*, which he had hoped to publish several years before its eventual appearance in 1747; but his health, grown more precarious during his last tour, nearly led to the abandonment of his studies. Rolle says: "But as in the course of his last Tour, his health had been considerably impaired, he was advised by his Friends totally to abandon his studies as incompatible wᵗʰ his Health. However disagreeable a Remedy this to one of his turn, He was actually about to comply with it, & the world was upon the point of being deprived of Polymetis, the chief object of his attention for several years past, & for wᶜʰ he had now been soliciting, & had obtained large & numerous Subscriptions, had not Dʳ Mead wᵐ he consulted interposed, prescribed to him a middle course, & advised him rather to apply moderately & at short intervals only to his studies, than entirely & at once to drop them." This wise counsel had the desired effect, though it is doubtful whether henceforth Spence ever enjoyed robust health.

Meanwhile, he had resumed his friendship with Pope, and apparently his association with the poet during the few remaining years of Pope's life was closer than ever. Twickenham was much more accessible from London than it had been from Oxford or Birchanger, and thither Spence repaired frequently, bearing mementoes from Italy for the grotto and receiving in return copious materials for his notebooks. It is impossible to state accurately how often he visited Twickenham or how long he remained on each occasion, but dated records of Pope's conversation make it possible to ascertain certain facts.[7] Thus in 1742 the two were together at least in April and again in August, and in 1743 in January, February, March, and December. Spence witnessed Pope's will on December 12 and was at Twickenham again in the succeeding January, February, and April. During May, 1744, when Pope was dying, Spence was in attendance almost constantly, and his presence resulted in the preservation of a detailed and touching account of the poet's last days.[8]

One can picture the scene as Spence hovered about the chair of the sick man, tending to his needs and listening to his talk—for almost to the end Pope's mind would clear for intervals—or reading a few pages from Longus or another book which he had brought in his pocket to pass the time while the patient was dozing. Pope faced his situation with fortitude and derived a melancholy pleasure from distributing copies of his "ethic epistles" to absent friends as he felt the end approaching. "I am," he observed, "like Socrates, distributing my morality among my friends, just as I am dying."

"I really had that thought," agreed Spence, "when I was last at Twitnam; and looked upon myself like Phaedo."

"Ay," smiled Pope, "but I can say very little that's wise to you now."

At times it seemed to him as if a curtain were hung before his eyes and he saw everything in the room through it. Objects lost their true colors. "The thing that I suffer most by," he complained, "is that I cannot think." The loss of his mind for an entire day caused him to express pathetic wonder that there could be such a thing as human vanity. His physician, Thomson, strove to encourage him by saying that his pulse was better; but Pope was not to be deceived. "Here am I," he replied, "dying of a hundred good symptoms." Later, writes Spence, he cried, " 'What's that?' pointing into the air, with a very steddy regard; and then looked down on me, and said (with a smile of pleasure, and with the greatest softness) 'T'was a vision.' " Dr.

Chiselden, the famous surgeon and long a friend of the poet, remembered a phrase from Shakespeare: "Like a fine ring of bells, jangled out of tune."[9]

Other friends were at Pope's side during the last days. Martha Blount and Warburton seem to have been present intermittently, though no remarks of theirs were recorded by Spence.[10] Hooke and Bolingbroke were faithful in attendance. "The greatest hero," observed Bolingbroke bitterly, "is nothing under a certain state of the nerves." And again, "There is so much trouble in coming into the world, and so much in going out of it, that 'tis hardly worth while to be here at all." He was sunk in the deepest melancholy. One morning he leaned against Pope's chair crying for a quarter of an hour like a child, saying repeatedly as he looked through tears at the dying poet, "O great God! What is man?" When Spence murmured that Pope was "always saying something kindly, between whiles, of his present and absent friends," and that his humanity seemed to have outlived his understanding, Bolingbroke replied emphatically, "It has so; I never knew a man that had a tenderer heart for his particular friends or a more general friendship for mankind." With growing emotion he continued, "I have known him these thirty year: and value myself more for that man's love and friendship than—" and his voice broke. Yet grief did not shake Bolingbroke's rigid agnosticism. When Chiselden sighed, "There is no hopes for him here; our only hopes must be—" Bolingbroke cut in with an impatient "Pshaw!" He went on, "We can only reason from what is: we can reason on actualities, but not on possibilities."

Pope's fevered mind dwelt much on the question of immortality. "I am so certain of the soul's being immortal," he whispered, "that I seem to feel it within me; as it were by intuition." Hooke selected an opportune moment to ask whether he would not die "as his father and mother had done" and whether a priest should not be summoned. The dying man replied that he did not suppose that was essential, but continued, "But it will look right: and I heartily thank you for putting me in mind of it." When the priest had come and gone, Pope said to Hooke: "There is nothing that is meritorious, but virtue and friendship; and friendship indeed is only a part of virtue." When Hooke whispered this at table to Bolingbroke, the latter replied aloud: "Why to be sure—that is the whole duty of man."

Pope fought against his infirmities, and on a day near the end, when everyone thought him on the point of death, he insisted upon being brought to the table where the assembled friends were dining—among them Miss Anne Arbuthnot, the daughter of Pope's old friend and physician. So wan and haggard he looked that Miss Arbuthnot exclaimed, aside: "Lord have mercy upon us! This is quite an Egyptian feast!" And Bolingbroke nodded sadly, "Sure Providence does this to mortify the whole human species!"

The faithful Spence was absent when the end finally came, after eleven on the evening of May 30. "But they did not know the exact time," he wrote; "for his Death was so easy that it was imperceptible to the standers by." And he closed the page with the fervent wish, "May our End be like his!" The thought may well have occurred to him, as it had done to that Phaedo to whom he had compared himself, "Such was the end of our friend, whom I may truly call the wisest, and justest, and best of all the men whom I have ever known." For in the mind of Spence, whatever others might think, such a tribute to the dead man was not undeserved.

The death of Pope meant for Spence not only the end of a most important friendship; it was to be followed by the abandonment of one of his most important literary plans —the production of a biography of the poet. That he intended the collections later known as the *Anecdotes* to be chiefly material for a life of Pope, no one can reasonably doubt: they begin with his early acquaintance with Pope, they are composed largely of entries contributed by or relating to the poet, and in the form in which they were left they close with his death. Yet Spence was unlucky enough —and, one must add, weak enough—to have his plan rudely shattered by the selfish force of a stronger personality. What had been the relationship between Spence and William Warburton during Pope's lifetime, one cannot say. The two men probably met shortly after Spence's return from abroad in 1741. Certain it is that Bolingbroke, whom Spence had long admired, resented Warburton's intrusion into the circle of Pope's intimate friends, and that there developed a deadly hostility between the two. Spence, too, may have been hurt by the enthusiasm which Pope expressed for this comparative newcomer, whose acquaintance he had made under circumstances interestingly parallel to those which had led to his friendship with Spence himself; but if so, Spence's modest and amicable nature prevented him from expressing annoyance.[11] After Pope's death the two men remained on friendly terms, though one guesses that they were never intimate. There are occasional records of Warburton's conversation in the journals for 1755–58, and, of course, Spence was sympathetic to him in his defense of Pope in 1749 against Bolingbroke and Mallet. On the other hand, his violent controversy with Spence's warm friend Lowth could hardly have endeared him to the anecdotist. As for Warburton, he once said to Spence: "He [Pope] deserv'd all that love from you; for I am sure that he lovd you very much: I have heard him say so often, & strongly."[12] But he himself actually thought meanly of Spence and on more than one occasion spoke with contempt of his mental powers. Writing to Hurd of the edition of Virgil which Joseph Warton, assisted by Spence and others, published in 1753, he confides: "The truth of the matter is, I suppose this edition of Virgil will be but a gallimaufry (from one concerned in the direction of it, *Spence*, who is an extreme poor creature, and has met his reward, as all such do)."[13] In another letter Spence is again a "poor creature."[14] With such a mean opinion of his rival, Warburton doubtless felt safe in claiming the right to produce the official biography of Pope as well as the official edition of the works.

His bold attempt was successful; but the pliancy with

73

which Spence yielded is puzzling. One wonders whether courtesy toward Warburton is the sole explanation—whether the difficulty or danger of the task was not in part responsible for his meek relinquishing of his purpose. At any rate, yield he did. Shortly before Pope's death he made the following parenthetical note about Warburton in the midst of a record of the latter's conversation: "Thinks of writing M^r P^s life, whenever ye world may have so great a loss; & I offer'd to give any lights I c^d toward it."[15] But Joseph Warton said that Spence later gave him the following more detailed account of his surrender to Warburton: "As they returned in the same carriage together from Twickenham, soon after the death of our Author, and joined in lamenting his death and celebrating his praises, Dr. Warburton said he intended to write his life; on which Mr. Spence, with his usual modesty and condescension, said, that he also had the same intentions; and had, from time to time, collected from Pope's own mouth, various particulars of his life, pursuits, and studies; but would readily give up to Dr. Warburton all his collections on this subject, and accordingly communicated them to him immediately."[16] The conversation here described must have taken place two months subsequent to the other; possibly Warton (or even Spence) made a mistake in the date, though the account seems too circumstantial for that. Of course, one can make the stories fit by assuming that Warburton made his announcement in April and then reiterated it (perhaps both to warn Spence off and to remind him of his promise of assistance) when the opportunity arose in June.

Spence made good his promise, though possibly he did not give the usurper the benefit of all his materials. Among Warburton's papers[17] are seven sheets of extracts which Spence apparently compiled from his collections and sent to Warburton. These extracts are by no means so exhaustive as he might have made them; but, on the other hand, many of them seem to be only summaries, and each entry is followed by a reference, presumably to a fuller account. Possibly these sheets were accompanied by a complete transcript of the *Anecdotes* and were meant to serve only as an index. At any rate, Warburton used much material from Spence in his edition of Pope (1751) and later supplied Owen Ruffhead with copious information from the same source.

That Spence never wrote a biography of Pope is a catastrophe. True, his materials have been printed elsewhere; but Spence, with his intimate knowledge of the poet's domestic life and a sympathetic attitude toward his character, might have welded those materials into a biography of great interest and charm as well as authority. Warburton, on the other hand, in addition to having known Pope only during the last five years of the poet's career, had been too much engrossed in his own affairs to make any sincere attempt to gather details of Pope's life; furthermore, he was to be extremely busy for the next few years and had neither time nor inclination to pursue his plan. And finally, he "was entangled by late friendships, *et recentibus odiis*. His prospect of elevation in the church . . . made him every day too great for his subject."[18] As a consequence, he did nothing for a time. There is abundant evidence to show that he had spread abroad the report that he was preparing a biography,[19] but none to indicate that he had even made a start upon the work. Thirty years later, however, he assisted Ruffhead and, according to report, "revised the life, as written by his locum-tenens, sheet by sheet."[20] Singer is justified in charging that "almost every anecdote of interest in that Life of Pope is derived from this collection [the *Anecdotes*], and always without acknowledgment."[21] Such being the case, there may have been method in the sluggishness which delayed the publication of Ruffhead's work until 1769, the year following the death of Spence. Ruffhead's book, though based on a wealth of authentic information, is disappointing, and students of Pope regret the circumstances which resulted in the poet's biography being composed twenty-five years after his death by Ruffhead rather than by Spence with his detailed knowledge and with nothing to hinder prompt publication.

There is no doubt that in a biography by Spence, Pope

would have appeared to much better advantage than he does in most works which have been written about him. Spence's feeling for him fell little short of idolatry, and Pope's influence upon Spence's life was tremendous. It is necessary, of course, to remember that of his sixty-nine years Spence passed at most only seventeen in intimacy with Pope and that, of those seventeen, he spent more than four abroad; but the years of friendship with the poet were not only the most important period of Spence's life but provided him with inspiration and memories for the remainder of it. Certainly, Pope played a greater role in the shaping of his mind and the direction of his career than did any other person or influence. Much of his time was devoted to the cultivation of the poet's friendship and the study of his intellectual and moral temper. Spence not only held his master in high regard as a man and a poet but, what seems strange, had a great respect for his learning. Though he pursued many interests outside of Pope's sphere and though his reputation among his contemporaries developed chiefly from these interests, he would probably have preferred to be known as "the friend of Pope," which is almost the sole capacity in which the world knows him today, than to be honored with any other title. And for faithful devotion, for sincere admiration of a superior, for single-minded interest in the concerns and the welfare of his hero, one cannot find in the history of English literature a parallel for Joseph Spence save perhaps in the person of James Boswell.

The years immediately following the death of Pope were busy ones for Spence. In addition to preparing *Polymetis* for the press, he published a number of minor writings, and he led as active a social life as the precarious state of his health permitted. During the Rebellion of 1745–46 he seems to have embarked for the first and last time upon the troubled sea of political writing. Frequent entries in his notebooks and other papers prove that he was strongly opposed to the Stuarts, particularly because of his fear of Catholic domination, and that he followed with interest the progress of Prince Charles's uprising.[22] Nichols, supported by Lowth, states that Spence published at least the first number of what was intended to be "an occasional paper" entitled *Plain Matter of Fact, or, a short Review of the Reigns of our Popish Princes since the Reformation; in order to shew what we are to expect if another should happen to reign over us.* Nichols had seen a copy of "Part I" dated 1748 and with Spence's name to it in manuscript as the author.[23] Lowth commented on Nichols' statement: " 'Plain Matter of fact,' etc. was Mr. Spence's. I think he wrote it during the Rebellion in 1745–6; and would have continued it, had the Rebellion continued. It was intended for a popular thing, and for the lower class of readers."[24] This testimony is corroborated by the appearance in the Spence Papers of a rough draft of what doubtless became *Plain Matter of Fact.* The paper is labeled "Part: 2. The Introduction," and contains a hasty review of English history from Mary Tudor to James II, attacking James I in particular for his belief "that Kings have a Right from Heav'n." And elsewhere[25] Spence makes a note reminding himself to send a copy of *Plain Matter of Fact* to a friend.

No copies of this pamphlet seem to be available—even Lowth did not know where to find one—but Lowth's remark that it "was intended for a popular thing, and for the lower class of readers" suggests that it possessed little literary merit. In spite of Nichols' assertion concerning the copy he had seen, Lowth's statement about Spence's plan to continue the paper if the rebellion continued makes one wonder whether 1746 rather than 1748 was not the date of publication.[26]

Other productions of Spence's pen found their way into print in the pages of Dodsley's periodical *The Museum: or, The Literary and Historical Register.* This fortnightly magazine was projected early in 1746, when Dodsley engaged Mark Akenside as editor, and ran a fairly distinguished course for thirty-nine numbers. Among its contributors were Joseph and Thomas Warton, William Collins, William Whitehead, Christopher Pitt, David Garrick, Stephen Duck, Lord Hervey, and Isaac Hawkins Browne, but none was more regular or more voluminous than Spence. Fourteen contributions in twelve numbers can be assigned to him, and it is possible that, in addition, he contributed some of the essays and reviews the authorship of which is uncertain.[27] He was intimately associated with Dodsley during these years in London, and Dodsley's biographer attributes to Spence an important share in the selection and assembly of the well-known *A Collection of Poems*,[28] of which the first three volumes were published in 1748. Included was Spence's poem *An Epistle from a Swiss Officer to his Friend at Rome*, reprinted, as were many pieces in the collection, from the *Museum*.[29]

This work is the best known of the poems of Spence, who dabbled in verse all his life. There is little doubt as to its authorship, since Lowth ascribed it to Spence[30] and it is reprinted under his name in *Bell's Classical Arrangement of Fugitive Poetry* (1789).[31] Written in rhymed couplets of loose construction, the poem is an exaltation of the freedom of a Swiss mountaineer as compared to the slavish magnificence of the life of a mercenary soldier at Rome. Scornfully the Alpine warrior resists his friend's efforts to draw him to Italy:

> Your Arguments that vainly strive to please,
> Your Arts, your Country, and your Palaces,
> What Signs of Roman grandeur still remain—
> Much have you said; and much have said in vain.
> Fine Pageants these for Slaves, to please the Eye;
> And Put the neatest Dress on Misery!

Bred up to liberty, the Swiss would make but "an awkward slave," and in lines of considerable force he contrasts the life of the mountain peasant with that of the Italian serf:

> Falsely you blame our barren Rocks and Plains,
> Happy in Freedom and Laborious Swains:
> Our Peasants cheerful to the Field Repair,
> And can enjoy the Labours of the Year;
> Whilst yours, beneath some Tree, with mournful Eyes,

Sees for some haughty Lord his Harvest rise:
Then silent, sighs; but stops his slavish Breath:
He silent sighs; for should he speak, 'tis Death.
Hence from our Field, the lazy Grain we call,
Too much for Want, for Luxury too small;
Whilst all Campania's rich inviting Soil
Scarce knows the Plowshare, or the Reaper's Toil.

The speaker goes on to contrast further the rugged life of the indigent but self-respecting Swiss with the indolent, subservient existence typical of Italy, and concludes with an apostrophe to his country:

Hear me, ye Rocks, ye Mountains, and ye Plains,
The happy Bounds of our Helvetian Swains!
In thee, my Country, will I fix my Seat;
Nor envy the poor Wretch that would be great:
My Life and Arms I dedicate to thee;—
For know, it is my Int'rest to be FREE.

Though artificial in phrasing and not always free from bathos, the poem at least shows Spence as a competent versifier.[32]

In the *Museum* for April 12, 1746,[33] appeared a little poem entitled *The three First Stanza's of the 24th Canto of Dante's Inferna made into a Song. In Imitation of the Earl of Surry's Stile.* It is attributed to Spence by both Nichols[34] and Joseph Warton.[35] These verses are worth reprinting here:

I

When in the opening of the youthful Year,
    Sol in *Aquarius* bathes his glistering Ray;
In early Morn the Fields all white appear,
    With hoary Frost is cover'd every Spray:
And every Herb and every Grass is shent,
All in the chill Imprisonment ypent.

II

The mean-clad Swain, forth issuing from his Cot,
    Looks sadly all around the whitening Waste;
And grieves that his poor Sheep, by Heaven forgot,
    Can find no Food, no tender Green to taste:
He beats his Breast as one distract, or mad;
And home returns, with pensive Look and sad.

III

There silent grieves. Then once again looks out,
  And sees the Groves and Meads quite alter'd are.
The Sun has cast his melting Rays about,
  And every Green appears more fresh and fair.
Then Hope returns, and Joy unknits his Brows,
And forth he leads his Flock the tender Grass to brouze.

IV

Thus when my Fair One views me with Disdain,
  My Heart is sunk within me, sad and dead;
My Spirits yield, and all my Soul's in Pain;
  I sit and sigh, and hang my drooping Head:
But if she smile, my Sadness melts away,
Each gloomy Thought clears up, and I'm all blithe and gay.

The only other published poems attributed to Spence
are congratulatory or elegiac verses penned upon the occasion of a birth, marriage, or death in the royal family, and
contributed to the various collections published at such
times by the University of Oxford. These odes—seven in
all—sprang from the circumstance of Spence's possession
of a professorship in the University, and they inevitably
lack spontaneity. Following the general pattern of laureate
odes, they abound in extravagant compliment and stereo-
typed epithet. It is interesting that, in spite of his assault
upon rhyme in the *Essay on Pope's Odyssey*,[36] Spence adhered to the rhymed couplet in four of his pieces and
adopted a rhyming stanza for a fifth, using blank verse in
only two. A fair sample of his product is the opening of the
poem celebrating the marriage of George III:

At length the gallant Navy from afar
Rises in prospect, with expanded wings
Improving the kind gale, so long delay'd;
And wins in pompous pride her easy way
To Albion's shore, charg'd with the precious freight
Of England's dearest hopes, and George's love.
Not so desir'd, nor with such treasure fraught,
Arrives the wealthy convoy, from the coast
Of Ceylon or Golconda; laden deep
With spicy drugs, barbaric gems, and gold.[37]

Nichols reprinted all of the pieces in his *Select Collection of Poems* in 1782, with a memoir and portrait of the author.[38]
Doubt has been cast upon Spence's authorship of certain of these Oxford poems. W. P. Courtney asserts without qualification that "of the seven poems . . . the second pair were by Rolle."[39] Both poems, however, are printed above Spence's name in the Oxford publications, and Courtney quotes no authority for his statement. Again, Joseph Warton, writing to his brother Thomas regarding the set of congratulatory poems on the marriage of George III (1761), observes: "The verses are many of them good. Above all, is not *Spence's* a noble copy, so proper and happy is the introducing our old Saxon connections. They were written and indeed owned by Dr. Lowth, so says Sturges, &c. here."[40] But this ascription to Lowth seems doubtful in view of the fact that Lowth himself assisted Nichols in the editing of Spence's poems in the *Select Collection* and made no allusion to the matter. Even if Spence were denied the authorship of all three disputed poems, however, the loss to his literary reputation would be negligible.

In addition to these published pieces, Spence wrote a number of poems which apparently never found their way into print. There exists a manuscript volume containing thirty-four poems, fifteen of them in Latin, written in Spence's hand.[41] Included are odes in imitation of Horace, translations and paraphrases of episodes from the classics and the Bible, complimentary epistles, and a seventeen-page *Art of Beauty*. One of the pieces is the *Epistle from a Swiss Officer to his Friend at Rome*, presumably the only one of the thirty-four to receive publication.

Of Spence's unpublished poems, the longest and most interesting is a mock-epic entitled *The Charliad* or *Charliade*.[42] As its title suggests, the poem was modeled on *The Dunciad*, and satire forms the basis of the work—satire leveled principally at the typical learned commentator, the author's pet aversion. Four of the men pilloried in *The Dunciad* (Cibber, Dennis, Theobald, and Bentley) are rallied in *The Charliad*, but the satire of Spence is neither so caustic nor so unflagging as that of Pope. The motive of the author is less the desire to wound than the desire to amuse; nonsense is invoked at the outset, and nonsense holds sway throughout. Absurdity is cultivated for its own sake, and Spence exhibits a taste for the ridiculous almost childish in its gusto.

It is impossible to assign a date to the poem, which obviously grew slowly over a long period of years. Underhill concluded "from internal evidence" that it was planned and executed subsequent to the death of Pope,[43] but there is no evidence to point definitely to such a conclusion. In a footnote is mentioned "the present year of our Lord 1731," and the work was probably begun by that time. Further, in the preface Spence describes the chairs of Pope and Swift in the Elysian kingdom as being vacant because their destined occupants are still sojourning on earth. On the other hand, it is probable that he continued to work on the poem during the leisure moments of his later years.

The Charliad begins with a brief "Advertisement to the Reader," followed by half a dozen mottoes "out of which every Man may choose that, which he finds most to his own Fancy." Next comes a lengthy disquisition entitled "Something instead of a Preface." Herein are detailed the particulars of a miraculous journey to the other world made by the hero of the subsequent poem. The fact that this preliminary narrative has nothing whatever to do with the poem proper is simply one of the many incongruities in which the author seems to delight. The hero, fallen into a trance, finds himself conducted through many adventures into the region where the spirits of the "Satyrogelists," or writers of satire, sit in joyful and often bibulous communion. The English worthies who are distinguished by mention include (in order) Tom Brown, Taylor the water-poet, Butler, Dryden, Garth, Pope, Buckingham, Prior, Halifax, and Swift. Pope's chair, explains the supernatural being who acts as guide, is being "kept for a person who, we are told, is the greatest Man now in your World. 'Twas order'd to be set apart for him several centuries ago, for

something[44] that he is to write in the year of our Aera
2611." Swift's chair, also vacant as yet, is placed with
those of Cervantes and Rabelais, and these three writers
are termed by the guide "the Chiefs of all our Society."
The hero recovers from his trance and calls upon all men
to believe what he has so marvelously experienced.

Now follows *The Charliad* itself, "an epic poem," divided
into three cantos and comprising two hundred and forty-
three lines. It begins with a mock invocation to Nonsense
and Mystery. Then are detailed the adventures of the
hero, Charlé, on his journey "from Gothic Isles" to Britain
and his welcome there by Bacchus and the Muses. After
being regaled upon such edibles as "a butter'd Harlequin
with toasted Cheese" and "a salted Laplander well sopt in
sack," the hero is favored with a long-winded and mysti-
fying discourse from Euterpe, whereupon he most discour-
teously falls asleep and is left wrapped "in Madrigals and
Straw." After seventy more lines of even less intelligible
nonsense, the author abruptly desists—none too soon.

Accompanying the poem is an explanatory letter purporting to be from John Dennis to "Lewis Tibbald," with
Theobald's reply, both extravagantly laudatory of *The
Charliad*, "that excellent poem." At the suggestion of Dennis, Theobald willingly undertakes the task of preparing
notes for the masterpiece; hence he is ostensibly the author
of the extensive and nonsensical footnotes, written in the
manner of Scriblerus himself. These lucubrations, which
occupy considerably more space than the poem and were
apparently the principal reason for its composition, are intended to parody the absurdity of dry-as-dusts in hazard-
ing far-fetched and often impossible interpretations of extremely unimportant passages.[45]

CHAPTER V

"Polymetis"

THOUGH during the years following his final return from abroad Spence found time to devote to lesser matters, his chief interest and preoccupation was the completion of the great work of his life, *Polymetis*. The idea of a production which should in some manner relate ancient literature and ancient art had been conceived in his mind at an early date. Possibly its inception occurred as early as 1721, when Addison's *Dialogues upon the Usefulness of Ancient Medals* appeared. Certainly to the theories which such a work would illustrate—though possibly not to the actual evolution of the work itself—Spence had devoted considerable thought prior to the writing of *An Essay on Pope's Odyssey*. In the *Essay* he says, for example, "Were you to give me full scope, I shou'd carry the resemblance between these Arts much farther than it has ever yet been carried: There is scarce a *Figure* or *Manner* in Poetry which I shou'd not imagine to have its tally in the Schools of the Painters."[1] And again: "It was chiefly from *two Poetical Epithets*, that *Phidias* design'd the countenance of his *Olympian Jupiter;* as, in Reverse, we often see the Person in his Epithet, from our being acquainted with some Statue, or Picture, to which it refers: Thus when *Apollo* is call'd the *Archer-God*, it recalls to our memory the representations we have so often seen of that Deity: the compleat Figure is rais'd up in the Mind, by touching upon that single circumstance."[2]

Whenever it was that the idea of a work relating poetry

and the plastic arts first occurred to him, Spence seems not to have begun his collections for the tremendous undertaking until his first visit to Florence in 1732. He strove to make his study as complete and authoritative as the materials available throughout Europe would permit him to make it. On the one hand, during the dozen or more years that the work was in preparation he read painstakingly the works of all the Roman poets from Ennius to Juvenal and of several of the prose writers from Varro to Macrobius, marking or copying out the most striking passages which in any way related to the gods, goddesses, heroes, and other imaginary beings received among the Roman people;[3] on the other hand, he gathered reproductions of the images of the same mythical beings as he found them represented in the art galleries and private collections of Italy, France, and England. The task was enormous. Spence's original design, indeed, had been to include in his discussion not only the allegorical spirits and deities of the ancients but, as Addison had done, many other aspects of Roman life which might be of use "toward making the classics more intelligible";[4] but he soon realized that such an undertaking would tax the powers of the most single-hearted and indefatigable scholar, and with more good sense than ambition he renounced his gigantic plans and restricted his endeavors to a narrower circle.

In preparing himself to discuss with authority "the remains of the antient artists," Spence displayed energy and diligence. His Continental tours enabled him to spend much time in the art centers of the world, and he devoted himself with fervor and persistence to the study and interpretation of the statues, relievos, medals, and gems to be found there. Rome supplied most of his subject matter in this portion of his work, as well as the inspiration for the entire project. The *Anecdotes* are full of references to Rome and its treasures. There he spent part of the year 1732 in company with Lord Middlesex, and he resided there with Lord Lincoln from December, 1740, to May, 1741. He shows familiarity with all the important art galleries, palaces, and gardens of the city, as well as with the private collections of many eminent connoisseurs. Florence ranks next in providing him with illustrations of his theories. There he spent nearly as much time as at Rome, and by his intimate knowledge of the art treasures of the city he proves his diligence and his zeal for his task. "I have paid," asserts Polymetis, his spokesman, "perhaps, a hundred visits to the Venus of Medici in person."[5] In Florence, as in Rome, he cultivated the acquaintance of the leading private collectors of antiques and, as is indicated in the *Anecdotes* and by references in *Polymetis* itself, lived on intimate terms with some of them. Venice and Turin, Versailles and Paris, rendered him further service in his researches. In London he of course had access to such scattered treasures as at that early date had found their way to England: he made use of the possessions of such private collectors as the Earl of Leicester, Lord Middlesex, Lady Betty Germain, and Dr. Richard Mead. If one adds a few medals in Spence's own possession and a number of plates copied from such works on the fine arts as those of Montfaucon,[6] Bartoli,[7] and Rossi,[8] one has catalogued the materials which supplied him not only with the plates and designs for his finished volume but with the background and the chief inspiration for his study.

It is well that Spence decided early to narrow his original extensive scheme and to limit himself to only one division of his vast subject, for even under those conditions he came perilously near to never bringing his work to completion. The ill-health which had almost led him to abandon the project after his return from abroad was not the only deterrent to the vigorous prosecution of his plans. As he drifted further into middle age, he came to yearn for a life unharried by the demands on time and energy involved in the production of such an ambitious work as *Polymetis*. He felt increasingly inclined to settle down in quiet retirement and to prosecute what labors he did undertake for his own amusement. Moreover, in the book itself there are manifest evidences of weariness. The clearest of these occurs toward the close of the work, when the loquacious Polymetis observes to his patient listeners: "You have proved that you have a great deal of patience, in attending me so long; thro' my temple of the Celestial Beings; that of the Constellations; the Beings of the Air; those of the Waters, and these of the Earth. We have now compleated our whole round; and I heartily wish you joy of it: for to say the truth, I begin to be a little tired of my office; as you may very well be, with hearing me."[9] Again, as he launches upon the last dialogue of the series, Polymetis exclaims, "Heaven be praised, we at length begin to come in sight of the shore!"[10]

The scope and much of the contents of *Polymetis* were known to Spence's friends long before the publication of the book. Gray had seen part of it in manuscript at Florence in 1740,[11] and the author had discussed his project with the art critics and collectors with whom he became intimate in Italy. On July 28, 1743, Walpole sent to Dr. Conyers Middleton "a print of a new work coming out by Mr. Spence, of which you must have heard, on the correspondence between the ancient sculptors and poets."[12] Spence had early realized that his work was of too expensive a nature to justify him in running the heavy financial risk involved, and accordingly, following the example of Pope, he issued proposals for publishing by subscription, the price to be one guinea on subscribing and another on receipt of the book. The work was advertised with the stipulation that unless five hundred copies were subscribed for, it would not be put into the press.[13] Well connected as he was, Spence apparently had no difficulty gathering subscriptions, with the result that long before the volume appeared he was assured of a handsome profit. When the work was ultimately published, the list of subscribers was one of which any author might have been proud. It contained 717 names, and since among them the subscribers took 99 extra copies the number of subscription volumes totaled 816. The name of the Prince of Wales headed the list, and among the subscribers were eighteen dukes, forty-five earls, and both archbishops. The Earl of Lincoln, the Earl of Middlesex, and John Morley Trevor each took twelve copies. The roll included such familiar names as those of Mark Akenside, Isaac Hawkins Browne, Lady Betty Germain, James Harris, Nathaniel Hooke, David Hume, Horace Mann, Edward Wortley Montagu, Alexander Pope, James Thomson, Horace Walpole, Daniel Webb, John Wilkes, and Edward Young.[14] The length of the list and the dignity and importance of many of the names therein testify to the extent of Spence's acquaintance among literary and aristocratic circles, to the respect in which he was held there, and probably to his diligence!

With large sums of subscription money collected and with the work long since announced as nearly completed, Spence must have felt increasing embarrassment as publication continued to be delayed. In the *Museum* for April 26, 1746, appeared, in the section devoted to "Literary Memoirs," a detailed account of the contents of the forthcoming production, with an introductory paragraph explaining that though "Mr. Spence has long promis'd the World his Work," the publication had been delayed, and would be "till next Winter," by the tardiness of the artist in executing the plates.[15] This article, though it purported to come "from a particular Friend of the Author's," was written by Spence himself, as is proved by the existence of a draft of the manuscript in his hand among his papers.[16] As if seeking to lessen the annoyance felt by the subscribers, he adds, "however this Delay has occasion'd his making several considerable Additions to the Work: and particulary [sic], four entire Dialogues at the Close of it."[17] This statement is of interest for its indication that the final chapters, criticizing modern artists, poets, and translators for their misuse of allegory, were not a part of the original design. The rest of the article is a concise summary of the content of the projected work.

Polymetis was finally published by Dodsley on February 5, 1747—the price, two and a half guineas.[18] The title-page read, *Polymetis: or, An Enquiry concerning the Agreement*

Between the Works of the Roman Poets, And the Remains of the Antient Artists. Being An Attempt to illustrate them mutually from one another. In Ten Books. By the Rev^d. Mr. Spence. The book made a handsome appearance, extending to 362 folio pages, well printed on good paper, and richly embellished with plates and drawings which, though not excellent, were quite satisfactory. As a frontispiece Spence used the only known portrait of himself, painted by Isaac Whood[19] and specially engraved by George Vertue.[20]

If *Polymetis* is considered as a product of the year 1747 it commands far higher praise than if it is judged by present-day standards, since for the criticism and interpretation of classical art the scholar of the twentieth century is much better equipped than was his fellow of the eighteenth. The multitude of discoveries made by the archeologists of two hundred years would alone be sufficient to establish the superiority of the modern scholar. Hence it is only fair to consider *Polymetis* first against an eighteenth-century background; in estimating its permanent value one must use a different perspective.

Although in his title-page Spence spoke in general terms of a comparison "between the works of the Roman poets and the remains of the antient artists," his researches did not extend so far as that phrase would lead the reader to expect. In his attempt to relate classical art and literature he was forced to restrict himself to "the imaginary beings" of Roman religion, resting content with merely outlining in the final dialogue the task which awaited the scholar who should carry the comparison into all provinces of ancient life and manners. He left his readers in no uncertainty as to the exact purpose of his work. Polymetis thus defines the end which the author wished to attain: "You, Philander, know that my principal view in making this collection was to compare the descriptions and expressions in the Roman poets that any way relate to the imaginary beings, with the works that remain to us of the old artists; and to please myself with the mutual lights they might give each to the other. I have often thought when in Italy, and at

89

Rome in particular, that they enjoy there the convenience of a sort of cotemporary comments on Virgil and Horace, in the nobler remains of the antient statuaries and painters. When you look on the old pictures or sculptures, you look on the works of men who thought much in the same train with the old poets. There was generally the greatest union in their designs: and where they are engaged on the same subjects, they must be the best explainers of one another. As we lie so far north from this last great seat of empire, we are placed out of the reach of consulting these finer remains of antiquity so much, and so frequently, as one could wish. The only way of supplying this defect to any degree among us, is by copies, prints, and drawings: and as I have long had this thought, my collection is at length grown very numerous; and indeed almost as full as I could desire it, as to the point which has all along been my particular aim."[21] His design, then, was to reflect a double light upon the life of Rome—to employ antiques in the interpretation of the ancient authors, particularly the poets, and to study the remains of the artists in the light shed by the classic writers. It should be observed that there is no confusion here between the art of poetry on the one hand and the plastic and pictorial arts on the other. Spence did, indeed, postulate a natural connection among all the polite arts. He placed upon his title-page a statement from Cicero vindicating his belief in such a mutual association: "Omnes artes, quae ad humanitatem pertinent, habent quoddam commune vinculum; & quasi cognatione quâdam inter se continentur."[22] But at least in the original enunciation of his purpose he did not sink into that confusion or identification of the arts for which Lessing was to condemn him so bitterly.[23] He simply maintained the self-evident truth that, since the ancient artists and poets lived in the same civilization, fell into much the same trains of thought, and were frequently employed upon the same or similar subjects, they may often serve to illustrate and explain one another; that, considering poetry, sculpture, and painting to be different ways of expressing the common experiences of humanity, the devotees of one art must of necessity throw light upon the work of contemporary devotees of the other two.

Two stumbling blocks Spence got round as best he could: his failure to concern himself with Greek as well as Latin poets and the awkwardness of the fact that many of the figures of the Roman deities had been formed by Greek artists. The first objection he answered by disclaiming any intention of treating the Greek poets simply because exigencies of time and space prevented such a course. He made no further attempt to defend himself on that score, admitting that *Polymetis* accomplished but a fraction of the labor that was to be done. The second objection he overrode without serious difficulty: almost all of the best statues in Italy had, indeed, been imported from Greece, but through a community of life and thought most of the Grecian deities became, as it were, naturalized in Rome: hence they must be considered illustrative of Roman civilization, where they became firmly intrenched, as well as of native Greek culture.

In the field of investigation which he had selected, Spence considered himself a discoverer—or at least a pioneer. On several occasions he speaks of the difficulties which he has encountered as a consequence of being practically the first writer to engage in a work of this kind. The most explicit and enlightening of these passages occurs in the preface: "Several of the best antient and modern writers have spoke of this connexion [between the arts], in general: but I do not know of any one, that has entered into any particular enquiry in relation to it; except Mr. Addison, in his Treatise on Medals. I wish that gentleman had gone much farther, than he has; or indeed that any one, tho' of much less taste than Mr. Addison, had made a track before me; for I should then have been enabled to find my way thro' so various a subject, with much more ease; and to have made my observations, with much less inaccuracy: but I entered upon it, as one does on a country newly discovered; without any paths made, and generally much embarassed. Had any work of this kind been published, before I went abroad; I could certainly have made this much more perfect, with extremely less pains: whereas all I can beg for it now is, that the difficulty of making one's way almost every where, may be duly considered; and that the many imperfections and errors which that must occasion, may meet with the indulgence that the case deserves."[24]

Spence concedes a claim to priority in the field, then, to only one work— Addison's *Dialogues upon the Usefulness of Ancient Medals*. Since he was beyond doubt more indebted to Addison than to any other author and since he candidly acknowledged that indebtedness, he could derive no possible advantage from denying obligations to other sources, if such there were; hence it is reasonable to accept his assertion that, so far as he was aware, Addison alone had attempted the subject before him. He observes, further, that Addison "seems rather to have only sailed along the coasts, than to have entered at all into the country."[25] But though this statement is true, Spence was more obliged to the *Dialogues upon the Usefulness of Ancient Medals* than his remark would lead one to believe. Entirely aside from the matter of the form into which he cast his work, he owed much to his eminent predecessor. It is difficult not to believe that the *Dialogues* sowed in his mind the seed of *Polymetis*. They almost certainly suggested the design of illustrating the works of the poets by means of the relics of ancient art. Addison devoted the second of his three dialogues to a comparison between the medalists and the poets in their respective delineations of the human virtues, their metaphorical emblems and compliments to the emperors, and their allegorical representation of nations, cities, and provinces. The work as a whole, though it does but "skirt the coasts" of the unexplored region, anticipated Spence in several important respects. Addison sustained the theory that there is a marked affinity between coins and poetry; that a medal may frequently clear up a passage in an old poet and that the poet may unriddle the devices on a medal; that since poetry is in some respects an art of designing as well as painting and sculpture are, the three may provide effective commentaries upon one another. Spence simply extended Addison's theories from medals alone to all the remains of ancient art, limited his investigation to the imaginary beings of the Romans and to the Roman poets,[26] and found his main design for *Polymetis* complete.

To the influence and example of Addison must also be ascribed significant features relating to the form and style of Spence's work. The similarity which first strikes the attention lies, of course, in Spence's use of the dialogue form. In this particular perhaps he borrowed more from his own *Essay on Pope's Odyssey* than from the *Dialogues*, but for the form of that essay itself he had been largely obliged to Addison; so that at least indirectly the *Dialogues* influenced his design. Moreover, in the setting for the conversations, in the personalities of the speakers, in the attempt to enliven the discourse with the spice of humor, in the expression of scorn for the narrowness and blundering stupidity of scholarly commentators, the *Dialogues* and *Polymetis* are so similar as to provide convincing evidence of borrowing on Spence's part. Finally, in Addison's raillery at modern medalists for dressing a king of England like Julius Caesar and for employing devices which have long since lost their metaphorical significance lies the germ of Spence's diatribe concerning "the defects of modern allegories."[27]

Undue importance, however, should not be attached to Addison's example. Spence developed the theories of the *Dialogues upon Medals* in directions unthought of by their author; for his illustrations both graphic and literary he himself was entirely responsible; and he fused with his main discourse a vein of poetic and artistic criticism which is wanting in Addison's work and which broadens the subject matter of *Polymetis* considerably beyond the narrower limits of the *Dialogues*. Further, Spence did not regard Addison as an authority to be followed without question or occasional opposition. He even distrusted his predecessor's interpretation of those medals to the study of which he had confined himself; for Signor Ficoroni, a talented Italian medalist and connoisseur, had confided to Spence at Rome: "Mr. Addison did not go into any depth in the study of medals: all the knowledge he had of that kind, I believe, he had from me; and I did not give him above twenty lessons upon that subject."[28] Indeed, it is clear that Spence considered Addison as an amateur rather than as an authority, and that he looked upon himself as the explorer of uncharted territory barely discovered in the *Dialogues*.

As for other possible sources for *Polymetis*, Spence seems to have been justified in claiming originality except for the example of Addison. To be sure, he drew upon such weighty compendia as those of Montfaucon, Graevius,[29] and Gronovius,[30] but only for occasional assistance in the assembling of his illustrative materials. Montfaucon, indeed, he criticizes on several occasions for the impracticable breadth of his design and for his irregular and faulty execution of it, as well as for his confusion of figures belonging to one category with those belonging to another.[31] Though Spence refers in his notes to a multitude of volumes treating of ancient art and poetry, his references reveal rather a wide acquaintance with literature of that type than a direct indebtedness to any one work or set of works. But in any attempt to determine the extent of his indebtedness to the inspiration of other minds there is one person to be taken into account—Alexander Pope. The poet had greeted the appearance of Addison's *Dialogues* with a tribute, entitled *To Mr. Addison, Occasioned by his Dialogues on Medals*, which supplied one motto for the title-page of *Polymetis*;[32] his *Epistle to Jervas* supplied another;[33] and his interest in the relationship among what he styled the "sister arts" of poetry, painting, and sculpture may well have impelled the pliant Spence to the studies which culminated in *Polymetis*. Assuredly, Pope furnished hints for certain details. One of his remarks quoted in the *Anecdotes*—"Virgil's great judgment appears in putting things together, and in his picking gold out of the dunghills of the old Roman writers"[34]—seems to be the source of what Spence has to say of Virgil's extensive borrowings.[35] Again, Pope appears to have been responsible for Spence's discussion of the absurdities of a too literal and frivolous interpretation of classic authors as illustrated by Otho Vaenius in his *Emblemata*.[36] That Pope directly proposed the idea of such a work as *Polymetis* is doubtful, but it would be strange if an intimate association of years with a man interested in the interrelation of poetry and the fine arts had no effect upon Spence—perhaps in more ways than appear on the surface.

For the rest, Spence had an intimate knowledge of a host of English and French treatises upon the fine arts and aesthetics in general, and though no one of the works in question deals with the precise subject of his book, he must have derived from them occasional suggestions. It is impossible to define exactly the limits of his indebtedness. It seems to be no more extensive than might be expected in the work of a man who has read widely on his subject and devoted thought to what he has read. He evidently knew both Dufresnoy and De Piles[37]—at least in the translation by Dryden, and Dryden's own preface had some effect upon his thought. Shaftesbury's *Characteristics* (1711) he had read and admired, and Addison's *Remarks on Several Parts of Italy* (1705) and the famous papers on aesthetics in the *Spectator*[38] probably increased his obligations to the author of the *Dialogues upon Medals*. Félibien[39] and Du Bos[40] may have had a share in the development of certain of Spence's ideas. The aesthetic treatise of the English James Harris,[41] though published three years before *Polymetis*, appeared at a time when Spence's work was practically completed and could have exerted little influence upon it.[42]

In assembling his materials, Spence adhered rigidly to the systematic program which he had mapped out. A thorough reading of all the Latin poets from Ennius through Juvenal and the works of certain prose writers provided him with a host of passages relating to the deities and other imaginary beings associated with Roman religion; his extensive travels, his keen interest in art treasures, and his colloquies with the connoisseurs of three nations supplied him with an equally copious body of illustrative material from the remains of the artists of antiquity. It remained to organize the information, to provide for the graphic illustrations of his book, and to weld the whole into a convincing proof of his original thesis—that the literature and the pictorial and plastic arts of the Romans may serve as the best possible commentary upon each other.

Spence selected the dialogue form as the best for his purpose. This form was, of course, highly popular in the seventeenth and eighteenth centuries in both England and France; but aside from the example of Addison, perhaps the chief reason for the choice was Spence's conviction that through the dialogue he might best achieve his primary aim—the just mingling of instruction with entertainment, the avoidance of that sullenness and severity which he felt too often accompanied contemporary studies of criticism and scholarship. In this attempt he considered himself a follower in the steps of Socrates, Horace, and the writers of the *Spectator*; and he speaks complacently, though with modesty, of his efforts to emulate their eminent example.[43] Moreover, by employing the dialogue form he hoped to avoid all appearance of arrogance, to unite the subdivisions of his work through connecting links of conversation, and to justify himself in the use of an easy, colloquial style rather than the stiff diction of formal discourse.

Spence could always write workman-like prose; on occasion he could even write stately or melodious prose; and in *Polymetis* his style is very pleasant. He had not, indeed, the imagination necessary to breathe life into the dead past, to carry readers back to the noisy Forum and let them perceive for themselves how the Romans thought and felt and acted: his statues are statues still. He had neither the skill to endow the actors in his quiet drama with distinct characters nor the power to convince the reader with a lightning flash of true insight. But his were the talents which make a pleasant companion or a composer of charming letters—urbanity, ease in writing, a graceful way of turning phrases, a faculty of drawing the reader into his confidence, transparency of meaning, and withal a trick of allowing his own genial good nature to show through the veil of his discourse.

Spence did not intend *Polymetis* to serve solely as an introduction to the comparative study of Roman art and letters; he cherished the design of blending a trenchant literary and aesthetic criticism with the execution of his primary undertaking. For this purpose he introduced chapters dealing solely with the history of Latin poetry, and others concerned with the comparative merits of ancient and modern artists and poets in their treatment of allegorical subjects.[44] So it is as a work of criticism as well as of classical research that the production upon which Spence hopefully rested his claim to literary immortality must be regarded.

Polymetis is divided into ten books, which are further subdivided into twenty-one dialogues. The author speaks through the medium of Polymetis, a gentleman "well known for his taste in the polite arts," who pilots his patient friends Philander and Mysagetes[45] through the temples in his gardens where he has housed his extensive collection of statues, bas-reliefs, medals, gems, and engravings. The conversation drifts to the erudite host's favorite topic— the aid rendered by these relics of antiquity in the study of the classic poets—and is conducted within that sphere, with occasional interruptions, throughout the whole of the book. By this device of an ordered progress, after the manner of students in a museum, through the shrines devoted to the different classes of Roman deities, Spence establishes a natural sequence for his discourse. He makes no statements in his own person, allowing the three companions to carry on the discussion without intrusion, and he never grows confused in his effort to make the book a series of dramatic dialogues instead of the exposition of the views of a single writer.

An important element in *Polymetis* is the helps with which

Spence has provided those of his readers who wish to do more than peruse the polite and instructive observations of the amiable friends. These are, first, detailed and scholarly footnotes in which the author, speaking now in his own person, elaborates the theories of the text, cites illustrative material from the classic writers and the confirming or dissenting opinions of contemporary scholars, discourses upon ancient painting and sculpture, explains difficult points in the mythology of the Latin poets, and chats entertainingly in the role of the experienced traveler who in the course of his wanderings has snapped up a host of unconsidered but interesting trifles. Moreover, there are complete indexes of all the "antiques" of which copies were inserted in the work, of the various representations of each imaginary figure, and of the passages in the Latin poets which might receive light from what was said in the course of the discussion.

In any work dealing with the fine arts, the graphic illustrations, of course, have much to do with the success and value of the production. In this respect Spence merits both praise and blame. He spared no effort to make the illustrations as complete and as helpful as possible; and his choice of materials was excellent for the purpose of exemplifying his statements by references to appropriate statues or medals. He took a justifiable pride in the care which he had exerted to make this part of his work valuable.[46] But the engraver whom he employed to copy the chosen works, Louis Pierre Boitard,[47] carried out his important assignment in what was generally considered to be a disappointing way.[48] The difficulties in the way of an accurate representation, however, were very great in Spence's day, and the beauty and exactness of the copies of ancient masterpieces found in modern works of this kind are naturally not to be expected in *Polymetis*.

Spence launches his work with an introductory book in which he first outlines the general design which he proposes to follow and then sketches the rise and fall of the poetic and the pictorial and plastic arts at Rome. To his survey of Latin poetry he devotes three dialogues—the first covering the poets from the beginning of Latin culture until the Augustan age, the second tracing those of the Augustan age itself, and the third tracing the gradual decline of poetic genius down to the time of Juvenal. The survey amounts to a concise history of Latin poetry. Spence's wide reading and his experience in Oxford lecture halls here stood him in good stead; not only does he show a thorough knowledge of the poets, but what he says in criticism of them is judicious and enlightening. His discussion of "the introduction, improvement, and fall" of the fine arts is confined to one dialogue and is considerably shorter than his treatment of the poetry—partly because there was less to be said on the subject, partly because he undoubtedly felt less at home here.

After this preliminary book of introduction and preparation begins the systematic survey of the "imaginary beings" of the Romans as represented by both poet and artist. Spence by no means cherished an ambition to revolutionize the study of ancient art and literature by the discoveries which he had made in the course of his investigations. Polymetis warns his expectant friends not to hope that every story told in marble or on a coin will explain the meaning of a poetical passage or that every sculptured image can be illuminated by light from a poetical source; he believes, rather, that the chief use of such a study as his is not so much the discovery of what lies hidden from the sight of men as the strengthening and beautifying of what they already know. His subject is the remains of classical art depicting the objects of religious veneration, especially as those remains may illustrate or be illustrated by the writings of the poets; but if he can trace no such interrelation in a given case, he by no means loses interest in the subject, for his heart is set not upon proving a hypothesis but upon understanding and appreciating the beauty inherited from Latin civilization.

Polymetis first discourses at some length upon the twelve great celestial deities of the Roman hierarchy—

Jupiter, Juno, Minerva, Neptune, Venus, Mars, Vulcan, Vesta, Apollo, Diana, Ceres, and Mercury. Then follows a discussion of the heroes whom the Romans supposed to have been received into the higher heavens and of the deities thought to preside over the virtues of men and the conduct of human life. In connection with this subject Spence took the opportunity to honor his friend Lowth by inserting that prelate's moral poem *The Choice of Hercules*.[49] Finally, after treating of the constellations, the planets, and the times and seasons, Polymetis brings to a close the central portion of his discourse by discussions of the deities and inhabitants of the air, the waters, the earth, and the lower world.

The concluding book of *Polymetis* is of more importance in connection with English literature—and perhaps more far-reaching in its influence—than any which precede it. According to Spence's article in the *Museum*,[50] four of its five dialogues were an afterthought, having been composed and appended while the plates for the book were being prepared. The dialogue headed "Of the Use of this sort of Enquiries, in general" repeats what Spence had said elsewhere concerning the utility of "antiques" in presenting to the eye a graphic picture of what the poets present to the mind and the assistance rendered by ancient authors in the interpretation of many of the sculptured remains of antiquity. He cites as a conclusive instance of the latter virtue the fact that the meaning of the magnificent Laocoön group would be unknown to us were it not for what Virgil and other Latin writers have said on the subject.[51] From this discussion it is but a step to the consideration of the exertions and the limitations of modern commentators upon the Latin poets. Spence derives enjoyment from the hits which he makes against a certain type of erudite but narrow critic.[52] He himself was a close and diligent student of the poets, but he pleads for clearness, conciseness, and simplicity as opposed to the labored display of superfluous erudition which so often goes wide of the mark. The universal use in schools of textbooks embodying two pages of learned comment for every page of text incites him to a spirited assault upon contemporary methods of education in England. To require an English youth to compose verses and deliver orations in Latin at the cost of an almost total neglect of training in his own language, to force an embryo lawyer or naval officer to become a classical scholar and a Latin poet, seems to Spence to be founding education upon a colossal blunder. Coming from a staunch Winchester and Oxford man, a former professor of poetry, and a devoted lover of Greek and Latin studies, this charge must have appeared of particular cogency to those of his contemporaries interested in education.

Turning at this point from the consideration of the allegorical fancies of the ancients to those of the moderns, Spence falls into criticism of the confusion and darkness which too commonly invest the allegories of modern artists and poets. Whereas the ancients universally expressed their meaning directly and by a single circumstance, the moderns frequently leave the observer in serious doubt as to their meaning. He instances his argument, first, by exposing the obscurity and occasional absurdity of two books intended as guides to the worker in allegorical subjects— the *Iconologia* of Ripa[53] and the *Emblemata* of Vaenius.[54] Next he cites the improprieties of modern painters in this respect, dwelling in particular upon Rubens but chiding also Dominiquin and even Raphael. The only remedy for this defect of modern art, opines Spence, is an immediate return on the part of the artists to the study of those who can best instruct them on this and other points—the ancients. Moreover, the artists are not alone in their failing. Indeed, the poets stand even more in need of a return to the contemplation of the regular and systematic treatment of allegory among the ancients. Even a poet of the loftiest genius and the best allegorist among modern writers— Spenser—may serve as a text to illustrate the errors of modern poets in this respect.[55] That poet's faults fall under three general heads—those which arise (1) from a confusion between the fables of heathenism and the truths of

Christianity, (2) from a misrepresentation of the allegories of the ancients, and (3) from something that is amiss in the allegories of his own contrivance. Of the first two types Spence has little to say, but he cites many just instances of the third. His complaints, though he may sometimes seem to be spurning at straws, are usually reasonable, but he by no means falls into the error of disregarding the beauty and the splendor of the *Faerie Queene* because of the obvious defects of Spenser's allegories; on the contrary, he expresses the warmest admiration for the poet and points out his inaccuracies solely because the fact that even the greatest modern allegorist errs so grossly testifies to the need for a speedy return on the part of poets to the study of the classic authors.[56] In this need they share with a class of writers who above all others should be familiar with the allegories of the Latin poets—the translators. For the exemplar of the defects of this class Spence chooses Dryden in his translation of Virgil, though he expresses great admiration for the translator himself, as he had done for Spenser, and professes to have chosen this work for the object of his critical attacks only because of its pre-eminence in the field. His principal quarrel with translators of the classics as represented by Dryden is that they grossly misrepresent the personages, dress, and mental attributes of allegorical figures, they mix natural and allegorical ways of speaking, they are insufficiently acquainted with the character and rank of the various deities, and, worst of all, they misunderstand the real intent and design of allegory as practiced by the Romans.

In a brief final dialogue Spence describes the manner in which an inquiry of the type conducted in *Polymetis* might profitably be extended to include many aspects of Roman life other than the narrow phase with which he himself had dealt. He expresses no desire, however, to carry the investigation further on his own account, realizing, he says, that the task is "too much for any one man, (at least, for such an one as I am,) to compleat it in its full extent."[57] And he seems to lay down his pen with relief.

Polymetis won immediate recognition among a limited class of readers. During the years following upon its publication the work was "the ornament of every choice library."[58] The large number of subscribers prominent in literary and aristocratic circles proves that Spence's long-heralded production won its way into the homes of many of the intellectual and social leaders of England, while it was bound to find a welcome among all readers interested in fine arts—whether in England or on the Continent. Spence had accomplished his design of mingling instruction with entertainment in such a way as to interest the average man who had no intimate knowledge of the subject matter. None felt inclined to criticize the style and execution of the work; with the exception of Gray, none found fault with the author's scholarship. Almost the only objections to *Polymetis* voiced within the few decades after its appearance were those of Lessing, leveled rather at certain of Spence's theories than at his conduct and management of the work.

Polymetis proved sufficiently successful to justify a second edition in 1755 and a third in 1774.[59] Singer wrote in 1819, "I believe it is not many years since, that it was thought a fourth edition might be acceptable to the public."[60] In 1764 an abridgment for use in schools was made by Nicholas Tindal.[61] This abridged version proved so popular that it passed through six editions between 1764 and 1802 and was only gradually superseded by Lemprière's *Classical Dictionary* (1788). Spence's original work was translated into German in 1773–76 in two octavo volumes.[62] Various portions of it have been reprinted—the dissertation upon Spenser's allegories in John Bell's *The Poets of Great Britain*;[63] Dialogue III, on the political character of the *Aeneid*, in *Miscellanea Virgiliana*;[64] the dialogues on Roman poetry and fine art as a separate volume in 1823;[65] and twenty pages of selections in the *Elegant Extracts* of Vicesimus Knox.[66]

The publication of *Polymetis* caused no excitement in the literary world. It was not the type of work to arouse either extravagant admiration or virulent opposition. Dodsley gave it encouragement in the *Museum* by printing a series of three articles upon it,[67] the first appearing as early as February 14, in the first issue following the publication of the book. The writer of the articles gives a detailed summary of the contents of each dialogue, commending Spence throughout but making little effort to draw attention to either the "beauties" or the "blemishes" of the work. After repeating Spence's suggestions to future scholars for completing the inquiry in several divisions, he concludes with this flattering tribute: "One only of these Divisions, would be a Work sufficient for one Author; at least, to execute it with that extensive Learning, Justness of Taste, and happy Clearness, for which the Work before us is so truly remarkable."[68] Shenstone, who had not been a subscriber,[69] received a copy of the book as a "genteel" present from a friend. He had known of Spence's intention to introduce Lowth's *Choice of Hercules* into the work, and since he had written a poem on the same theme, he was particularly interested in the manner in which Spence had managed the introduction.[70] Walpole, who had probably read part of *Polymetis* in manuscript, subscribed for five copies and evinced a lively interest in the publication of the book. One of his extra copies he sent to Gray, who returned thanks by letter and engaged in extensive comment therein upon Spence's work.[71] Though he confesses, almost grudgingly, that the attractive appearance of the book inclines him to regard it with more favor than he had been willing to accord to the half-finished manuscript which he had seen at Florence,[72] he takes vigorous exception to Spence's total neglect of the Greek poets—which neglect he terms the "one fundamental Fault, from whence most of the little Faults throughout the whole arise."[73] He lets fall an insinuation that Spence's decision to restrict his studies to the Latin poets alone was due to the scantiness of his knowledge of Greek language and literature. He avers further not only that the volume is what Spence admits it to be—rather a beginning than a completed work—

but that it is "a Beginning at the wrong End."[74] In conclusion he serves up for Walpole's delectation a few mistakes in matters of detail which afford him opportunity to
cast discredit upon Spence's scholarship.[75] There is no
denying that Gray's chief objection is a valid one; *Polymetis* would have been a much more valuable work if the
author had gone for his exemplifications to the Greek
poets—the fountainhead of Roman mythology. But, on
the other hand, it seems hardly fair to criticize a man for
not doing what he frankly apologizes for neglecting.
Lowth expressed resentment against Gray in a letter to
John Nichols in 1782, observing that the poet criticized
Spence for not performing "what he never undertook; nay,
what he expressly declared that he did not undertake."[76]
Lowth held a high opinion of *Polymetis*—a judgment possibly swayed by his attachment to the author. In a note to
his twelfth praelection on Hebrew poetry (1753) he wrote:
"Haec autem vide accurate et scienter explicata a Viro
Doctissimo *Josepho* Spence in Opere erudito juxta atque
eleganti cui titulus *Polymetis. . . .*"[77] At Spence's request
he carried several copies of the book with him into Italy in
1749—they must have formed a burdensome article of
luggage—and presented them to various friends of the
author there. He reported to Spence that one of these
friends, Signor Camillo Paderni, had been so much pleased
with the work that he had presented it to the King of
Naples "as an Example proper to be follow'd for the beauty
of the Paper, Impression &c. in the Work which they are
now going to put to the press."[78] Joseph Warton was another friend who thought highly of *Polymetis*. He made extensive use of it in his edition of Virgil (1753) and was
moved by Spence's criticism of Dryden to employ Pitt's
version of the *Aeneid* rather than that of the older and
more famous poet.[79] Edward Gibbon, who had condemned
the *Essay on Pope's Odyssey*,[80] shared the admiration of
Lowth and Warton for their friend's later work. In remarks to the reader of his *Essai sur l'Étude de la Littérature*
(1759) he observes: "Je ne suis point entré dans la carrière

immense des beaux-arts, des beautés qu'ils empruntent de la littérature, et de celles qu'ils lui rendent. Que ne suis-je un Caylus ou un Spence!" Then at Spence's name he adds a footnote: "Auteur d'un ouvrage nommé Polymetis. La mythologie des poëtes y est combinée avec celle des sculpteurs. Cet ouvrage plein de goût et de savoir mériteroit d'être plus connu en France."[81]

Nicholas Tindal, the abridger and to a large extent the popularizer of *Polymetis*, was naturally anxious to put the work in a good light, but his claims for his version of "this valuable treasure of classical learning" are nevertheless of interest: "In short, by studying this compendium, the reader may learn the rise, growth, and fall of the polite arts among the Romans—the just characters of the Latin poets, and their works—the figures and other appearances of their deities—He may gain a true notion of the allegories of the ancients, and of their machinery, or the interposition of the gods—consequently he may acquire a true taste of the beauties of poetry, painting, and sculpture, and be enabled to judge of the propriety and impropriety of the modern allegories, and the excellencies and defects of our authors, translators, and artists."[82]

Upon the genesis of a critical document extremely important for the subsequent literature of western Europe— the *Laokoon* of Lessing—*Polymetis* had a vital influence. True, that influence was negative, in that Spence provided Lessing with hypotheses for contradiction and spirited opposition, but it was nonetheless important. The historian of the Society of Dilettanti took pride in the fact that a treatise by a member of that brotherhood "had the good fortune to act upon the general mind and culture of Europe, producing effects out of proportion to any critical or scientific value of its own."[83] This observation shadows forth one of the perils to which Spence was exposed by unwittingly furnishing a target for the attacks of a greater man than himself: his work came to be considered of interest less for itself than for the onslaught made upon it by Lessing, and many readers were destined to know it only at second hand—and very imperfectly—through *Laokoon*. Such notoriety, the cynical may suggest, is preferable to oblivion. But there was a yet greater danger to Spence lurking in Lessing's use of *Polymetis*. The German was by nature a controversialist. His favorite method was dialectic, the evolution of true principles in the course of an assault upon the false. Consequently, he was frequently led to be unjust to his opponents, whose cause he could present as he willed. This is what happened in the case of Spence. *Polymetis* doubtless merited many of the critical shafts which are leveled at it in *Laokoon*, but the work would have fared much better had Lessing not allowed zeal for his own emancipatory ideas to warp his judgment of the case of his opponent.

Lessing has no quarrel with Spence's main thesis that the remains of ancient poetry and of ancient art may be mutually and helpfully illustrative; but he objects to the narrow blindness which, he asserts, carried the English writer to absurd lengths in the application of his theories: "Diese Uebereinstimmungen können bey zeitverwandten Künstlern und Dichtern, über Dinge, welche nicht mehr vorhanden sind, zu wechselsweisen Erläuterungen führen; allein dergleichen Erläuterungen dadurch aufzustutzen suchen, dass man aus dem Zufalle Vorsatz macht, und besonders dem Poeten bey jeder Kleinigkeit ein Augenmerk auf diese Statue, oder auf jenes Gemählde andichtet, heisst ihm einen sehr zweydeutigen Dienst erweisen. Und nicht allein ihm, sondern auch dem Leser, dem man die schönste Stelle dadurch, wenn Gott will, sehr deutlich, aber auch trefflich frostig macht."[84] He accords to Spence a considerable measure of praise both for his learning and for the worthiness of his design: "Spence schrieb seinen Polymetis mit vieler klassischen Gelehrsamkeit, und in einer sehr vertrauten Bekanntschaft mit den übergebliebenen Werken der alten Kunst. Seinen Vorsatz, aus diesen die römischen Dichter zu erklären, und aus den Dichtern hinwiederum Aufschlüsse für noch unerklärte alte Kunstwerke herzuhohlen, hat er öfters glücklich erreicht."[85] But because Spence, according to Lessing, seeks behind every trifling stroke of the poet a reference to some work of art, his book "für jeden Leser von Geschmack ein ganz unerträgliches Buch seyn muss."[86] Lessing concedes that in many instances Spence has been of service in explaining difficult passages in the poets or interpreting perplexing figures in statues or on medals, but he rebels at the suggestion that Tibullus must have had a picture in mind when he described the loveliness of Apollo,[87] that Statius in his description of Vulcan needed a picture to tell him that labor wearies and heat reddens,[88] that Virgil's beautiful account of a river overflowing its banks and tearing down the bridge that spans it had reference to some work of art wherein the river god was represented as actually demolishing the bridge.[89] He ridicules Spence for believing poetry and painting to have been so closely connected in classic times as to go hand in hand, the poet and the painter never losing sight of each other, and for seeking ingenious explanations of incongruities in the representations of various deities in poetry, on the one hand, and in painting or sculpture, on the other. Such a disagreement is found in the depiction of the muses, where Spence thinks it odd that the allegorical devices employed by the artist to distinguish the muses from each other do not appear in the poets—forgetting that poetry is not restricted to the dumb language of the canvas and the marble.[90]

Spence cannot be defended against certain thrusts of Lessing's rapier. He did go too far in mechanically attributing to the example of works of painting and sculpture many of the simplest and most inevitable details in the descriptions of the poets. He was at fault in ignoring "dass die Poesie die weitere Kunst ist; dass ihr Schönheiten zu Gebothe stehen, welche die Mahlerei nicht zu erreichen vermag; dass sie öfters Ursachen haben kann, die unmahlerischen Schönheiten den mahlerischen vorzuziehen."[91] But, as Irving Babbitt says of all the authors pilloried in *Laokoon*, "At the same time, if we study these writers directly, we shall be surprised to find how much more sensible they are than we should ever suppose from Lessing's attacks."[92] And Spence presents a much better appearance between the covers of his own book than he does in the pages of *Laokoon*. He by no means identifies painting and poetry so fully as Lessing charged. The original proposition from which he started was no more than that poets should be read and studied with an eye to the realities of life which surround them and by which their works may be vividly illustrated. He is not so unimaginative as to expect the poets to describe Urania, for instance, always with wand in hand and the heavenly globe before her, which is the notion Lessing attributes to him.[93] Of the description of Apollo by Tibullus,[94] he observes merely that in it he suspects the poet of having borrowed several pictorial elements from some work of art. Moreover, he concedes to the poet the power to do one thing not within the power of the artist: to imitate the transitoriness of motion —precisely the thing which Lessing maintains for him.[95] Spence's dictum on the eyes and look of Venus contradicts Lessing's assertion that he possessed no conception of the wider and nobler potentialities of poetry as compared with sculpture and painting: "The sculptor can only give you the proportions of things, and one single attitude of a person in any one statue or relievo. The painter can do the same, and add the natural colours as they appear on the surfaces of things; and by the management of lights and shades, may fling them into their proper distances. The poet can describe all that either of the others express by shape, or colours; and can farther put the figure into a succession of different motions in the same description. So that of the three sister-arts of imitation, poetry (in this at least) has the advantage over both the others; as it has more power, and can take a larger compass than either of them. This must have given the poets an advantage, in describing the quick and uncertain motions of Venus's eyes; and occasions our meeting with some expressions in them, which cannot be explained either from statues, or paintings."[96] In view of this passage it is interesting to speculate upon what Spence thought or would have thought of *Laokoon*, which appeared two years before his death but which he may never have seen. In spite of Polymetis' statement that "scarce any thing can be good in a poetical description; which would appear absurd, if represented in a statue, or picture,"[97] it seems certain that if Lessing and Spence could have discussed the latter's theories together, the German would have found the Englishman much more in accord with the ideas of *Laokoon* than a reader of that work would suspect.

After the death of its author, *Polymetis* sank gradually into the oblivion which was its destiny. The decline, however, was by no means sudden. In 1766 Lessing had referred to the book as a famous English work,[98] and not many years later a German edition and a third English edition were published. Further, the abridgment by Tindal continued to find wide acceptance as a textbook. But the ultimate result was inevitable. By the early part of the next century an interested observer could say, "In regard to Spence's Polymetis, I can only say, that it was thought the name of the Author would have supported it. But it has sunk by its own weight; and, I will venture to add, will never rise again. That and Jortin's Erasmus were two books that (I know not how) will be lost to posterity, though the writers themselves had much merit."[99]

Readers of the last century and a half have for the most part been content to let Spence's work rest undisturbed. There was at least one important exception, however, in the person of John Keats. During at least one period of the future poet's youth, *Polymetis* was among the books which were for him "constantly recurrent sources of attraction,"[100] and a number of scholars "have called attention to specific correspondences between lines from Keats and passages or engravings in the *Polymetis*."[101]

William Goodhugh cast another dissenting vote against the popular judgment in his *Library Manual* (1827), when he asked: "Where can be found compositions uniting the politeness of the gentleman with the attainments of the

scholar, blended in juster proportions, than in the Polymetis of Spence, the Athenian letters, the Dialogues of
Lord Lyttelton and Bishop Hurd, and the papers of the
Adventurer and the Observer?"[102] Vicesimus Knox, too,
believed that the work deserved a better fate.[103] But these
were voices crying in the wilderness. The attitude of nine-
teenth-century scholarship in general is not unfairly
summed up by the curt reference to *Polymetis* in Von Müller's monumental *Handbuch der klassischen Altertums-
Wissenschaft*, where the writer[104] mentions Spence's attempt at aesthetic appreciation of ancient art "durch
seinen allerdings unzureichenden Versuch, einen Zusam-
menhang der Kunstwerke mit den Dichtern nachzuweisen
... der dadurch misslang, dass nur römische Dichter
herangezogen und die Grenzen beider Gattungen nicht
scharf gezogen wurden."[105]

Two modern scholars—Irving Babbitt[106] and, more especially, W. G. Howard[107]—believe that Spence has been
handled too roughly by Lessing and his followers and that
Polymetis possesses far more merit than is generally realized. Saintsbury accords the book a measure of usefulness,[108] while Seccombe sees in it an important indication
of a powerful revival of curiosity in the remote past just as
Hurd's *Letters on Chivalry and Romance* (1762) were later
to give impetus to an interest in the Middle Ages.[109]

To pass final judgment upon *Polymetis* is difficult. The
neglect which the book has suffered offers silent testimony
that the world has considered it of little permanent value,
but there is no doubt that it was the most significant of a
large number of not unimportant eighteenth-century
treatises which developed a detailed parallelism between
poetry and the pictorial and plastic arts, assuming their
standards to be more or less interchangeable. Such Lessing
proved Spence's work to be when he selected it for attack
in *Laokoon*, and, as such, *Polymetis* possesses historical
importance. Spence's fundamental idea—that of illustrating the ancient poets and artists by the light which they
unquestionably shed upon each other—was shrewd and

useful enough; he brought to his work a wide knowledge both of Latin poetry and of the remains of ancient art known in his day; his judgment, both literary and artistic, is usually unexceptionable; and he presented the results of his investigation in a graceful, easy style. In many ways his achievement was a considerable one. On the other hand, regarding *Polymetis* from the point of view of the twentieth-century scholar, in the light of the archeological discoveries and the advancement in archeological science made during the last two centuries, one finds Spence's work inadequate. To the two chief weaknesses pointed out by his contemporaries—neglect of the Greek poets and confusion of the arts—must be added others. He could not, of course, take into consideration the art treasures which, unknown to his generation, still lay buried in the earth. But more serious is the charge that he made no inquiry as to the age of a work; that he did not recognize ancient art as a result of the gradual development of successive types which more or less fully represent successive periods of national culture and thought; that he made no distinction between schools or between types of art—one antique, whether painting, statue, frieze, gem, or coin, was as good as another for his design of illustration. And it is for such reasons rather than for those voiced by Lessing that *Polymetis* is destined "never to rise again."

CHAPTER VI
At Byfleet

WITH the death of Pope and the publication of *Polymetis*, two of the most engrossing interests of Spence's life came to an end. Though Spence was to live for more than twenty years longer, there is nothing in his later career to give the focus provided earlier by his association with the poet and his protracted studies for *Polymetis*. It is true that he continued to interest himself in the manuscript records which were later to become the *Anecdotes*, and repeatedly sought confirmation of various entries from persons in a position to supply it; but the fact that Warburton had pre-empted the field of Pope biography must have lessened Spence's interest in his own materials. He seems to have arrived early at the conclusion that they should be published posthumously if at all.

The remainder of his life Spence filled with a happy pursuit of his hobby of gardening, with unremitting activity in behalf of indigent and deserving acquaintances, with a series of minor writings, and with the cultivation of a host of friendships in literary and aristocratic circles.[1] At this turning point in his career came a change in residence from London to the country. Rolle explains the step thus: ". . . in due time, his taste for the Country & for Natural Beauties strongly returning, he thought of purchasing a few acres of ground, & a small House Somewhere in the Country.

"Upon mentioning this intention to his great Friend Ld Lincoln casually only; He very generously offered him such a House at Byfleet in Surry, &, wch was a great addition indeed to its value, near his Lordships own Seat at Oatlands."

Spence gave a more detailed account to Massingberd in a letter of April 14, 1748, and was moved to philosophical reflections upon the occasion: "Some weeks ago, I was saying to Ld Lincoln, that as I had got a little money by my book, I had a great mind to buy a little House with a great Garden, & a few acres of Meadow Ground about it; to plant, live there in ye Summer, & come to Lodgings here when I had a mind to it in the Winter. He told me directly, that he was very glad I had mention'd it to him; because he c^d save my laying out any money that way: having an empty house, within two mile of Oatlands (his own seat) with about an acre of Garden Ground, & five of Meadow laying all round ye Garden; that he s^d be glad to have us so near him, & that it was much at my service. The name of the place is Byfleet; as rural as anything in Yorkshire, (for I went last week with his L^p to see it,) at the hither end of a little village; two mile from the Thames; but on the River Wye, wch is navigable to it. Next month, I am to carry my Mother & Cosin to see it; & if they like it as well as I do, the next Spring I suppose we shall move, (with our Bag & Baggage) to this little Retirement. You see I am so far from thinking of Bishopricks, that I am preparing to fly from the world; & to chuse out a quiet spot for the 10 or 12 year, that Heaven may add to my life. However, I leave the world in charity with all men; & almost without a wish for anything better in it: & indeed so I ought to do, for this is quite enough to make a man of my turn easy & happy. When I steal from Byfleet to my Winter Lodgings, I shall laugh at the fools you talk of, instead of being angry with their follies, (for Monkies were certainly made for our Diversion, rather than for our Wrath,) converse with a few sensible friends; & do every thing to make the rest of my life, as easy, & as useful, as I can. This you may reckon among my moral Epistles."

Spence held to his plan of not moving his household to

Byfleet until the spring of 1749, but he himself spent considerable time there in the preceding summer and autumn. As early as May 22, 1748, he drew up a plan of the Byfleet property for use in projecting alterations,[2] and on October 22 in the same year Dodsley addressed him in a fashion to indicate that by that date he was busy "improving" the grounds of his new home: "While you are planting the Groves, directing the Walks, and forming ye Bowers that are in all probability to afford You a Retreat for the whole of your future Life; you seem like a man arriv'd at the end of his Labours, and just beginning to enjoy the fruits of them."[3] Spence himself twice dated the period of his life spent at Byfleet as commencing in 1748,[4] but a letter of June 16, 1749, to Massingberd makes it clear that he did not move there *en famille* until May of the latter year.

At his new home,[5] where he spent the greater part of his time during his remaining twenty years, Spence led a tranquil life, though hardly an idle one. His mother, aged seventy-nine in 1749, and his cousin Mrs. Collier were members of his household until their deaths, after which he seems to have lived alone except for servants. As at Birchanger, he devoted much time to gardening, a pursuit which now became his chief interest. Information concerning his developments at Byfleet is found in abundance throughout the Spence Papers. In one place[6] he describes how, having found his little ground "all confin'd, Gloomy, Regular, & Flat," he has conducted extensive alterations with a view to making it appear "less Flat, quite Irregular, light & open." The area at that time was between sixteen and seventeen acres,[7] and this he formed into gardens and fields, with the flatness broken by knolls and terraces and the regularity overcome by groves. Flower beds and hedgerows garnished the whole, and here and there a view opened to the surrounding hills. A winding walk of sand all round enabled the proprietor to make the circuit of his grounds in half an hour. He took advantage of the surrounding landscape to make parts of it appear as a continuation of his own domain. Further, he was the leader of a sort of community project to beautify the countryside by plantations, with the result that an area of ten or twelve square miles was artificially planted. He constructed a walk which led halfway to the seat of Lord Lincoln at Oatlands, and Lincoln co-operated by completing the walk and effecting other improvements at his friend's suggestion.

Upon his gardens at Byfleet Spence expended, according to Rolle, a large share of the money arising from the publication of *Polymetis*.[8] Shortly before Spence's death they were described by a visitor as "adorned with every beauty the situation will bear; his ponds filled with gold-fish, and his woods filled with nightingales, and all kinds of melodious songsters."[9] Like Shenstone, he commemorated his friends by dedicating seats and views to them.[10] His improvements made the little estate one of the show places of Surrey, and his enthusiastic interest in the beautification of "every rude & uncultivated Spot"[11] in the district won him the gratitude of his neighbors. Eighty years after his death, one end of near-by St. George's Hill was still known as "Spence's Point," where a certain fir tree was shown to visitors as the first planted in that vicinity by Spence. At that time (1859) it could be said of Spence that "all the people in Byfleet seem to have heard of him from their forefathers, and speak of his vast improvements in the neighborhood of Byfleet."[12]

Spence's interest in gardening had from his early manhood led him to read widely on the subject and to seek out and visit every show place near which his travels in Great Britain or on the Continent carried him. Scattered throughout his published and unpublished papers are innumerable notes on such reading and on the estates which he visited. Beginning with his return from abroad in 1742 he began to be consulted by persons desirous of improving their grounds according to the new fashion, and in an unprofessional capacity he exerted no small influence upon the changing styles in landscape gardening. Rolle says that in this art Spence became "so celebrated, & his character herein so well setled & established, that his Decisions upon any controverted point of this Sort, were generally implicitly Submitted to & acquiesced in; as carrying a kind of stamp of Conviction with them: who indeed had Hardiness enough, to doubt of the Propriety of any little intended alteration, after it was known to have been Suggested by Mr Spence!" And a young lady who visited Spence at Byfleet wrote enthusiastically to her fiancé that her host was "well-known in the literary world as an author, a perfect critic in poetry, painting, and gardening; I mean the Landskip garden, which is a kind of painting. It was he and Pope, and another or two of his friends, who introduced the present taste in gardening, and rescued them from the imprisonment of high walls and clipt hedges."[13] Among the Spence Papers is a sheaf of plans and hints concerning the gardens and estates of gentlemen whose properties Spence visited and to some of whom he acted as adviser. He had early developed in his pupil Lord Lincoln a taste for gardening, and he assisted the Earl in the improvement of his grounds at Oatlands and also acted in an advisory capacity at Clumber. His suggestions were welcomed by the Duke of Manchester at Kimbolton and Lord Wentworth at Kirkby; at the request of the owners he drew up hints for the improvement of Raby, the seat of the Earl of Darlington, and Knole, home of the Sackvilles; and the owners of dozens of lesser estates benefited by his advice.

The rich fund of material which he had accumulated through study and observation as well as practice, Spence intended to make use of in at least one publication on the subject of gardens past and present. Evidence of such a plan abounds in his papers. One manuscript, entitled "Heads; for Garden-Letters," is a brief history of ornamental gardening, beginning with the "fabulous gardens" of antiquity and proceeding through the Asiatic, Greek, Roman, Italian, and French fashions to the English, with a final chapter entitled "Rules for Gardening." The introduction begins: "You have often smiled at me, when you have heard me say; that among many other blessings, not generally taken notice of, I often thank Heaven, 'That I was born in the Age in which the true taste in Gardning has first prevail'd.' You seem'd to doubt whether what I said was true. I dont forget your not only bringing in the Gardens of Versailles & Marli, & those of Tivoli & Frescati against me; but your going back so far as to the Pensil-Gardens at Babylon: & even to the Gardens of Adonis, & the Hesperides. I am not afraid of a comparison with any of these; as far as we can know anything of them: & if I am apprehensive at all, it is from another quarter; that you have never yet mention'd. Take care that you do not draw me into a History of Gardens, ever since the Fall. As it happens, I have a good deal of leisure upon my hands at present; & as I find I must be forced to do it one time or other, in order to convince you; I dont see why I may not as well set about it immediately, as at any more distant time." The treatise which follows upon this imposing preamble is disappointing. It comprises fewer than sixty small pages, and only the English gardens are discussed in any detail. References to Pope and to Southcote abound in the English section, but the manuscript is obviously only the barest outline of an ambitious production.

Another paper is apparently the first of a series of projected letters on gardening. It begins:

My Dear S^R.

It was my being so often and so much of the time in his garden with your very good friend Mr. Pope in the last sixteen years of his life and my seeing your Gardens, and some others of the best taste, so happily introduced among us in the present century, that first made me a Lover of Gardening. . . .

In his journal for 1758 Spence is found toying with a title for his projected work: "Tempe; or, Letters relating to Gardens, in all Ages: &, more particularly to the Method of making the Grounds & Country pleasing all around one, so happily introduc'd of late among us." "Tempe" was to be a general name "like Evelyn's Sylva," and the

motto was to be Martial's "Rure vero barbaroque laeta-
tur."

Since Spence never completed his plans for publication,
the best exposition of his theories of ornamental gardening
is to be found in a copy of a letter which he wrote on September 9, 1751, to the Rev. Mr. Wheeler, a Somersetshire
friend and garden enthusiast.[14] This rather elaborate treatise begins as follows: "When you set me to write about
Gardening, You Set me upon a thing that I love extreamly;
but as to any large tract of ground, there is no saying any
thing in particular, without being upon the Spot; & having
consider'd it well, & often: Some General Rules one might
mention; but after all, nine parts in ten depend upon the
application. Yet I will just mention some that I follow'd
my Self." Spence then discusses in order sixteen "general
rules," which may be condensed and summarized as follows: "consult the genius of the place," follow nature, conceal the bounds by the use of groves and sunk or invisible
fences, contrive the outer parts so as to make them unite
with the landscape beyond, mingle the useful and the ornamental, and study variety. Everything, he continues, is
summed up in Pope's couplet

> He gains all points, who pleasingly confounds,
> Surprises, varies, and conceals the bounds.[15]

"And in conversation," Spence adds, "I have heard him
include it in one single word, Variety."[16]

Spence's interest in the gardens of his friends and the
renowned estates of England combined with his gregarious
temperament and his fondness for travel to make his residence at Byfleet anything but the undisturbed retirement
of a rural retreat. When he was at Byfleet, he seems to have
driven frequently the twenty miles to London. The prox-
imity of Oatlands kept him in constant association with
Lord Lincoln; in 1752 Stephen Duck, granted the living of
Byfleet, became an almost daily associate; and Spence occasionally saw his Gothic neighbor at Strawberry Hill.
Among the other well-known men with whom he associ-

ated during this period were David Garrick, Edward Moore, Robert Dodsley, Samuel Richardson, Joseph Warton, Lord Radnor, William Warburton, William Shenstone, Robert Lowth, Bennet Langton, Edward Young, the Duke of Manchester, and Lords Darlington, Middlesex, and Wentworth.[17] In a letter of 1754 to Joseph Warton, Spence describes a typical period of travels and visitors: "I have either been out upon some journey, or full of visitors at home, for this whole summer. I had first a long journey into the North; two or three days after my return hither, I was invited to Mr. Herbert's, in Brook-street, for a fortnight: and on my road from thence met with a message to desire that I wou'd attend Lord Lincoln to Cheltenham Wells, in Glocestershire; that took up five or six weeks; and when that was over, Captain Rolle . . . was so good as to come hither. So all my time has been entirely taken up very agreeably indeed. . . ."[18]

The expedition to Cheltenham, incidentally, was in a sense a renewal of Spence's former relationship of companion-governor to Lord Lincoln, who was drinking the waters for his health. From Cheltenham, Spence wrote frequent letters to the Duke of Newcastle reporting on Lincoln's progress,[19] and it would appear that he was there partly at Newcastle's request.

The mention of Samuel Richardson among the friends of Spence's Byfleet period leads to a discussion of one of the anecdotist's most interesting literary relationships. There is evidence to indicate that the friendship between the two men was very close. When Spence wrote his account of the poet Blacklock in 1754 he observed: "I myself can have the Pleasure at present of reckoning two or three, in the little circle of my own most intimate Friends, who have been rais'd purely by their literary Merit and good Characters, from inconsiderable or no Circumstances, to considerable or at least very easy ones."[20] To this passage he added a note stating that the persons he had in mind were "Mr. *Duck*, Mr. *Dodsley*; and Mr. *Richardson*." Since he classed all three among his "most intimate Friends" and

since Duck and Dodsley are known certainly to have belonged in that category, there is every reason to believe
that Richardson was a member of the "little circle." It
seems probable that Spence met Richardson late in 1747
or very early in 1748. He met Colley Cibber in early January, 1748,[21] and the following passage from an undated letter to Massingberd proves that his first meeting with
Richardson occurred about the same time: "You know I
was always a mighty man for getting acquainted with
authors: I have lately faln flounce in with no less than four
new ones: the author of Pamela; the Writer of a Comedy,
which is to appear the 13th of next Month;[22] a very pretty
young Lady, that writes verses; & old Colly Cibber. Old
Colly is himself a Comedy; the Comedy-writer a very
agreable man, & his piece one of the best that has ever ap-
peard on our Stage; the Lady is as pretty & as genteel, as
she is sensible; & M[r] Richardson is one of the most worthy
hearted men, that ever I knew in my life."

There is extant a letter from Richardson to Spence, dated October 30, 1749, in which the novelist speaks of dis-
rupted plans for a visit and assumes that "dear Mr.
Spence" will "make North End his Town house, not only
now, but whenever he shall come to Town."[23] If, as seems
certain, the "Mr. Richardson" whom Spence saw fourteen
times during the years 1756–58 was the novelist, those
visits indicate some closeness of association.[24] Three letters
of 1758–59 from Spence to Richardson show the two men
on very good terms and indicate that Richardson (at his
friend's request) took a salutary interest in young Harry
(or Hall) Lawman, Spence's cousin.[25] But the most interesting piece of evidence is a lengthy letter from Spence to
Richardson, dated January 21, 1748, which shows Spence
standing in the interesting relationship of critic to the
novelist.

Richardson had apparently delivered to Spence, who at
that time was still living in London, some of the forthcoming numbers of *Clarissa*,[26] soliciting his opinion thereon.
After speaking of the pleasure which the reading has given

him, Spence continues thus: "I have a moral feeling for you, of another sort; on seeing how much you suffer from the contrariety of advices that have been given you. Such a multitude of opinions can only serve to confuse your own judgment, which I verily believe would direct you better, without any help, than with so much.

"I wish you would take up a resolution (which perhaps may be new to you) of neither trusting others, nor distrusting yourself, too much. If you bundle up the opinions of bad judges in your head, they will only be so much lumber in your way; and even the opinions of good judges, in general, when they come to decide about particulars in your Clarissa, are to be suspected.

"Have they sufficiently considered your design and manner of writing in that piece? Do they know the connections and dependencies of one part upon another? Are they acquainted with your various ends in writing it; your unravellings of the story; and your winding up of the whole? Without these lights, a very good judge may give a very wrong opinion about the parts that compose it. Another defect in those that are called the best judges is, that they generally go by rules of art; whereas your's is absolutely a work of nature. One might, for instance, as well judge of the beauties of a prospect by the rules of architecture, as of your Clarissa by the laws of novels and romances.

"A piece quite of a new kind must have new rules, if any; but the best of all is, following nature and common sense.

"Nature, I think, you have followed more variously, and at the same time more closely, than any one I know. For Heaven's sake, let not those sworn enemies of all good works (the critics) destroy the beauties you have created. If you indulge them in all their wicked will, they will cut every tree in your garden into a bird or a beast.

"What I have just said will hold stronger against lopping. You love the Scriptures. There, you know, a good man is said to be like a tree by the rivers of water. You are, as yet, flourishing in all your verdure; for God's sake, don't let them make a pollard of you! Upon reading the contents of the whole, I am more and more convinced that much ought not to be parted with. Pruning is always proper. If you see a dead branch, or a straggling bough, that offends your eye, cut it away; but do not labour to find out faults where they do not meet you."[27]

This is all sound advice, and especially pertinent in view of Richardson's tendency to yield too pliantly to suggestions of his innumerable correspondents in shaping the course of his narratives. The letter is interesting also as showing Spence's impatience with those who applied "rules of art" to a work of inspiration; clearly, Spence looked upon Richardson as a "child of nature." The comparison between literature and gardening is also significant.[28]

After the death of Richardson in 1760, Spence apparently considered writing a memoir of him. Such at least is the supposition raised by the following sentence in a letter (September 3, 1761) from the Rev. John Jones, close friend of Edward Young: "He [Young] told me lately, that if he could see you, he would, or at least can, furnish you with ample materials, nor do I doubt but they will be pertinent, *relating to ye life of his late friend Mr. Richardson, the poetical Prose-writer.*"[29]

At the time of Spence's only known contact with Colley Cibber, the ancient enemy of Spence's idol Pope was seventy-seven years old and living in retirement. "Old Colly," Spence told Massingberd, "is himself a Comedy."[30] They seem to have talked on January 10, 1748,[31] probably in London, and the conversation ran largely on Pope: the incident described in Cibber's famous *Letter* to the poet, Cibber's conviction that Pope was the principal author of *The What d'ye Call It,* and his confirmation of Pope's charge against Addison of "bearing no Rival, enduring none but flatterers, transl^g the greater part of T^s first Iliad & publish^g it with a design to have overset P^s."

Another person with Pope associations—of a different kind!—Spence talked with in the following year. This was Martha Blount. It is reasonable to assume that Spence had met her more than once at Twickenham during Pope's lifetime, but the assumption cannot be proved. No surviving records of conversation with her can be dated before the poet's death.[32] Spence did, however, spend some hours with her on May 18 and 27, 1749, when, as might be expected, Pope was the chief topic of discussion. Spence took the opportunity to question her concerning her earliest acquaintance with Pope, while she dilated with some bitterness and at considerable length upon her quarrel with the Allens. To the meeting on May 27 Spence brought a manuscript copy of the *Anecdotes* and read aloud at least some of the entries relating to Pope. The result was "several things confirm'd, & some few alter'd."[33] On the verso pages of the copy which Spence used on this occasion, "Conf^d by Mrs. B." is a frequent entry.[34]

One of the topics discussed was the attack which had then just been made upon Pope's memory in the "Advertisement" to Bolingbroke's *Letters on the Spirit of Patriotism, on the Idea of a Patriot King, and on the State of Parties at the Accession of King George the First.*[35] This bitter invective is generally attributed to David Mallet, the editor, but possibly was written by Bolingbroke himself. To the charge that Pope had secretly superintended an earlier and unauthorized printing of Bolingbroke's work, friends of the poet were quick to make angry retorts, and there ensued a brief pamphlet war. Among Pope's defenders loomed the figure of the truculent Warburton, and he is usually the only person identified as having taken part in the contest on the poet's behalf. But it would have been strange if Spence, peace-lover though he was, had kept silence when Pope's integrity was questioned in a posthumous attack, and he is probably the anonymous author of a pamphlet published by Griffiths and entitled *An Apology For the Late Mr. Pope; On Occasion of the Editor's Preface To The Three Letters, lately Published, On the Spirit of Patriotism; On the Idea of a Patriot King; and On the State of Parties at the Accession of King George the First.* This essay originally appeared in French in Griffiths' *Magazin de Londres,*[36] and the English version followed in pamphlet form a few days later.[37]

The chief piece of evidence pointing to Spence's author-ship comes from Walpole. In the course of a discussion of the whole controversy he writes to Mann: ". . . if one had a mind to defend Pope, should not one ask if anybody ever blamed Virgil's executors for not burning the *Æneid*, as he ordered them?" To this passage Walpole later appended a note: "This thought was borrowed by Mr. Spence, in a pamphlet published on this occasion in defence of Pope."[38] Now the author of *An Apology for the Late Mr. Pope* de-velops this identical argument: "The will of the dead is at least as sacred as that of the living. Virgil, on his death-bed, made it his solemn request to Plotius Tucca and Vari-us, to consign his Aeneid to the flame, or not give it to the public but perfected, which amounted to the same; for who was there so hardy as to put a hand to it? Yet these trusty friends neither executed the one, nor the other; they proba-bly considered this violation of their trust, as a greater act of piety, than destroying a work so deserving of immortali-ty. All nations, all ages have confirmed this judgment of theirs. No one has at least hitherto thought of making it a subject of reproach to them; or of seeing in it any reason to impeach their character, as it is handed down to us, em-balmed in the following verses of the greatest and most amiable of poets.

'Plotius et Varius, sinuessae, Virgiliusque,
Occurrunt animae quales neque CANDIDIORES
Tena tulit, neque queis me fit devinctior alter.' Hor."

Whether the argument was "borrowed by Mr. Spence" or arrived at independently by him, its appearance in the pamphlet, taken with Walpole's statement, seems to iden-tify the essay as coming from Spence's pen.

The identification is supported by internal evidence. Not only does the writer show a veneration for Pope which sounds very much like that expressed again and again by Spence, but he has a high opinion of Bolingbroke and is obviously desirous of exculpating Pope without being un-duly severe upon the philosopher. Moreover, in the pam-phlet there are phrases which seem like echoes of the conversation which Spence had with Martha Blount on the subject at this very time. For example, the writer of the apology states that Pope was "never greedy of riches," and apparently on May 27 Spence observed to Miss Blount: "Mʳ Pope's not being richer may be easily accounted for. He never had any love for money; & tho' he was never extravagant, he always delighted when he had any to spare to make use of it; in giving, lending, building, & gardening."[39] Again, the writer says that Bolingbroke was "the loved, the revered choice of his [Pope's] head and heart," and that the poet could not be guilty toward his friend except "through an excess of veneration and esteem." On May 18 Spence told Miss Blount that he had heard Pope speak of "some work of Lord Bolingbroke's, which that lord designed to suppress: he spoke of it as too valuable to the world to be so used; and said he would not suffer it to be lost to it."[40] The lady "had immediately the same thought relating to that affair," and said that "she could take her oath that it was done out of his excessive esteem for the writer and his abilities."[41]

Finally, throughout the pamphlet the writer shows skill in defending Pope against the aspersions of Mallet's "Advertisement," and the more one studies the arguments used and compares them with remarks found in Spence's acknowledged writings, the more one comes to feel that Spence is indeed the author of the apology.[42]

Early in 1752[43] Dodsley published for Spence the little work entitled *Crito: or, a Dialogue on Beauty*, purporting to come from the pen of Sir Harry Beaumont, a pseudonym which Spence employed for the first time on this occasion.[44] A second edition was advertised on October 31 of the same year,[45] and the little treatise was reprinted in Dodsley's collection of *Fugitive Pieces* in 1761.[46]

After the *Essay on Pope's Odyssey*, *Polymetis*, and the *Anecdotes*, *Crito* is by all odds the most important of Spence's works. It fully justifies the assertion that Spence is "a man to whom historians of esthetics owe more respectful attention than they seem to have given him."[47]

Moreover, if an admirer of Spence were asked to select the one piece of writing on which he would most confidently rest Spence's reputation as a stylist, he would choose *Crito*. Modern readers would be surprised at the ease, the grace, the urbanity of the little book, and would acknowledge the persuasiveness of Spence's reasoning and the truth of his conclusions. In the *Essay on Pope's Odyssey* there are dreary stretches, in *Polymetis* the prolixity of the discussion induces weariness, but in reading *Crito* one does not find his attention flagging. Here Spence is not only at his best as a critic but comes closest to attaining the goal he always set himself as a writer: to write in a manner which should charm his readers at the same time that it "improved" them, which should interest as well as instruct.

Crito, like the *Essay* and *Polymetis*, is written in dialogue form. But evidently Spence had benefited by practice and experience, for in *Crito* the conversation is handled more expertly than in the earlier works: it is far more realistic. The friends are once more three in number, once more gentlemen eminent for taste and erudition who converse in the pleasant gardens of a country estate. After the usual narrative introduction, Crito, the chief speaker, begins by limiting the discussion to a single aspect of beauty, because, he says, "Every Object that is pleasing to the Eye, when looked upon, or delightful to the Mind, on Recollection, may be called beautiful; so that Beauty, in general, may stretch as wide as the visible Creation. . . ."[48] For the sake of brevity, therefore, he will confine himself "to visible Beauty; and of that, to such only as may be called personal, or human Beauty; and that again, to such as is natural or real, and not such as is only national or customary. . . ."[49] Within these bounds he finds four constituent parts of beauty—color, form, expression, and grace, the first two being the body and the two latter the soul of beauty.[50] Color, though the lowest of all the constituent parts of beauty, is the most striking and the most observed; it requires less of judgment than any of the other three. Crito discourses briefly upon the pleasure to be derived from observing the lovely blending and variety of colors in the human face and body. In treating of this subject, as well as every other topic discussed in the dialogue, Spence draws upon the Latin writers for illustrations in much the same manner as he had done in *Polymetis*. If he speaks of the necessity of health to beauty, he cites the authority of Cicero;[51] if he dwells upon the interplay of red and white in the complexion of a girl, he calls upon Virgil, Ovid, and Tibullus for confirmation of his opinion.[52] Under the heading of form, Crito considers the symmetry of the body, the turn and shape of each part, and the attitude. The beauty of form is superior to that of color, and he greatly regrets that modern fashions in clothing obscure so much of the beauty of the human body.

By expression, which is common to all persons and faces, Crito means the exhibition of the emotions or passions— the changes of the mind as they are made visible to the eye by look or gesture. This beauty of the emotions, expressed chiefly through the eyes, the eyebrows, and the mouth, is much superior to that of either color or form, for a woman with a soft complexion, the finest features, and an enchanting shape, but without anything of the mind expressed in her face, is as insipid and unmoving as a waxen figure; the emotions may give beauty without the assistance of color or form and can take it away where color and form have united to bestow it.

In his treatment of grace, which he terms the fourth constituent of human beauty, Spence has been revealed[53] as an innovator in aesthetics and a forerunner of Kames[54] and Lessing. In *Laokoon* Lessing wrote: "Ein andrer Weg, auf welchem die Poesie die Kunst in Schilderung körperlicher Schönheit wiederum einholet, ist dieser, dass die Schönheit in Reitz verwandelt. Reitz ist Schönheit in Bewegung. . . ."[55] Lessing was long thought to have been the first to define grace as beauty in motion,[56] but in 1856 Guhrauer[57] demonstrated that the idea had been expressed by Kames,[58] and Blümner[59] proved that not only

Kames but Webb[60] and Hagedorn[61] had associated grace
and motion, though he still claimed a certain priority for
Lessing in that the idea "durch ihn erst entwickelt und in
die Aesthetik eingeführt worden ist." Wilhelm Neumann,
in 1894, was the first to do justice to Spence by showing
that he was "der Vater dieses Begriffes," or at least that
he enunciated it before any of the other writers named:
"Früher, als sie alle, und vielleicht nicht ohne Einfluss
auch auf Home, ist ein kleines Werkchen, dem wir hier
Gerechtigkeit widerfahren lassen wollen, durch Anführung
der unsern Gegenstand berührenden Stellen. Es ist ein
Büchlein von Henry Beaumont: Crito or a dialogue on
beauty. Die zweite Auflage des populären Schriftchens,
nach der ich citiere, erschien bereits um Jahre 1742."[62]

Spence does indeed definitely associate grace with motion:[63] "Though Grace is so difficult to be accounted for in
general; yet I have observ'd Two particular things, which
(I think) hold universally in relation to it.

"The First is: 'That there is no Grace, without Motion;'
by which I mean, without some genteel or pleasing Motion,
either of the whole Body, or of some Limb, or, at least, of
some Feature. And it may be hence, that Lord *Bacon* (and,
perhaps, *Horace*), call Grace, by the Name of decent Motion; just as if they were equivalent Terms.

"*Virgil* in one Place points out the Majesty of *Juno*, and
in another the graceful Air of *Apollo*, by only saying, that
they move; and possibly he means no more, when he makes
the Motion of *Venus* the principal thing, by which
Æneas discovers her under all her Disguise. . . ."[64]

In thus defining grace as a quality of motion and insep-
arably connected with it, Spence does not in *Crito* take the
further step of contrasting the powers of painter and poet
by showing that motion—and hence grace—defy the art
of the painter and that, since "Reitz ist Schönheit in Bewegung," it is "eben darum dem Mahler weniger bequem als
dem Dichter."[65] But this step he had practically taken in
Polymetis in the passage showing that the graceful twin-

kling of the eyes of Venus can be represented by poetry alone.[66] So not only in his definition of grace but also in his restriction of that quality to poetry alone among the arts, Spence anticipates Lessing.

The discussion of grace forms the most interesting part of *Crito*. The second principle which Spence enunciates in regard to it—the first being, of course, that there can be no grace without motion—is " 'That there can be no Grace, with Impropriety;' or, in other Words, that nothing can be graceful, that is not adapted to the Characters of the Person."[67] After demonstrating the truth of both axioms, he finds himself yet at a loss to express the "je ne sais quoi" which he feels to be an inherent part of grace but which nobody can explain; and rather than attempt a narrow definition he is content with a few general observations upon this most baffling quality of human beauty: "Whatever are the Causes of it, this is certain, that Grace is the chief of all the constituent Parts of Beauty; and so much so, that it seems to be the only one which is absolutely and universally admired: All the rest are only relative. One likes a brunette Beauty better than a fair one; I may love a little Woman, and you a large one, best; a Person of a mild Temper will be fond of the gentler Passions in the Face, and one of a bolder Cast may chuse to have more Vivacity and more vigorous Passions exprest there: But Grace is found in few, and is pleasing to all.

"Grace, like Poetry, must be born with a Person; and is never, wholly, to be acquired by Art. . . .

"Grace has nothing to do with the lowest Part of Beauty, or Color; very little with Shape, and very much with the Passions; for it is she who gives their highest Zest, and the most delicious Part of their Pleasingness to the Expressions of each of them.

"All the other Parts of Beauty are pleasing in some Degree, but Grace is Pleasingness itself. . . ."[68]

In the remaining pages of *Crito* Spence offers upon the subject of beauty some random observations which have occurred to him. The beauty of any person may be measured, he believes, by a scale similar to that which De Piles employs to judge the comparative excellence of painters.[69] Setting the highest excellence in color at ten, in form at twenty, in expression at thirty, and in grace at forty, he would rank all of England's most celebrated beauties according to their merit in each particular; though the highest possible reckoning is thus one hundred, the utmost that he will concede to the most beautiful lady of his acquaintance is seventy-three![70] Like beauty, the ability to judge with discretion is meted out to mankind in very unequal proportions, and a man may be influenced to a false opinion by any one of a number of causes: love for a particular woman, a similarity in temperament or person, ideas of utility rather than of beauty, and difference in national tastes—as exemplified in the stoutness of Rubens' women ("His very *Graces* are all fat") and the highly rouged cheeks of the ladies of France. Though individual or national prejudice is more strongly operative in the articles of form and color than in those of expression and grace, even the most awkward child may appear graceful to its parents, and every motion and air of a beloved person may be pleasing to the lover. Finally, after a few words upon the beauties of the earth, of the heavens, of animals, and of the entire universe, Spence concludes with a moral exordium upon the loveliness of the good life: "And yet all the Profusion of Beauty I have been speaking of, and even that of the whole Universe taken together, is but of a weaker Nature in Comparison of the Beauty of Virtue. . . . People, to be beautiful, should endeavour to be virtuous; and should avoid Vice, and all the worst Sort of Passions, as they would fly Deformity. I wish the more beautiful Half of the human Creation, in particular, were thoroughly sensible of this great Truth; 'That the readiest way to be beautiful, is to be good;' and such of them as are more solicitous about choosing and adjusting what they wear, and how that will appear, than about forming their Minds, and regulating their disagreeable Passions, will really fall under the Censure I mentioned before, from one of the

Latin Poets; and shew too plainly to all the World, that they, in their own Hearts, consider their Dress as the better Part of themselves. . . ."[71]

A study of the sources whence were derived the materials for *Crito* results in the paradoxical conclusion that the little volume was both imitative and original. Spence himself said of it: "If the former part of it may be thought now & then too warm, the latter must attone [*sic*] for it: which grows, especially toward the end, very like a Sermon. The matter was all taken formerly from the Life; & indeed it was not near so well to be studied in Books: & if it had, I have never met with any treatise on that subject, that cou'd have much helpt me. The Quotations which will appear at the bottom of some of the pages, were got in some time after I had written the whole; to confirm some particulars, asserted in it."[72] And on another occasion he told Massingberd: "Since I wrote it, I have read over two other Dialogues on Beauty; one by Plato, & the other by one of our Countrymen in imitation of him: But they are both metaphysical, & so do not interfere at all with mine; which is all from Fact, or the most obvious reflections arising from facts."[73] Now in spite of these assertions, what looks like the sources of many of Spence's ideas and even of some of his phrasing may be traced; yet the little book as a whole produces the effect of a stimulating freshness. Spence may have gone to Shaftesbury for suggestions. Bacon's essay "On Beauty" he knew thoroughly, and it is probable that he was indebted to that source rather than to Shaftesbury for his association of grace with motion.[74] To De Piles he was under obligation for his scale of beauty as well as for several minor points. He employed[75] Félibien's *Entretiens* in his discussion of what constitutes the beauty of the human form, while Le Brun's *Conférence sur l'expression générale et particulière des passions* was probably of service in the section devoted to the expression of emotion in the human face. But it was chiefly in the Latin classics, in which he was so thoroughly steeped, that Spence found inspiration—often, no doubt, without realiz-

ing it. Indeed, *Crito* might be called a sympathetic reinterpretation of the ideas of the classical writers upon human
beauty (particularly feminine), written with a zest and
pleasant grace which invest it with originality.

That *Crito* met with a favorable reception is indicated
to some extent by the appearance of a second edition in the
year of publication. The Duchess of Somerset called the
attention of Lady Luxborough to the work,[76] but evidently
that lady did not read it until a year or so after its initial
appearance, when Shenstone sent her copies of *Crito* and
Spence's *Moralities*. In a letter of May 12, 1753, she wrote
to the poet: "The *Moralities* and *Crito* I send back: the
former is certainly *trite*-issimo; the latter is the reverse."[77]
In the *London Magazine* for March, 1752, appeared an
anonymous poem, "To Sir Harry Beaumont: On Publishing his Dialogue on Beauty," which begins:

> Beauty was wont to dazzle and surprize;
> A mingled blaze of charms to vulgar eyes:
> Man found its radiant efflux fire the blood;
> Heart-felt, 'tis true, but never understood:
> You first dispel the cloud that hid its charms;
> Show, how its influence every bosom warms:
> By you distinct its powers are all exprest;
> Each in its proper, native brightness, drest.[78]

The anonymous author then proceeds (with some extravagance!) to compare Spence's achievements in aesthetics
with those of Newton in physics. As early as 1755, *Crito*
received the distinction of translation into French,[79] and a
portion was again translated in 1769.[80]

As has already been suggested, Spence merits a position
of more importance in the history of aesthetics than has
yet been accorded him. To be sure, his *Crito* did not exert
an influence comparable to that of Kames's *Elements of
Criticism* or of Burke's *On the Sublime and Beautiful*, but
it does not deserve the neglect which has fallen to its lot.
Lessing himself could have profited by a reading of the dialogue, which seems to have been unknown to him. Kames
almost certainly used it.[81] On the writing of another trea-

tise of some importance in the history of aesthetics Spence's
work exercised a shaping influence. Daniel Webb in 1760
dedicated his *An Inquiry into the Beauties of Painting* to
"the author of *Crito*" in words which indicate that Spence
was considered eminently worthy of receiving such a distinction from a writer upon aesthetics:

SIR,

The most accurate observer of the beauties of nature, must be the
best judge of their imitations; and the same elegance of imagination
which forms the painter, must enlighten the critic. It was natural for
me, under this persuasion, to address my observations on Painting to
the author of *Crito*.

How ingenious are men in colouring their passions! thus have I
heightened self-love into a love of justice: For, what could be more
advantageous to me, than to have it known, that Mr. *Spence* ap-
proves me as a writer, and acknowledges me as a friend? What success
I may have in the former character, must depend on futurity; but I am
in possession of all the credit of the latter, while you permit me to declare, in this publick manner, That I am, Reverend Sir, with the truest
respect, your most obliged, most obedient, and most humble servant,

DANIEL WEBB

Webb adopted Spence's characteristic doctrines as expressed not only in *Crito* but also in *Polymetis*. Webb's
"there is no grace without motion" is, of course, repetition,
his illustrations are frequently borrowed from Spence,[82]
and he probably used the dialogue form because of his
predecessor's example. Moreover, when Webb says of a
descriptive passage in Virgil, "I am persuaded, the poet
must have had in his eye, some celebrated picture in this
style,"[83] it is as though Polymetis himself were speaking.

Spence's treatment of one idea in *Crito*—the "scale of excellence" borrowed from De Piles—may have influenced
the compilation of similar scales throughout the second
half of the century. Among the many writers to employ
this popular device were Goldsmith, in his *Citizen of the
World*, and Sterne, in *Tristram Shandy*; and in the latter
case there is a contemporary charge of indebtedness to
Spence. Speaking of his famous mock dedication, Sterne
observes to his patron: "My Lord, if you examine it over

again, it is far from being a gross piece of daubing, as some dedications are. The design, your Lordship sees, is good,— the colouring transparent,—the drawing not amiss; or to speak more like a man of science,—and measure my piece in the painter's scale, divided into 20,—I believe, my Lord, the outlines will turn out as 12,—the composition as 9,— the colouring as 6,—the expression 13 and a half,—and the design,—if I may be allowed, my Lord, to understand my own design, and supposing absolute perfection in designing, to be as 20,—I think it cannot well fall short of 19."[84] Though, of course, it cannot be proved that Sterne derived his idea directly from Spence, such a charge is made in a pamphlet entitled *The Clockmaker's Outcry against the Author of the Life and Opinions of Tristram Shandy*,[85] which appeared shortly after the publication of the first two volumes of Sterne's work. There one of the outraged clockmakers denounces the book incident by incident, asserting that even the death of Yorick was "intirely borrowed." Another ventures to make an exception in favor of the clever "scale of beauty," but sharp comes the retort that nobody should be so ignorant as not to know that the scale was lifted from the ingenious Mr. Spence's *Crito, or Dialogue on Beauty*.

Crito, like *Polymetis*, has "sunk" (though hardly by its own weight) into obscurity; but for its urbane style, its lucid interpretation of classic ideas on beauty, its enunciation of important aesthetic axioms, and its influence upon contemporary and later thought, it deserves to "rise again" into the consciousness of students of the eighteenth century.[86]

Another publication of the year 1752 was a result of that interest in gardening which Spence had renewed upon his removal to Byfleet. Though only a translation instead of the original work for which during many years he had been making collections, it nevertheless exerted considerable influence upon English gardening. This was Jean-Denis Attiret's *A Particular Account of the Emperor of China's Gardens near Pekin*, issued by Dodsley on December 4, 1752,[87]

as "translated by Sir Harry Beaumont." Attiret, an artist
of some ability and a man of intellect, had been sent by the
French Jesuits as a missionary to China and lived for
twenty-five years at the court of the Emperor Kien-Long
at Pekin.[88] On his arrival at the court he had dispatched
to a Jesuit friend a long letter describing the life and manners there and stressing particularly the beauty and magnificence of the gardens surrounding the palace. The letter
was published in 1749 in *Lettres édifiantes écrites des mis-
sions*, and Spence's translation brought it for the first time
to the notice of the English public. The work appeared at
a propitious moment. The formal, straight-lined, architec-
tural garden was gradually losing favor in England under
the impact of attacks by Shaftesbury, Addison, Pope,
Kent, and Spence himself. In Attiret's description of the
Yuen-ming-yuen, Spence perceived a similarity in taste to
the natural style of gardening which was gaining increasing vogue in England. There is no doubt that Chinese theories of gardening, made known to Europe chiefly through
the letters of Jesuit missionaries such as Attiret, were to
give a decided impetus to emancipation from the formal
style, and Spence's part in the process was not small.[89]
Walpole, the historian of the new movement, paid a compliment to Spence at the same time that he professed to
find no similarity between the Chinese and the English
fashions: "The late Mr. Joseph Spence, who had both
taste and zeal for the present style, was so persuaded of the
Chinese emperor's pleasure-ground being laid out on principles resembling ours, that he translated and published,
under the name of sir Harry Beaumont, a particular account of that enclosure from the collection of the letters of
the Jesuits. I have looked it over, and, except a determined
irregularity, can find nothing in it that gives me any idea
of attention being paid to nature."[90] Notwithstanding
Walpole's skepticism, however, Attiret's description justifies Spence's opinion that English gardeners might learn
much from China, and the effect of the whole is distinctly
in favor of the natural style which Spence hoped to ad-

vance: "They go from one of the Valleys to another, not by formal strait Walks as in *Europe;* but by various Turnings and Windings, adorned on the Sides with little Pavillions and charming Grottos; and each of these Valleys is diversified from all the rest, both by their manner of laying out the Ground, and in the Structure and Disposition of its Buildings.

"All the Risings and Hills are sprinkled with Trees; and particularly with Flowering Trees, which are here very common. The Sides of the Canals, or lesser Streams, are not faced (as they are with us) with smooth Stone, and in a strait Line; but look rude and rustic, with different Pieces of Rock, some of which jut out, and others recede inwards; and are placed with so much Art, that you would take it to be the Work of Nature. In some Parts the Water is wide, in others narrow; here it serpentises, and there spreads away, as if it was really pushed off by the Hills and Rocks. The Banks are sprinkled with Flowers, which rise up even through the Hollows in the Rock work, as if they had been produced there naturally. They have a great Variety of them, for every Season of the Year."[91]

A recent writer believes that to Spence "horticulture seemed a natural branch of painting, and thus the garden artist was a garden poet as well."[92] If Spence made this association, he may have exerted an influence upon Thomas Whately,[93] whose theories accorded to gardening a high place among the pictorial arts. Evidence that Spence did at least relate horticulture with painting is found in the remarks of his young friend Elizabeth Cartwright, who, after terming him "a perfect critic in poetry, painting, and gardening," adds by way of explanation: "I mean the Landskip garden, which is a kind of painting. It was he and Pope, and another or two of his friends, who introduced the present taste in gardening, and rescued them from the imprisonment of high walls and clipt hedges."[94] No doubt the young girl's classification of landscape gardening as "a kind of painting" was an echo of the words of the "perfect critic."

All in all, enough can be learned from scattered sources about Spence's ideas on the art of gardening to indicate that his contemplated treatise on the subject would probably have been of some importance as the expression of an acknowledged authority and would have exerted some influence upon contemporary and later practice.

To this period belongs an episode which shows Spence in intimate relation with Garrick and Edward Moore. Early in 1753 there came to the ears of Lowth at Winchester a rumor which puzzled him. He wrote to Dodsley on January 16: "I saw 'tother day in a Letter from Mʳ. Garrick, that Mʳ. Spence acknowleges [*sic*] himself to be the Author of yᵉ *Gamester*, a Dramatic piece now in rehersal [*sic*] at Drury Lane. Pray explain this to me if you can."[95] Lowth, who would probably have known in advance if Spence had written anything for the stage, was confident that there was an error somewhere. He was correct, but the "error" was the result of strategy. *The Gamester* had, of course, been written by Moore, who had sound reasons for hesitating to acknowledge it: "The author had reason to think, that his enemies formed a party against *Gil Blas*, and to prevent a renewal of hostilities, was advised to have recourse to a stratagem. Mr. Spence, the admired author of an Essay on Pope's Odyssey, was the intimate friend of Mr. Moore. He gave his consent, that it should be circulated in whispers, that the *Gamester* was the production of his leisure hours. The story was believed, and had the desired effect."[96] Under Spence's name the play met with applause at its opening on February 7, 1753, and Moore was so far encouraged as to assume the laurels of authorship after the third night. The move was premature, however, for as soon as the identity of the real author became known the tragedy "was loudly condemned by many who had been its warm admirers while Moore's name was concealed."[97] The friendship with Moore which this little artifice would imply is confirmed by repeated appearances of Moore's name in Spence's journals. Of course, Moore was an intimate of Spence's close friend Dodsley, and it may well be that Spence is the author of one or more of the un-assigned papers in *The World*, the sprightly periodical edited by Moore and published by Dodsley from 1753 to 1756. In the latter year Spence was among the subscribers to Moore's complete works.

Garrick is mentioned frequently in the journals of 1755–58, and there is a record of a dinner at which he and Spence, as well as Edmund Burke and Bennet Langton, were fellow-guests. Dodsley wrote to Richard Berenger on January 10, 1758: ". . . You judged extreamly well, or rather were inspir'd with a prophetic spirit, when you imagin'd the society of Wits and choice spirits might be very numerous at *Tully's Head;* for the day after I heard from you, I had no less than a round dozen of them din'd with me. The two Mr Wartons, Mr Spence, Mr Burke, Mr Cooper, Mr Langton, Mr Gataker, Mr Bedingfield, and Mr Garrick were of the party. . . ."[98] Garrick was among the many friends in whose gardens Spence took an active interest. He wrote to Massingberd on May 9, 1755: "Garrick's ground too is pretty well furnisht with [ever-greens]. This has been an excellent year with him; & this, & the next (if as succesful) I hope will clear all his Ex-pences of Purchasing, Building, & Ornamenting." Burke had paid Spence a graceful compliment in his *Philosophical Inquiry into the Origin of our Ideas of the Sublime and Beautiful*,[99] and Langton and Spence were intimate friends. Langton seems to have thought highly of Spence, for he took pains to assure Boswell that a contemptuous judg-ment expressed concerning the anecdotist by Johnson was hasty and not the result of conviction.[100] From him John-son learned Spence's opinions concerning the respective shares of Broome and Fenton in the translation of the *Odyssey*,[101] and he once related to Johnson a Popeian anec-dote which he had derived from Spence.[102] Among the Spence Papers there is further evidence of intimacy with Langton, including the draft of a letter to Langton on the death of his brother Ferne, and there are frequent refer-ences to him in Spence's letters to Massingberd. In a letter of October 27, 1763, for example, Spence describes thus a recent visit of Langton to Byfleet: "Mʳ Langton favour'd me with his good Company here, longer than he ever had done before, but not so long as I cou'd have wisht. He went from hence the 19th instant; & promis'd to return the 21st: but I have expected him in vain, ever since. He is an amazing man; but what may perhaps amaze you most, is that he went to bed regularly every night, before Eleven; came to Breakfast at 9: & to Dinner, constantly, at two. I still hope to see him here again soon; he having left his Portmanteau, & several other things here." Earlier, Langton seems to have made a proposal which would have resulted in an advancement for Spence but which was declined with thanks. Spence wrote to Massingberd on September 14, 1753: "You judg'd very rightly, as to my opinion of Mʳ Langton's kind Proposal: I am very much oblig'd to that Gentleman, for his good thoughts of me; but I live now in so easy & so satisfy'd a way, that I dont care to have any thing (upon any consideration whatever) to disturb it: so that my Answer must be the same as I have giv'n upon other occasions, of the same kind, since my Retirement; a great many Thanks, & an absolute Declining of the Favour. I ought to have said this sooner; but you knew me so well, that I thought your Answer was almost as good as my own."

Sir John Hawkins alludes to a meeting between Spence and Johnson,[103] and it is reasonable to assume that with such mutual friends as Dodsley, Garrick, Langton, and Richardson, to name only a few, they must have been in company at least occasionally. Johnson's recorded utterances about Spence, though for the most part rather unfriendly, have an air of authority which suggests some acquaintance between the two. Long after Spence's death Johnson was to make important use of the manuscript *Anecdotes* in his *Lives of the English Poets.*[104]

Spence's next publication after his translation of Attiret was the little work entitled *Moralities: or, Essays, Letters, Fables; and Translations,* issued by Dodsley in April, 1753,[105] under the pseudonym of Sir Harry Beaumont. The contents comprise chiefly the majority of Spence's contributions to the defunct *Museum*, though there are included pieces apparently written subsequent to the cessation of that periodical. In all, there are some thirty brief items, all in prose and having in common one obvious characteristic: they invariably point a moral. The subtitle accurately indicates the divisions into which the pieces fall. Though Lady Luxborough's opinion that the book is "*trite*-issimo"[106] is perhaps an exaggeration, it is only an exaggeration of the truth. Though the moral tone of the pieces is high and they are sometimes not unentertaining, little more can be said for them.

The essays are fairly represented by the moral history of Florio, who suffers his native sense to be overcome by his good nature and his modesty. Acting on the principle that "one ought always to fall in with the Humour of the Company, which one happens to meet with," he goes from bad to worse until finally in assisting a drunken friend who, unknown to Florio, has grossly insulted a lady, he kills the lady's husband and is led off to prison, where he passes the rest of his days lamenting his folly. In perhaps the most interesting piece in the book, "A true and exact Narrative of several Events, that happen'd in a War between two Nations of Emmets," Spence gives evidence of a surprising curiosity regarding natural history and makes a painstaking study of the habits of ants with almost the eye and the pen of a Thoreau.

Of the letters, one "to Sir Charles Easy in Town, from the Parson of his Parish in the Country," deplores the evils of gaming;[107] another provides counsel for "a very Good-natured Lady, that is married to a very Ill-natured Man"; and there is a series of letters (exchanged between a mother and her daughter lately gone into service) that is reminiscent of *Pamela*.[108] There is also a long dialogue freely translated from Erasmus and teaching a "sure Method for procuring Happiness in the Married State." This dialogue had appeared in the *Museum*,[109] and the version in the *Moralities* is purged of several "rogueish" passages which apparently were tolerable so long as the piece was anonymous but which were too gross to be permitted to appear under the name of the moral Sir Harry Beaumont.

The fables, twenty in number, are mostly in the Aesopian tradition. Though sometimes amusing, they are obvious and unoriginal. Two selected at random will serve to illustrate Spence's purpose: A small boy having lost his bright new shilling, his officious old nurse hurries to his aid and with her broom sweeps zealously over the spot where the coin has fallen, but fails in her search. At this the impatient child falls to upbraiding her, complaining that had she not interfered the coin might possibly have been found, but that the devil himself could not find it under the heap of dust which she had swept together. "The Moral of this Fable," adds Spence, "is humbly recommended as a Matter worthy the Speculation of those learned Gentlemen, the Commentators; who, no doubt, will have Sagacity enough to discover it."[110] Again, a prosperous physician has a dream in which Death sits at his bedside; but the specter hastens to explain that he has not come to summon the dreamer to the grave. For, he explains, "In killing you, I should kill but one; whereas, if you continue to live and practise for some Years longer, I know that you will kill your Thousands, and your Ten Thousands, for me."[111]

The translations, uniformly more serious and elevated in tone, are placed separately in the second part of the book. They begin with a free paraphrase of "Our Saviour's Sermon on the Mount," derived chiefly from the account in the Gospel of Matthew but augmented by verses from the Gospel of Luke. This piece is of particular interest because it seems to have been the first step toward a projected "harmony of the Gospels." In a prefatory note to the paper as it was published in the *Museum*,[112] the then anonymous author wrote: "I Have long since had some Thoughts of a Work, which (cou'd I finish it agreeably to the Idea I have of it) might be a very necessary and very useful one. It may be called, *The Harmony of the Gospels: Or, the Life and Doctrines of our B. Saviour, collected from the four Evan-*

gelists; wrote regularly, and in the common Stile of our own Histories. What I should endeavour in such a Work wou'd be to follow the real Sense, but not the Words or Manner of the Original: and to give it in such Language, as might render it more intelligible than it usually is, to a common *English* Reader. I herewith send you, *Our Saviour's Sermon on the Mount*, done in the Manner which I should propose to follow throughout the Work. If you think it worth while to hand it to the Publick, it wou'd oblige a constant Reader of your Paper; and if I find that it is not too much, or too generally disapproved of; I may possibly go on with the whole, in the same Manner." If Spence did entertain the design of proceeding with this project, he fortunately decided not to do so—perhaps because of the apathy or disapproval of "the public," perhaps because of his own loss of interest.

The second translation is a prose version of "The Choice of Hercules" from Xenophon.[113] Spence had published in *Polymetis* Lowth's English verse translation of the same passage. The book concludes with "The Picture of Human Life: Translated from the Greek of Cebes; a Disciple of Socrates," a moral apologue extremely popular throughout the eighteenth century. Spence's translation is the longest of the pieces in his book and the most insistently moral, reiterating the counsel which is indeed the keynote of the whole volume: "Get an Habit of doing right, whatever Pains it costs you; and let no Difficulties deter you, in the Way to Virtue. . . ."[114]

The *Moralities* represent better than any other of his works one side of Spence's character. The tendency toward sentimental, prosaic moralizing which shows faintly in the *Essay on Pope's Odyssey* and *Polymetis* and appears more clearly in *Crito* here comes into full view and is the central motif. Spence writes in the role of the "good Sir Beaumont," the sage "Phesoj Ecneps" whom James Ridley was to venerate,[115] the "man of God" of whom Alexander Dick spoke.[116] If the literary merit of the work is but small, its ethics are above praise! The pedestrian style and the lack of originality are in part accounted for by the fact that Spence was "writing down" to his public. The *Museum*, for which many of the pieces were prepared,[117] was intended as a popular periodical; and Spence originally planned to observe in a preface to the *Moralities* "ye difference of stile —difficulty, to write low enough for ye lower sort of people."[118]

Though it was as the "elegant" author of *Polymetis* that Spence was best known to his own generation, he enjoyed during his declining years a considerable reputation as a moralist. Thomas Hooke, his intimate friend and the son of the historian Nathaniel Hooke, inscribed to him some flattering verses written soon after the appearance of the *Moralities:*

> You good Sr Beaumont! were by Heav'n design'd
> T'adorn and cultivate the Human Mind:
> To teach the Great, how Greatness to employ,
> Beam like your noble Friend, the heart-felt joy!
> With views divine their riches to dispense,
> And win true Glory by Munificence:
> The spotless Maid, preserv'd from cruel harms,
> Warm'd by your precepts, seeks fair Virtue's charms.
> You show not virtue with a frowning mien,
> But simple as herself, and as your soul, serene.[119]

The book was translated into German in 1761 under the title of *Abhandlungen, Briefe, Geschichte, und Fabeln aus der Sittenlehre*, but it is safe to say that by the close of the century both Beaumont and his *Moralities* were forgotten.[120]

In another production of 1753, Joseph Warton's edition of Virgil,[121] Spence played the part of counselor to the editor as well as contributing to the notes. Though Warburton, who himself contributed a "Dissertation on the Sixth Book of the Æneid," affected to fear that the work would prove to be but "a gallimaufry" because Spence was "concerned in the direction of it,"[122] Warton himself gratefully acknowledged his debt to Spence in the advertisement prefixed to his first volume: ". . . Besides these assistances,

I must inform the reader, that Mr. Spence hath promoted this undertaking with that warmth and readiness with which he always serves his friends, by communicating to me a great number of manuscript notes of the late Mr. Holdsworth, author of Muscipula, &c: who by residing many years in Italy, and by making Virgil his constant companion in his travels, had an opportunity of being very exact in his observations on his favorite author. Many of them, that are local, and relate to the soil, the climate and customs of Italy, will I believe be found extremely curious and useful. Mr. Spence likewise obliged me with several excellent remarks of his own, made when he was abroad, that were never yet published, and with some few of Mr. Pope's. His Polymetis also hath greatly enriched the following collection...."[123] Warton stated that his decision to print Pitt's translation of the *Aeneid* rather than the more famous version by Dryden was the result of the errors in Dryden's translation which Spence, "a very candid writer, and one who entertains the highest opinion of his [Dryden's] genius,"[124] had disclosed in the chapters on allegory in *Polymetis*.

The friendship between Warton and Spence, which had probably begun many years prior to the publication of Warton's *Virgil*, continued without interruption until Spence's death. In his edition of Pope (1797) Warton wrote of Spence as follows: ". . . To this learned and amiable man, on whose friendship I set the greatest value, am I indebted for most of the anecdotes relating to Pope mentioned in this edition, which he communicated to me when I was making him a visit, 1754, at Byfleet in Surrey...."[125] John Wooll, Warton's friend and biographer, attributed to this visit an important function in Warton's intellectual development, averring rather extravagantly that under Spence's roof "was laid the foundation of those critical disquisitions which proved his [Warton's] competency of deciding on the merits of modern, as his Virgil had before done on those of ancient poetry."[126] Aside from the natural compatibility of their temperaments, the two scholars found a common meeting ground in their mutual interest in Pope as well as in their affection for Winchester College, where both had been bred. Spence remained intensely loyal to his old school, while Warton was a master there for thirty-eight years.[127] In the year of his death Spence referred to Warton as "the ingenious and learned schoolmaster of Winchester College, my particular friend."[128] On his part, Warton became a defender of Spence's posthumous reputation and on more than one occasion spoke up in his behalf to deprecate the unflattering remarks of Johnson and other critics.[129]

CHAPTER VII

Durham and the Closing Years

A FEW years after Spence's death it was written of him: "He was so high in patronage, that it is pretty certain he might have obtained a mitre, if his ambition had prompted him to solicit one."[1] Whatever the reason, Spence never became a bishop, but in 1754 he received the last of the series of valuable preferments which kept his life free from financial stress. Dr. Richard Trevor, formerly Bishop of St. David's and since 1752 Bishop of Durham, granted him the first prebend which fell to his disposal, and in March, 1754, Spence journeyed to Durham to be installed as prebendary of the seventh stall.[2] On March 21 he subscribed before Bishop Trevor to the Thirty-nine Articles,[3] he was formally installed on May 24,[4] and on the following Sunday (May 26) he read the appointed prayers in the Cathedral. Though Byfleet was to remain his principal place of residence, he spent much of his time during the next twelve years at Durham, where he developed a circle of friends and seized the opportunity to engage in his favorite pursuit of gardening among new surroundings. The grounds of ruined Finchale Priory, four miles north of Durham by lane and path, were part of his prebendal estate,[5] and he soon set about the improvement of what he termed his "wild Abbey-Grounds."[6] During his periods of residence at Durham he apparently passed most of his leisure time at Finchale, where he made "a good room in the farm-house near the abbey, with a bow window overhanging the murmuring streams of the Were, and looking upon the sweet sequestered walks of Cocken, but turning its back upon the venerable ruins."[7] The "round" of his completed garden was about five hundred feet.

During his closing years, in the midst of professional and social activities—whether at Byfleet, Durham, Great Horwood, or London—Spence repeatedly found occasion to continue that liberality and willingness to assist persons in distress which his friends never tired of praising. Rolle, for example, writes that Spence contented himself "wth very moderate enjoyments or gratifications f^{m} his Fortune, except indeed what he felt, & wch were the greatest of all to him, from benefiting of others by it; as if he had stood Possess'd of it as steward only for the Service of Mankind, he constantly applied a great part, to the Purposes of charity & good offices.

"In confering those, tho men of Genius, & of Literary merit in particular, & for whom he had the most congenial affection, were sure not to be forgotten; yet were his aims much more Liberal & unconfined, for as Distress of every Sort had always its claim upon him, so the softening this as much as possible to men in general became his chief Passion, & his great Object was the doing them Good.

"It was this friendly Propensity towards mankind, & this perpetual Bent to general Benevolence, that seem'd to have distinguish'd him from others, & may be looked upon as forming a kind of Specific character of Mr Spence."

Rolle's admiration was shared by other friends, notably Lowth, Gloster Ridley, and Sir Alexander Dick. One of the most impressive tributes to Spence's Christian charity came from the pen of young James Ridley, son of Gloster and the promising author of a series of highly romantic adventures entitled *Tales of the Genii* (1764). In the course of the work Ridley took occasion to pay tribute to certain friends of his father and himself, and one of the most elaborate of the eulogies is that rendered to Spence. The anecdotist is celebrated in the ninth tale under the not very obscure anagram of Phesoj Ecneps, the Dervise of the

Groves, who had been the early tutor and adviser of Mirglip, the faultless hero. Ridley's praise is spoken with oriental enthusiasm: "But reverend Sage, said *Mirglip*, thou hast taught thy Guest but half thy Virtues; for know, O noble Stranger, there's not a Family within ten Leagues of this plain Cottage, but feels the good Effect of *Phesoj Ecneps* Presence; the Youth of either Sex he places under proper Tutors and Directors, and makes the rising Progeny of *Persia* both loyal to their Prince, and duteous to their God. . . ."[8]

In addition to such testimony from his friends and that of his published works, evidence of Spence's unfailing charity abounds in his journals.[9] There are frequent notes such as "Promis'd, to Prentise out S^s two children; if I live, till they are fit for it";[10] "Mr Kinderly, at Norwich, can frequently dispose of Boys, for 5£ if Cloathd . . . as Journey-men weavers";[11] a memorandum that he must try to get something for "Mr Benson, the Blind Minister of Crowland in Lincolnshire";[12] reference to a note from "Mr Richardson" concerning "Rev^d Mr. Bennet Schoolmaster, at Hoddesdon in Hertfordshire; a very worthy man, & under difficulties from his worthiness."[13] So strong was his desire to help others that he cautioned himself against it in the following reflection, which sounds a little smug but is probably quite sincere: "Benevolence is more of a Passion, than of a Virtue in me; & ought to be watcht, almost as much as a Vice; (to keep it, either from Impertinence, or Impropriety.)"[14]

That benevolence toward men "of Literary merit in particular"[15] which Rolle mentions led Spence to the publication in November, 1754, of a pamphlet entitled *An Account of the Life, Character, and Poems of Mr. Blacklock; Student of Philosophy, in the University of Edinburgh*.[16] Thomas Blacklock, born the son of a poor tradesman at Annan, had lost his sight in infancy from smallpox. Through the charity of persons who interested themselves in him he was enabled to study at the grammar school of Edinburgh and then at the University there. In 1746 he published an octavo edition of his poems, and a second edition appeared in 1753–54. Spence's curiosity was aroused by what he heard of Blacklock, and he made a study of the poet's works with a view to ascertaining how a man blind from the cradle could produce poetry as rational as that of a writer possessed of normal sight. No doubt Spence was sincerely interested in this example of the force of genius surmounting great physical barriers, but he and Dodsley, who published the pamphlet, were primarily concerned with increasing the reputation of the blind author and helping the sale of his poems.[17] At the time he prepared the sketch, Spence had not met Blacklock and was forced to derive information about the poet's biography at second hand; but of his "moral and poetical character" he felt himself qualified to speak, evincing a detailed knowledge which shows that he had studied his subject with great interest. After this opening gun he began laying plans, in cooperation with Dodsley, for a London edition of the poems, to be published by subscription.

It appears that David Hume, at that time hard at work on his *History of Great Britain*, had been the means of interesting Dodsley and Spence in the writings and hardships of Blacklock. He had been affected by the gentle character and sad fate of the blind poet, as Spence was to be later, and had interceded in Blacklock's behalf with several influential persons. Writing to a friend, Dr. John Clephane, on September 1, 1754, he describes Blacklock's situation and his poetry, praises the volume of *Miscellanies* which the poet had recently published, and then continues as follows: "I sent up half-a-dozen [copies of Blacklock's volume] to Dodsley, desiring him to keep one, and to distribute the rest among men of taste of his acquaintance. I find they have been much approved of, and that Mr. Spence, in particular, has entertained thoughts of printing a new edition by subscription, for the benefit of the author. You are an acquaintance of Mr. Spence: encourage, I beseech you, so benevolent a thought, and promote it everywhere by your recommendation."[18] Six weeks later Hume decided to address himself directly to Spence, and wrote a lengthy letter beginning as follows:

SIR

The agreeable Productions, with which you have entertain'd the Public, have long given me a Desire of being known to you: But this Desire has been much encreas'd by my finding you engage so warmly in protecting a Man of Merit, so helpless as Mr Blacklocke. I hope you will indulge me in the *Liberty I have taken of writing to you.* I shall very willingly communicate all the particulars I know; of him; tho' others, by their longer Acquaintaince [*sic*] with him, are better qualify'd for this Undertaking.[19]

Then follows a discussion of Blacklock's character, learning, and deserts, with an appeal to Spence to forward his subscription project with all possible zeal. The letter concludes with this sentence: "I shall be very glad if the employing my Name in your Account of Mr Blacklocke can be of any Service."

One wonders whether Hume may have had a double motive in addressing Spence. Undoubtedly he was interested in Blacklock's welfare and wished to further it, but Spence had already set on foot his subscription plan and did not seem to need urging. It is not impossible that Hume cherished the hope of receiving public notice of his patronage. His assistance of Blacklock had been a worthy enterprise, and Spence's respectful commendation of his energy in such a cause would have brought him favorable notice. If such had been Hume's hope, however—and possibly the suggestion is unjust[20]—he was fated to disappointment. In the pamphlet edition of the *Account of Blacklock* Spence does indeed mention Hume and bases the biographical portion partly on a letter which Hume had written to Dodsley;[21] but in the version prefixed to the subscription volume Hume is not mentioned. Hume makes rather ugly charges against Spence in a letter to Clephane dated April 20, 1756. After commenting upon the appearance of the subscription volume and acknowledging "Spence's industry in so good a work," he continues thus: ". . . there is a circumstance of his conduct that will entertain you. In the Edinburgh edition there was a stanza to this effect:

JOSEPH SPENCE

> The wise in every age conclude,
> What Pyrrho taught and Hume renewed,
> That Dogmatists are fools.

"Mr. Spence would not undertake to promote a London subscription, unless my name, as well as Lord Shaftesbury's, (who was mentioned in another place,) were erased: the author frankly gave up Shaftesbury, but said that he would forfeit all the profit he might expect from a subscription, rather than relinquish the small tribute of praise which he had paid to a man whom he was more indebted to than to all the world beside. I heard by chance of this controversy, and wrote to Mr. Spence, that, without farther consulting the author, I, who was chiefly concerned, would take upon me to empower him to alter the stanza where I was mentioned. He did so, and farther, having prefixed the life of the author, he took occasion to mention some people to whom he had been obliged, but is careful not to name me; judging rightly that such good deeds were only *splendida peccata*, and that till they were sanctified by the grace of God they would be of no benefit to salvation."[22]

Reference to the text proves that the names of Hume and Shaftesbury have indeed been deleted,[23] but Spence's motive in urging the deletions was unquestionably the defensible one of concern for the sale of Blacklock's volume. Hume and Shaftesbury—particularly Hume—were not in good repute, and Spence would have been justified in feeling that the insertion of tributes to them might reduce sales. Nevertheless, if Hume's account of the episode is true, Spence's conduct does seem small. It must be kept in mind, however, that the action seems out of accord with his character and that but one side of the story has been heard.[24]

Spence divided his account of Blacklock into four sections, dealing, respectively, with the poet's biography, his moral character, his poetical character, and his manner of describing visible objects. He pays tribute to the sweetness and virtue of Blacklock's nature; so much, indeed, does he esteem the poet's "moral character" that when he turns from it to the "poetical character," though he admires Blacklock's talent, he is regretfully sensible of a decided fall. He points out the "beauties" of the verse much as he had done those of Pope's *Odyssey*—but in reading this praise of mediocre poetry one must remember that Spence was out to put Blacklock in a good light and to swell the forthcoming subscription list.

In the fourth section, entitled "Of his describing Visible Objects," and termed "much the most difficult Part" of the undertaking, Spence seeks to discover and explain how the blind poet could so well describe external objects which it was impossible for him ever to have seen. He suggests that Blacklock really has as true and clear a perception of objects as does the normal man, though a perception attained through other means than that of sight; hence his employment of description is as accurate as that of a seeing poet. His conception of the sun, for example, is not the same as ours, which is largely associated with the idea of light, but it is equally definite and clear. It is a conception expressed in terms of thought as well as of the sense of feeling, and when Blacklock speaks in what appears as metaphor he is really speaking in language to him quite natural and unadorned; hence the peculiar vividness of many of his descriptions.

This rather fantastic theory was later rudely rejected by Johnson. "That foolish fellow, Spence," he remarked to Boswell, "has laboured to explain philosophically how Blacklock may have done, by means of his own faculties, what it is impossible he should do."[25] But in 1756 young Edmund Burke had discussed Spence's conclusions more sympathetically. Speaking of Blacklock in the *Philosophical Inquiry into the Origin of our Ideas of the Sublime and Beautiful,* he said: "Few men blessed with the most perfect sight can describe visual objects with more spirit and justness than this blind man; which cannot possibly be attributed to his having a clearer conception of the things he describes than is common to other persons. Mr. Spence, in an elegant preface which he has written to the works of this poet, reasons very ingeniously, and, I imagine, for the most part, very rightly, upon the cause of this extraordinary phenomenon. . . ."[26]

The publication of the *Account of Blacklock* was the opening gun in a campaign, managed jointly by Spence and Dodsley, to obtain for Blacklock sufficient funds to secure him against destitution. Spence had closed his little sketch of the poet with this artful appeal: "What an Object, what a happy Opportunity is here, for any one who is capable of it, (either from his Affluence or his Power,) to acquire a good deal of solid and unenvied Reputation, by raising a Person of this Turn and of such extraordinary Desert, to some Situation where he may be above Want; or rather by which he might be enabled, in some degree, to exert and enjoy the beneficent, and noble Dictates, of his Soul!"[27] The next step was to plan the publication of a subscription volume and secure enough subscriptions to warrant going ahead with the project. The best account of the procedure followed is found in a letter which Spence wrote at this time to his old acquaintance John Conybeare, Bishop of Bristol, in an effort to interest the Bishop in the forthcoming publication. This letter, written at Byfleet on January 11, 1755, is obviously only one of many of its type which Spence must have distributed among his friends throughout England.[28]

Spence begins with an explanation of Blacklock's situation, in which he makes use of some information derived from Hume's letter of October 15, 1754.[29] He gives Dodsley credit for conceiving the idea of a subscription volume, and he speaks of his own pamphlet as being aimed at making Blacklock "somewhat more known in this part of our Island." After describing the publication, in November, 1754, of Dodsley's proposals—"for a Guinea large paper, & Half a Guinea the small"—he continues as follows: "I then went to Town: where (after a fortnight sollicitation) I had the pleasure of paying in above 50 Subscriptions, the day before I came away; & but three Half Guinea ones in that number.

"But, at the same time, I had the Mortification to find, that my notable Treatise had had very little effect. Like the honest Mr Abraham Adams, I had concluded that all good People only wanted to have a man of so much worth pointed out to them, in such necessitous circumstances; & that they wou'd all run to help him, immediately; but I found myself as much mistaken, as that Gentleman generally was, in his humane Conclusions. For all the Subscriptions, that came in whilst I was in Town, seem to have been got by the meer dint of Personal Application: there is scarce the name of a single Volunteer, among them.

"As I found this to be the Case; on my return home, I resolv'd to trouble each of my Best Friends with a Letter, to beg their good word to any very worthy & charitable Persons, whom they might meet with, either in their Visits, or at their Tables; for their help toward relieving so great & so uncommon a subject for Charity.

"Will Your Lordship give me leave not to omit you, in the number of these Friends? & can You pardon me for this tedious Narrative? I know Your love of doing good; & hope that will plead for my excuse. . . ."

That Spence's friends, willingly or unwillingly, yielded to his solicitations is proved by the subscription list prefixed to the published volume, for among the names listed are those of such persons as the Bishop of Durham, Stephen Duck, Nicholas Herbert, the Earl and Countess of Lincoln, Robert Lowth, the Duke of Manchester, William Burrell Massingberd, the Earl of Middlesex, the Duke and Duchess of Newcastle, Gloster Ridley, Edward Rolle, Edward Rudge, and Lord Wentworth. Hume subscribed, of course, as did Spence and his mother. In addition, "Sir Harry Beaumont" took four large-paper copies and, oddly enough, a "Mrs. Beaumont" took one![30]

Before the publication of the subscription volume Spence saw to it that he was prepared to write about

Blacklock with more authority than when he had composed his first sketch. Thus he could begin his revised and expanded account as follows: "In the former edition of this little narrative, I complained of want of lights in relation to the person who is the subject of it; but at present, there is no occasion for my repeating that complaint: I have since been favour'd not only with several letters, but with a kind visit from him, of some weeks, when I was in the north of *England;* which will enable me to give not indeed a much longer account of him, (for that is not necessary), but one much less defective than my former."[31] The subscription volume was published in February, 1756,[32] with the following title: *Poems by Mr. Thomas Blacklock. To which is Prefix'd, An Account of the Life, Character, and Writings, of the Author, By the Reverend Mr. Spence, Late Professor of Poetry, at Oxford.* A second and a third edition had been published by the end of May,[33] but a letter from Dodsley to Blacklock on July 16, 1757, seems to imply that the sale was disappointingly slow. Dodsley says: "I heartily wish I could give you as good an account of the sale of your poems as they deserve, but to say the truth they sell but very slowly; & I will send any number you please to Scotland whenever you direct me to whom I must send them. As to settling the account, I beg you will not be in haste about it, I should be very sorry to send you an account without a ballance in your favour. . . ."[34]

Blacklock sank back into the neglect and obscurity whence he had momentarily and partially ascended, but the efforts which Spence and Dodsley had made in his behalf must have provided some relief from the poverty which had previously afflicted him. Spence retained interest in him until his own death, continuing to extend at least his personal charity to the man whom he had befriended. When he and Dodsley journeyed together through the Lowlands of Scotland in July, 1758, they visited Blacklock for a day or two,[35] and Alexander Dick, in a letter to Spence of August 25, 1765, replying to an anxious request for information, relates details of the satisfactory circumstances of Blacklock and his wife, concluding: "Your intended humanity to them will I dare say be very seasonable, & I presume will be the last they will need to set them well on their feet."[36]

Blacklock, like Duck, was always prepared to express gratitude to his benefactor. His most elaborate tribute is embodied in a poem addressed to Spence in 1759, describing the effects of the mention of Spence's name upon the poet as he lay in an apathy from which he could be roused by no other means:

> Thus exorcis'd, to Lethe's dismal shore
> Fled Indolence, and sought her haunts of yore,
> With all her train forsook the poet's breast,
> And left the man completely dispossess'd.
> If to your very name, by bounteous heav'n,
> Such blest, restoring influence has been giv'n,
> How must your sweet approach, your aspect kind,
> Your soul-reviving converse, warm the mind![37]

A more explicit acknowledgment of Spence's favors is found in *Paraclesis; or, Consolations Deduced from Natural and Revealed Religion: in Two Dissertations. The First supposed to have been composed by Cicero; now rendered into English: The Last originally written By Thomas Blacklock, D.D.*[38] The second dissertation was dedicated to Spence. The dedication, dated October 9, 1767, begins as follows:

REVEREND SIR,

How agreeable to me is this public opportunity of expressing the sentiments of a heart overflowing with gratitude for the many favours it has received from you. It is to your kind patronage that I owe my introduction into the republic of letters, and to your benevolence, in some measure, my present comfortable situation. But as this subject can no way interest the generality of readers, and would, I believe, hurt your delicacy, if I give scope to my pen; I will therefore leave unsaid the greatest part of what the warmth of my sensibility suggests upon this occasion. Allow me only to add, that an Essay on the Evidence and Consolation of Christianity could not, with greater propriety, be dedicated to any one than the Reverend Mr Spence, who is so distinguished for all the virtues that adorn the Christian character. . . .

Because of the existence of the journals for 1755–58, it is possible to trace Spence's course in greater detail during those years than during any other period except that of his Continental travels. His memoranda show that he spent a considerable portion of every year traveling and paying or receiving visits, while at the same time he continued, not only at Durham but also at Byfleet and occasionally at Great Horwood, to be active in the pulpit. In 1755 he spent the months until May chiefly at Byfleet, his life varied by the usual round of visits and visitors. He then made his regular trip to Durham, where he officially began his residence on May 30 and remained until late in August.[39] On his return journey he visited Lord Wentworth at Kirkby and paused at Great Horwood, and then passed the rest of the year and the early months of 1756 at Byfleet and in London. It is probable that his mother died during this period.[40] In June he again set out for the north, pursuing a circuitous route no doubt designed to enable him to stop with as many friends as possible. On June 16 and 17 he "did not get to bed till aftᵣ Sunrise," a strange procedure for a man who supposedly had to be careful of his health. From July until the following February (1757) he was in Durham and its neighborhood, returning thence in a slow progress to Byfleet. On September 19 he wrote to Massingberd that he had just returned to Byfleet "after a Ramble of about 2 Months, thorough half a Score of Counties," and on January 17, 1758, that he had spent "two Months at Kimbolton, making (or rather destroying) the Duke of Manchester's Garden; came thence with him to London, staid there a fortnight, & am but just return'd to this Place."

In 1758 he varied his itinerary by venturing upon a Scottish tour in the company of Dodsley. The publisher, of course, had been his close friend for years, and the two were to remain on the best of terms until Dodsley's death in 1764. Though Spence had been in Italy when Dodsley had first gained prominence as the author of *A Muse in Livery* (1732) and had made the acquaintance of Pope, the two no doubt met soon after Spence's return. In Dodsley, Spence discovered two qualifications, either of which would have insured his regard: the poetic footman was another example of natural genius manifesting itself in an unfavorable environment, and he was a man in whom Pope was interested. Spence played an active part in forwarding his new friend's progress: Dodsley's biographer calls Spence "the most loyal and the most devoted" of the publisher's many friends.[41] Nichols quotes a "snarling quatrain" from one of Curll's scurrilous attacks on Pope (1737):

> 'Tis kind indeed a *Livery Muse* to aid,
> Who scribbles Farces to augment his trade:
> Where You and Spence and Glover drive the nail,
> The Devil's in it if the plot should fail.[42]

Spence made Dodsley the sole publisher of his own works, and in 1736 he edited Sackville's *Gorboduc* for Dodsley and Pope.[43] He was a subscriber to Dodsley's *Collection of Old Plays* (1744–45) and may very well have been one of the "most judicious" friends who, according to Dodsley's proposals for his edition, had promised him "their best Assistance in this Work."[44] He had, of course, been one of the most frequent contributors to the *Museum* (1746–47) and had probably helped Dodsley materially in the compilation of the *Collection of Poems* (1748–58).[45] The friendship had been strengthened by the collaboration of the two men in behalf of Blacklock.

Two letters from Dodsley to Spence have been preserved: one, dated October 22, 1748, enviously contrasts Spence's rural quiet and happiness at Byfleet with the publisher's immersion in the cares of business; the other, undated, but evidently belonging to 1751,[46] contains a song entitled "Mutual Love," to be sung at Vauxhall, the authorship of which Dodsley intended to conceal from all except the trusted Spence.[47]

The Scottish tour was planned far in advance and the itinerary carefully mapped out.[48] Dodsley wished to include a visit with his friend Shenstone at the Leasowes, near Birmingham. Apparently Spence and Shenstone had never met,[49] though on an earlier occasion Spence had planned to visit the Leasowes at Dodsley's suggestion and

had been unable to keep his appointment.[50] Dodsley felt
that the two would have much in common. First, however,
a stop was to be made at Spence's living at Great Horwood.
The trip was begun on June 16 or 17, and the travelers apparently arrived at the Leasowes on the twenty-second. It
was inevitable that two gardening enthusiasts should take
pleasure in each other's society. Shenstone wrote to Graves
that he had found Spence "extremely polite, friendly,
chearful, and master of an infinite fund of subjects for
agreeable conversation,"[51] and he later exclaimed to the
same correspondent: "Mr. Spence, the very man *you*
would like, and who would like *you*, of all mankind."[52]
Spence, charmed by the beauty of the Leasowes and much
interested in Shenstone's "improvements," set down an
account of the plan of the grounds.[53] At Shenstone's request he chose a particular oak tree for a seat, which the
poet then caused to be inscribed in the following fashion:

"EXIMIO NOSTRO CRITONI
CUI DICARI VELLET
MUSARUM OMNIUM ET GRATIARUM CHORUS
DICAT AMICITIA"[54].

When Dodsley and Spence left the Leasowes after a week's
visit,[55] the latter carried with him the manuscript of Shenstone's *Elegies* and, after his arrival at Durham, sent them
back "with a sheet or two of criticisms, and an handsome
letter."[56] Shenstone wrote Graves that had his affairs permitted he would have accompanied his friends into Scotland,[57] and he had given his promise to visit Byfleet the
following May.[58]

Dodsley and Spence continued their leisurely progress
northward through Liverpool and Lancaster to the Lakes,
where they spent several days before crossing the Border
on July 7. At Dumfries they talked again with Blacklock.
After a drive of a hundred miles "through bad Roads, over
Mountains, by Cottages composed of Dirt, and a barren,
bleak country," the travelers became enthusiastic over the
scenery as they approached Edinburgh, and the Scottish

capital itself prompted Spence to write almost lyrically of its beauty to Shenstone.[59] Thence the course lay through Dunbar, Berwick, Alnwick, and Morpeth to Durham, where they arrived July 17. Dodsley, like many another visitor before and since, was impressed by the romantic beauty of the city and was particularly enchanted by the ruins at Finchale.[60] After a brief sojourn, however, he turned his face toward London and the cares of business, while Spence remained to perform his duties at the Cathedral.[61]

At Durham, as at Byfleet, Spence never found time heavy on his hands. He wrote to Shenstone on August 19 that "Visits, and returning Visits, and Business" had occupied the month since his arrival, and he added: "I am now set down to writing Letters, which I verily believe will take up another Month, for, on casting up my Accounts of that Kind, I found myself no less than forty-seven in Debt; a Number, for which I am sure you must pity me."[62]

He began his official three-week period of residence on August 21, spent some time in the fall "a' Gardning" at Kimbolton, and set out upon his southward journey in December.

Spence and Shenstone corresponded intermittently for a time, but on Shenstone's side the correspondence was impeded by a dilatoriness which caused him to blush for his own neglect. Concerning Spence he exclaimed to Graves: "How much am I interested in the preservation of his friendship!—and yet, such is my *destiny* (for I can give it no other name), I have never wrote to him *since*."[63] Yet he continued to delay writing, for writing to Dodsley on March 31, 1759, he said of Spence: "—how I blush, whilst I recollect that Name! And yet, were it not for my *own* Omissions, it must revive *only* my most *favourite* Ideas. Surely 'tis written in the Book of Fate, that I shall discharge my Debt within a Post or two; for Fate evidently enough interferes, or I could never have been so long silent. I am almost ashamed to desire my humble Respects to him, and yet it is impossible for me to suppress my Feelings."[64] Time after time he disappointed the hopes of Dodsley and Spence that he would join them—in London in February, 1759,[65] at Byfleet in May, at Bath in the autumn.[66] He continued to be remiss in his correspondence with Spence, and Dodsley chided him for his bad manners: "Notwithstanding you have taken Pains to forfeit all Claim to Favour from Mr. Spence, I am very well satisfied, the Letter you promise will effectually cancel all your Offences: I shall go down to him in about a Month, (you see I give you Time enough) enclose it to me, and I will carry it to him, with one of your small Plans, to which I will put References. . . ."[67] This letter evidently accomplished the desired result, for a month later Dodsley wrote to Shenstone: "I have Compliments to you from Mr. Spence, and he is much obliged to you for the Survey of your Farm."[68]

To the year 1759 belongs a publication which exhibits Spence once more in the role of benefactor and indicates that he was still on terms of intimacy with Horace Walpole. In the summer of 1753, during his annual visit to Great Horwood, Spence had become interested through a neighboring clergyman in Robert Hill, "the learned tailor of Buckingham." Though at this time he was with Hill for only part of one day, Spence decided to make him the subject of a *Letter to the Rev.^d Mr. G[loster] R[idley]*, which was published at the end of the year.[69] This brief pamphlet, like the similar accounts of Duck and Blacklock, was intended to bring its subject to the notice of the public. Hill, who no doubt appealed to Spence as another example of the force of nature displaying its power in a humble and uneducated mind, had received practically no schooling but by amazing persistence and dogged application had acquired, during the brief hours of respite from his labors, some knowledge of Greek, Latin, and Hebrew. Blessed with an excellent mechanical memory, he had completely mastered the few dozen books to which he had access, and had gained some attention for his curious feats of learning. In 1753 he had printed a small volume of *Observations* upon Bishop Berkeley's *Essay on Spirit*, as well as *Some Considerations on the Divinity of the Holy Ghost.* Following the publication of the *Letter* concerning this "modest, good Sort of Man," Spence continued to interest himself in Hill and apparently aided him financially for several years.[70] Then by 1758 he had decided to assist his newest protégé by a different method.

During his visit to Florence in 1740 Spence had listened to tales of the noted Antonio Magliabecchi, librarian to the Great Duke and famed for his scholarship and prodigious memory. It struck him now that there was some resemblance between Magliabecchi and Hill, and he determined to spread the renown of the Buckingham tailor by comparing his feats to those of the much more widely known Florentine. Accordingly, he referred to his notes on Magliabecchi and apparently had Hill travel to Byfleet expressly for the purpose of supplying information concerning his life and studies. This visit, which lasted for a fortnight, occurred in April,[71] and was thus described by Spence in a letter of May 3 to Richardson: ". . . when I am so very busy in writing the Life, not of a Hebrew Jew, but of a Hebrew Tailor; who was with me, for a fortnight, lately; & whom I sent off from me, with a Hundred & Fifty Pound-weight of Fathers, & Polemic Divinity."[72] Apparently the two were also together in June on the occasion of Spence's visit to Great Horwood with Dodsley.[73] Walpole had offered the use of the press at Strawberry Hill, and early in 1759 appeared the curious little work entitled *A Parallel; In the manner of Plutarch: Between a most celebrated Man of Florence; And One, scarce ever heard of, in England. By the Reverend Mr. Spence.*, to be sold by Dodsley "For the Benefit of Mr. Hill." Walpole records that the printing of seven hundred copies was begun October 2, 1758, and finished on November 11, and that the day of publication was February 2, 1759.[74] According to him, six hundred copies were sold in a fortnight.[75] A second edition was promptly printed by Dodsley,[76] who also reprinted the work two years later (1761) in his *Fugitive Pieces.*[77]

In *A Parallel* Spence made somewhat more pretense to

literary merit than he had done in his pamphlets on Duck and Blacklock. Less abrupt and colloquial than in those sketches, his style approaches more closely to the polish attained in the *Essay on Pope's Odyssey*, *Polymetis*, and *Crito*. No doubt he considered that a book from the aristocratic press at Strawberry Hill deserved greater pains than the Grub Street pamphlet on Duck or the appeal on behalf of Blacklock. After sketching the life and achievements of each of his subjects in separate sections of the work, he devotes a final chapter to a comparison between them. He concludes as follows: "Upon the whole; I think we may fairly conclude, that they are both equal in merit, as to their industry and application to their studies; each seeming to apply to them, as much as he could: But of the two Mr. Hill is the more sensible and better man; and Magliabecchi, the more extraordinary, the more applauded, and the more fortunate."[78]

The comparison with Magliabecchi "in the manner of Plutarch" was of course simply a device to make the book more readable and to provide a plausible excuse for the charitable project. For the modern reader the account of the noted Italian scholar—"the universal library"—holds far greater interest than the sketch of the English tailor and the rather forced comparison between the two. To the accounts of Magliabecchi which he had derived at first hand at Florence,[79] Spence added information from the few available printed sources. It is clear that during the years which had passed between Magliabecchi's death in 1714 and the writing of *A Parallel*, tradition had exaggerated the achievements of the Italian's phenomenal memory. Spence himself doubts the authenticity of some of the amazing incidents which he relates, and cautions his readers that some allowance must be made for the habitual Italian tendency to overstatement. Nevertheless, Magliabecchi must indeed have possessed a remarkable mind, and the tale of his rise from a fruitseller's shop to the position of librarian to the Duke of Florence, together with instances of his mental capacity, still has a certain interest.

Not so much can be said of the section devoted to the biography of Hill. The Buckingham tailor, though he deserved praise for his hard-won mastery of linguistic knowledge, was far below the level of genius, and his moral fiber seems to have needed strengthening. The comparison between the two scholars is drawn aptly enough; indeed, it must be conceded that Spence performed the task of bringing Hill to public notice in a way which commands respect when one bears in mind the difficulty of the undertaking. Yet Walpole's comment on *A Parallel* is not unjust. He wrote to Chute: "Mr. Spence's *Magliabechi* is published to-day from Strawberry. I believe you saw it, and shall have it; but 'tis not worth sending you on purpose. However, it is full good enough for the generality of readers."[80]

The extent of the financial success of the project is not certain, but the sale of six hundred copies in two weeks and the prompt appearance of a second edition indicate some measure of success. Spence had appended an advertisement asking for donations to relieve Hill's distress and listing a number of persons (including Richardson and Dodsley) who would act as agents in receiving such gifts, and to the reprint in *Fugitive Pieces* in 1761 was attached a list of approximately one hundred benefactors of Hill, together with the sum that each had subscribed. Among the contributors were Spence, Langton, Lowth, and Young, but the subscriptions amounted in all to less than £100.

Probably Spence continued to see Hill on his annual visits to Great Horwood, but no record of their association after 1759 has survived. Hill outlived his patron, dying in 1777 after having adhered to the end to his original occupation of tailoring.

In March, 1759, Spence passed a few days in the company of Edward Young, whom he had known at least since 1729, when Young wrote to him introducing James Thomson.[81] Now in his middle seventies, the poet was living in retirement at Welwyn in Hertfordshire. The meeting almost certainly took place at Welwyn, which lies not far from Great Horwood. Notes of Young's conversation, dated March 23–28, are preserved in the Spence Papers.[82] There is also an interesting bill from the Post House, at Stamford in Lincolnshire, on the back of which Spence has jotted anecdotes from Young and the Rev. Mr. John Jones, Young's friend and companion at Welwyn. As he had done with Martha Blount a decade earlier, Spence read to the aged poet at least some sections of the manuscript *Anecdotes*.[83]

Mr. Jones wrote to Spence on September 3, 1761: "I have many times wondered why you never called upon us again at Wellwyn. Dr. Young, I am sure, would have been *glad to have seen you*, & will still be so, every time you pass through this little Hamlet."[84] It is not certain whether Spence ever visited the poet again, though a sheet in the Spence Papers headed "fro Dr Young" and dated February 7–11, 1765, would seem to indicate that the two were together at that time. Young died later in the same year.

In August, 1759, Spence journeyed through Dorchester, Weymouth, Exeter, Glastonbury, and Wells to Bath, where he passed some time in the early autumn with Dodsley and William Whitehead, Cibber's successor in the laureateship. The little coterie was no doubt joined by Richard Graves, good friend of both Dodsley and Shenstone, and rector at near-by Claverton.[85] Probably one of the topics of discussion was the projected *Select Fables*, which Dodsley had now had in mind for a year, and to which Graves was a minor contributor. The idea had been suggested originally by Lowth during Dodsley's visit to Durham with Spence in the summer of 1758,[86] and Dodsley was encouraged and possibly assisted by Spence, who in his *Moralities* had published a number of "modern fables." There is reason to believe that Spence was the author of the "Life of Aesop" prefixed to the work in its later editions. In the original production Dodsley had used a biographical account translated and altered from that of Meziriac and supplied with notes summarizing later scholarly opinion on the subject. But, deeming this "not so full and satisfactory as it might have been," he induced "a learned and ingenious friend" to consult the ancient authorities on Aesop and write a new sketch of his life.[87] Accordingly, the revised biography appeared in all the subsequent editions, of which there were many. That the "learned and ingenious friend" was Spence is suggested by Shenstone's remark to Graves on May 2, 1761, shortly after the publication of the first edition: "Mr. Spence offers him [Dodsley] to write the *life* afresh. . . ."[88]

Spence continued to be an active traveler. On February 27, 1762, he wrote to Massingberd from Edwinstowe in Nottinghamshire: "I begin now to be quite of the Household with my good Patron [Lord Lincoln]; & attend him generally, at Oatlands; London; & now, on his Rambles." On his annual trip to the north he was accustomed to pay visits on the way to Lord Wentworth at Kirkby and Massingberd at Ormesby. Other friends whom he visited regularly were Nicholas Herbert, of Suffolk, and Edward Rudge, of Oxfordshire. From Durham he journeyed many times across the Border to visit Sir Alexander Dick, the friend of Boswell, at Prestonfield, near Edinburgh, where he suggested, as usual, a number of "excellent Improvements" in the estate, to the admiration of the gardener, James.[89] Here he seems to have met Hume and William Robertson,[90] and he so charmed the household that the members said to one another: "When shall we see again the man of God in our family?"[91] He left a record of one journey from Durham to Edinburgh in September, 1760, during which he proved himself an indefatigable sightseer,[92] and he toured the western counties again in the summer of 1763.[93] Lowth visited him at Byfleet, and the two were frequently in company at Durham, where Lowth (also a prebend of the Cathedral) maintained a residence at Sedgefield. Rolle was apparently at Byfleet at least once each year, and Spence often visited London "for 5 or 6 days at a time."[94]

It is probable that Spence was of considerable help to Dodsley in preparing the edition of Shenstone's works

which appeared in April, 1764.[95] In the summer of that
year the two old friends again set out on a northern tour,
destined to be the last they would ever take together. The
melancholy story of this journey is derived chiefly from
letters which passed between the travelers and a young
Derbyshire woman named Elizabeth Cartwright, talented,
vivacious, and not a little flattered at her friendship with
two men so eminent in the literary world. Dodsley had
maintained a correspondence with her for several years,
and in 1763 she had paid him and his sister a visit in London.[96] She had some literary aspirations[97] and was a skilled
performer of parlor tricks, one of which was the cutting of
elaborate paper landscapes. In her correspondence with
Dodsley the first mention of Spence occurs when Dodsley
tells her that he has received her "exceeding pretty landscape for Mr. Spence, and by his order have got it framed
in the same manner that mine is."[98] The next day Spence
himself sent his thanks to the artist, and added: "Poor
Dodsley was not well, or I should have scolded him more
than I did for that omission.[99] He complained, for the first
time I ever heard him in my whole life, of low spirits. Have
not you left a dart in one side of him?"[100] The itinerary of
1764 was planned to include a visit to Miss Cartwright and
her parents at Duffield, near Birmingham. Dodsley was to
join Spence at Byfleet in June, whence they planned to
proceed to Great Horwood, then to Duffield, and finally on
to Durham. On April 28 Dodsley wrote to Miss Cartwright: "Mr. Spence talks of setting out about the middle
of June, and of staying a week or ten days at his Living on
the road, and a day or two at Lord Wentworth's, but for
his servants you need give yourself no trouble, for he will
have none with him but John, who may lie at the Public
House at the Bridge. We shall have no horses but those on
hire, and get rid of at every post. As to Mr. Spence and I,
if it would not be too troublesome, we shall chuse to be at
your house, which will want neither hills, nor rivers, nor
lawns, to make it agreeable. I flatter myself we shall find
there somewhat much more agreeable than all these. We

shall certainly go by Matlock, where I did purpose to stay a few days, while Mr. Spence made his visit to the Duke; but of this we shall better determine when we are upon the spot."[101]

On June 12 Spence wrote to Miss Cartwright concerning their plans. Dodsley had arrived on the ninth, and the friends were to set out on the thirteenth for Great Horwood, whence they would depart on the eighteenth, Dodsley to go direct to Duffield while Spence stopped for a few days with Lord Wentworth at Kirkby.[102] He added: "I have been in a perpetual round of business, and visits, and visitors for a long time, which have kept me in (what I heartily abhor) a continual hurry. Pray forgive me, or rather pity me."[103] Apparently the journey proceeded according to plan, and on July 24 Spence wrote to Miss Cartwright from Durham as follows: "Mr. Dodsley, who is pure well for a man in his condition, joins me in hearty thanks to you and all the good family for all your goodness to us at Duffield, and in all services to all Friends there. We came on so leisurely that we did not get hither till the 17th., in the evening, and on the Road I had prevail'd on my very honest cripple of a companion to promise me that he would attempt to walk round my garden here (which is about 500 feet) once every day for the first week, twice for the second, and so on, to four times a day, which would have been towards half a mile. But all this fine scheme was defeated the very first morning after our arrival, for on making the experiment of one round only, Mr. Dodsley was so excessively fatigued, that I have never been able to get him to venture on a second. I am now endeavouring to make it practicable by preparing three resting-places for him: one is a chair placed in a sort of grotto hollowed under the house; the other is by a little turning seat on a small knoll that takes in a prospect of the Country, and particularly the London Road; and the third is a bench with a foot board, quite covered and surrounded with a little grove. Now, if he will take 'Gil Blas' or any other good book in his hand, he may walk from one of these seats to another, and read as long as he pleases at each, and by this means may very well be in the air an hour or two whenever he pleases. The seat on the knoll is not yet finished, but as soon as it is, and the weather is inviting, I hope for better success in this experiment than we had in the former. At least they will be more serviceable to me every time I come here, for already, without having the gout, and by mere dint of old age, I find frequent Resting places to be very agreeable things to myself. Mr. Dodsley begs you would return his visit to you at London, and, whenever you do so, I beg you would come together for a good long visit to me at Bifleet. I am already your much obliged and affectionate humble servant,

Jo. SPENCE"[104]

Spence's good intentions toward Dodsley came to nothing, for the patient grew slowly weaker, and on September 23 he died. He was buried in the cemetery attached to Durham Cathedral, and Spence composed the following inscription for the tombstone:

If you have any respect
for uncommon industry & merit,
Regard this Place
in which are interred the Remains
of
Mr Robert Dodsley;
who, as an Author, raised himself
much above what cou'd have been expected
from one in his rank of life
and without learned Education.
And who, as a Man, was scarce
exceeded by any in Integrity of Heart
& Purity of manners & Conversation.
He left this life for a better
Sept 23ᵈ 1764 in the 61 year of his Age.[105]

To this year belongs the publication of James Ridley's *Tales of the Genii*, in which Spence was so flatteringly celebrated.[106] Spence took a pardonable interest in this work of the son of his old friend Gloster Ridley and apparently had made his usual efforts to bring the budding author to the favorable notice of his circle of friends.[107] He also addressed to young Ridley a letter written in the style of the *Tales of the Genii*, eulogizing Ridley's work and the virtue of his moral instruction. After expressing hopes for the future success of the ill-fated author, who was to die in the following year, Spence concludes: "These are the prayers of Phesoj Ecneps, the 'Dervise of the Groves,' for the most moral and most illuminated of the sons of men."[108]

In the summer of 1765 Spence made "an agreeable jaunt" to Clumber in company with Lord Lincoln,[109] and probably to the same summer belongs a visit paid to him at Byfleet by Miss Cartwright.[110] In April, 1766, he was again with Lord Lincoln at Clumber, and in the following summer he made what was to be his last journey to Durham. He probably followed his usual route through Great Horwood to Lord Wentworth's at Kirkby, where he suffered a light stroke. Concerning this disaster he wrote philosophically to Miss Cartwright on July 2: "I was favoured with dear Miss Cartwright's most obliging letter yesterday, in the evening, and hope to wait upon her on my way to Durham, though it may be two or three days later than I talked of in my first. How uncertain is everything in this world! Four days after I wrote to you I was seized with a paralytic stroke; it thinned me pretty much for a day or two, but every day since I have been growing better and better.

"If I have not a second stroke, I think of proceeding Northwards from hence, on the 10th instant; but who can tell what to-morrow may produce? Pray don't be at all concerned for me. I find by the first experiment that if this is the way that I am to go out of the world by, it would be a death to be envied, as being entirely without pain, and have thank't Heaven most heartily for it several times since its first visit to me."[111]

Having made a partial recovery, he proceeded slowly to Durham, but his health was so precarious that he made application to the King for a dispensation from attending to his duties at the Cathedral, and also took occasion to make his will on August 4 at Lowth's residence at Sedgefield. The dispensation was granted on August 21,[112] and accordingly he set out for Byfleet earlier than was his custom, pausing at Clumber on the way. In the autumn Miss Cartwright was married to Mr. John Coltman, and the couple spent a portion of their honeymoon at Byfleet.[113]

Meanwhile, Spence was occupying many of his leisure hours by preparing for the press the Virgilian studies of the late Edward Holdsworth, whom he had known intimately in Italy. At Holdsworth's death in 1746 all his papers relating to Virgil had been placed in Spence's hands for publication. Some of his notes had appeared in Warton's edition of Virgil in 1753,[114] but Spence continued to assemble and organize his dead friend's remarks on the Latin poet, a labor of love as well as duty, since he himself had admired and studied Virgil since boyhood. Ill-health, however, all but prevented completion of his design, and he was forced to call upon Lowth for aid with the final burdensome details of publication.[115] The work finally appeared in February, 1768, under the following title: *Remarks and Dissertations on Virgil; With some other Classical Observations: By the late Mr. Holdsworth. Published, with several Notes, and Additional Remarks, by Mr. Spence.*

The contents of the volume were not derived entirely from Holdsworth's papers, but came in part from Spence's own notes. "The Editor's Advertisement" gives the following explanation: "Several other observations of Mr. Holdsworth, in this kind, I had been acquainted with, many years before his death: I first having had the happiness of meeting with him at Florence in 1732; and of being favoured with a great degree of his intimacy and friendship. He soon communicated his design, and particular thoughts on Virgil to me, with the greatest freedom. I took notes down on paper, that I might not lose his thoughts; which were so very valuable to me. I went further; I procured an interleaved Virgil, and endeavoured to follow him, as well as I was able: and this occasioned my own observations, which I beg pardon for mixing in the same work with his. I have less reason to make any excuse for those of some friends, of particular worth and eminence, which are inserted in this work." Since Spence ascribed each note to its source, one can readily determine the extent of his own contribution. Particularly in the sections devoted to the *Eclogues* and the *Aeneid*, his remarks are numerous. They concern a wide variety of topics—questions of local geography, illustrations from statues and gems, interpretation of the text, details of Roman civilization—and bear the mark of Spence's scholarship and good sense. He followed faithfully the rules which in *Polymetis*[116] he had quoted as a guide for commentators: that since the difficulties which arise in our reading of the classics are due chiefly to our ignorance either of the sense in which a word was used formerly or of some opinion or custom familiar to the ancients, the editor should limit himself in the first instance to accurate determination of the meaning of the word and in the second to brief explanation of the thought or idea hinted at. He occasionally lapsed into the sin of digression, but in general his practice accorded with his theory.

The volume consists of sections devoted to miscellaneous observations upon the *Eclogues*, *Georgics*, and *Aeneid*, preceded by a Latin "vita" and followed by five dissertations from the pen of Holdsworth, a glossary of words and one of places mentioned, and Holdsworth's Latin poem *Muscipula*.[117] The preparation of the work for the press was a heavy task for Spence, and there is pathos in the picture of one aged and infirm scholar expending his final energies in preserving the writings of another already in his grave. The book apparently met with no more than mediocre success,[118] though Spence was remembered as a Virgilian scholar for some years after his death.[119]

The final months of Spence's life were apparently spent in quiet at Byfleet. When James Boswell set out for London in the spring of 1768 in company with Dr. John Armstrong,[120] he carried with him a letter to Spence from their common friend Sir Alexander Dick, and planned to pay the anecdotist a visit.[121] He was kept so busy in the city, however, that the projected trip to Byfleet was postponed several times, until finally he wrote Dick to say that he was forwarding the letter to Spence and that he and Armstrong would follow it as soon as he could get away from London.[122] When Spence died a few months later, Boswell wrote Dick a perfunctorily sympathetic letter, which does not settle whether the visit ever occurred.[123] One would like to think that the two men did meet—one whose contemplated biography of Pope was never written, the other whose plans concerning the biography of Johnson were to receive splendid fulfilment. Boswell later saw the *Anecdotes* when they were in Johnson's possession, and in view of his projected work he must have examined them with interest.

On August 12 Spence wrote to Elizabeth Cartwright Coltman to congratulate her upon the birth of her first child, offering to stand godfather by proxy.[124] Eight days later, on the evening of Saturday, August 20, he started for a stroll through his beloved gardens at Byfleet. An hour later he was discovered lying dead, face downward in the water at the edge of a small pond.[125] The water was shallow—not deep enough to cover his hand, or any part of his body[126]—and it seems clear that the apoplexy which had been toying with him for several years had at last ended the game.[127] A rumor spread, however, that Spence, like his protégé Duck, had drowned himself. This scandal annoyed Ridley and Lowth, and they took pains to contradict it. Ridley assured Lord Lincoln that the report was untrue, and Lowth some years later expressed resentment against "certain ill-natured people" who fostered it. "He could not have chosen that place so improperly," the Bishop wrote to Nichols, "where there were other places near at hand quite fit for such a purpose."[128]

Upon hearing of Spence's death, Ridley hastened to Byfleet to superintend his friend's affairs.[129] After reading the will, he wrote at once to his fellow-executors, Lowth and

Rolle, and to the authorities at New College. The coroner's inquest[130] was held on August 23, and on the following day the body was interred in the Church of St. Mary in Byfleet, where Spence had often occupied the pulpit.

The will mentioned no relatives closer than Spence's "Cosin Mrs. Mary Lawman Widow," daughter of his father's sister, for whom an annuity of £12 was provided, and another "Cosin Joseph Spence Berry," who was left £50 "to bind him Apprentice to some good Trade or to help set him up in some good Trade or both according to his Father's Judgment."[131] There were legacies of £100 each to the Fund for Superannuates at Winchester College, to his goddaughter, Martha Lowth (daughter of Robert), and to his godson, William Massingberd. To Mrs. Coltman went the pictures and framed prints,[132] and two servants received £20 each. His "three dearest friends," Lowth, Ridley, and Rolle, were asked to serve as executors and were named residuary legatees. A codicil, annexed January 6, 1768, provided for £50 each to be given to Mrs. Hooke of Birkby, Yorkshire,[133] and to the Rev. Mr. Sheppard of Weybridge, while the legacy to the servant John Elliot was raised to £100. Then on February 26, having made a present to Mrs. Hooke, Spence canceled the codicil in so far as it related to her legacy.[134]

The executors were disturbed to find that Spence's estate would fall considerably short of what they had expected—indeed, at first, Ridley and Rolle felt little inclined to act as executors. There were difficulties with Mrs. Lawman, who on September 14 had written requesting a little advance "to put myself into morning." She added: "I think ye memory of so Larned a man ought never to be forgot"! After an annuity had been purchased for her, she requested that it be sold for cash, and the executors were troubled by numerous letters from her—and her attorney! By May 11, 1771, all the dead man's affairs had been settled, and the executors signed a statement that the estate had amounted to £1,813 15s. 10d. and the disbursements for legacies and other obligations to £1,103 15s.

10*d*.[135] The remainder of £710 was divided equally among the executors.[136]

It was agreed that a memorial tablet should be erected in the Church of St. Mary at Byfleet. Rolle sketched an epitaph which did not meet with the approval of Lowth. The Bishop wrote another, which, with the approval of the pliant Rolle and a few additions from Ridley, was finally adopted and was inscribed on a plain tablet of white marble placed in the chancel of the church.[137] It reads:

> To the Memory
> of Joseph Spence M.A.
> Regius Professor of Modern History
> In the University of Oxford
> Prebendary of Durham,
> and Rector of Great Horwood Bucks.
> In whom Learning, Genius, and Shining Talents,
> Tempered with Judgement,
> and softned by the most exquisite sweetness of manners,
> were greatly excelled
> by those truely Christian Graces,
> Humanity ever ready to assist the distressed,
> Constant and extensive Charity to the Poor,
> and unbounded Benevolence to all.
> He died Aug.st xx.th MDCCLXVIII,
> In the LXX.th Year of his Age.

CHAPTER VIII

The "Anecdotes"

SPENCE'S executors were aware that for many years
their friend had collected observations and anecdotes
from the conversation of Pope and others, and that he had
made an extensive manuscript compilation which, according to Rolle, "used to be left open & for the entertainment
of his Friends."[1] Whether they knew that he had planned
the eventual publication of these materials, one cannot be
sure; but they were disturbed to find that on March 24,
1767, he had concluded with James Dodsley articles of
agreement involving his manuscript remains. The most
significant section of this document reads: "The said M^r
Spence doth hereby, for himself his Executors Administrators & Assigns sell and assign to the said James Dodsley
his Executors Administrators & Assigns the sole Right of
all the Copies which he the said Mr Spence hath not yet
published, and which the Executors of the said Mr Spence
shall judge proper to be published."[2] As a "consideration
for the particulars contained" in this section of the agreement, Dodsley contracted to pay £100. No doubt it was
understood between Spence and the publisher that the
manuscript of the *Anecdotes* was the principal item involved. At least, Dodsley lost no time in laying claim to
it, for on September 5 Ridley noted:[3] "Mr Dodsley says,
he owes £100 of the agreement, but has a bill of something
more than 12 p^{ds} desires the Copy of the Ancedotes [*sic*] as
soon as possible." Apparently Ridley communicated at
once with Lowth concerning this request, for on Septem-

ber 17 Lowth wrote to him: "The Anecdotes, I think, sh^d not be published with^t much previous consideration. They are partly forestalled by what has been communicated to B^p Warburton and Dr Warton; and in ye whole they are such, y^t I much doubt, whether they sh^d be published at all. Pray examine them & consider of it." Lord Lincoln, too, told Ridley on August 18 that he "desired we w^d not suffer the Conversazions to be printed." Ridley commented in his memoranda: "I told his Lordship I apprehended y^t was out of our power, Mr Spence having bargained with Dodsley for it." The more the executors thought about the matter, however, the less inclined they were to allow publication. They could, of course, take refuge in the clause of the agreement wherein the approval of the executors was stipulated as a condition of any posthumous publication. Further, Spence had expressed in his will the desire "that nothing farther of mine may be printed except it be by the Joint Judgment and Approbation of my said Executors." Their judgment confirmed by that of Lord Lincoln, the executors decided finally to suppress the collection, and Lowth was commissioned to convey the decision to Dodsley. Apparently the matter was settled amicably. Lowth, no doubt replying to a query from Ridley, wrote on June 11, 1769: "The whole that I said to Dodsley was, that we sh^d not suffer the Anecdotes to be published, and y^t therefore his engagement to pay 100 ££ for y^t article w^d be void." Under a list of debts and legacies noted in Ridley's memoranda appears the following remark: "Mr Dodsley claims a promise from Mr Spence to publish his Book of Conversations, on the payment of 100 p^{ds} The Executors have a power by Will to prevent the publication of any of his MSS. nor are any to be published without the consent of all the three executors." In the margin this point is marked "settled." And apparently the final step in the negotiations with Dodsley is alluded to in a list of receipts and expenses drawn up May 11, 1771, when something over £15 was devoted to the "balance of Dodsley's account." This sum no doubt covered Dodsley's claim described by Ridley on September 5, 1768.[4]

Though the reservations in both the will and the contract with Dodsley show that Spence hesitated to commit himself irretrievably, there is no doubt that he expected the *Anecdotes* to be published after his death. He once considered the publication of far more personal and less interesting materials—his letters from abroad—and the manuscripts of the *Anecdotes* show a care in editing and arrangement which indicated plans for publication. Furthermore, Spence had written on the cover of one manuscript the following significant note:

"All the people well acquainted with Mr. Pope, looked on him as a most friendly, open, charitable, and generous-hearted man;—all the world almost, that did not know him, were got into a mode of having very different ideas of him: how proper this makes it to publish these Anecdotes after my death."[5] Whatever his intentions, however, his collections were destined not to appear—in full and under his own name—until more than half a century after his death.[6]

Having decided upon suppression, Lowth, Ridley, and Rolle had next to determine the fate of the manuscripts. It seemed logical that Lord Lincoln, now become second Duke of Newcastle-under-Lyme,[7] should be given possession of one copy of the collection, and accordingly they presented him with four vellum-bound volumes containing a neat copy of the *Anecdotes*.[8] In the first volume, opposite the title-page, they wrote the following paragraph, dated May 15, 1771, four days after the final settlement with Dodsley: "The Bp. of Oxford, D.[r] Ridley, & Mr. Rolle, Executors of the late M.[r] Spence, present their most respectful Compliments to The Duke of Newcastle; & beg his Grace's Acceptance of the MS fair Copy of M.[r] Spence's Anecdotes. They did not think it adviseable to publish this Work; & they were confirmed in this opinion, as they had reason to believe, that it concurred with his Grace's judgement. But that it may not run the hazard of being lost, or of falling into improper hands, they beg leave to commit it to his Grace's custody; & they propose to act in the same manner, (with his Grace's approbation) in regard to any

other of his Papers, which they shall think it right to preserve: being persuaded, that in so doing they shall act most
agreeably to Mr. Spence's sentiments, & shall place his
Literary Remains in those hands, to which his love, respect, & gratitude, would certainly have directed them."[9]
That the promise concerning Spence's remaining papers
was not fulfilled will appear later. But until the publication
of Singer's edition in 1820 the Newcastle manuscript was
generally supposed to be the only copy of the *Anecdotes* in
existence—even Warton appears to have been ignorant of
any other.

In the long interim of their suppression Spence's collections did not remain a sealed book. They enjoyed a sort of
paradoxical existence and were "consulted, like the Sibyl-
line papers of old Rome, only upon extraordinary occasions."[10] While Spence was yet living, of course, Warburton and Warton had enjoyed some use of his materials, and
many of the anecdotes relating to Pope and other English
writers accordingly appeared in Warburton's edition of
Pope (1751) and Warton's edition (1797), as well as in
Ruffhead's biography of the poet (1769) and in Warton's
Essay on the Genius and Writings of Pope (1756, 1782).
When Johnson was writing his *Lives of the English Poets*
(1779, 1781), he applied to the Duke of Newcastle through
the medium of Sir Lucas Pepys for permission to consult
the *Anecdotes*. The Duke generously placed the manuscript at his disposal, and Johnson drew upon it materially
in writing his biography of Pope as well as those of Dryden,
Addison, Tickell, and others. He kept the manuscript by
him for some time, during which some of his friends took
the opportunity of turning over the pages and perhaps of
making notes therefrom for their own purposes.[11] Johnson's
acknowledgment of his debt was far from handsome—even
Boswell deplored the Doctor's brusqueness and his failure
to mention the Duke's name.[12] "Great assistance," wrote
Johnson, "has been given me by Mr. Spence's Collections,
of which I consider the communication as a favour worthy
of publick acknowledgment."[13] Apparently Newcastle was

offended by the curtness of the statement, and the manuscript was "somewhat indignantly closed."[14] Some years later, however, Malone had sufficient influence to gain temporary possession of it. He wrote to the Earl of Charlemont on November 7, 1794: "I have lately, by the favour of the duke of Newcastle, got an invaluable treasure, Spence's Anecdotes, which contain many curious particulars of Pope, Dryden, and other of our poets. I expect to draw much from them for a life of the latter, which I meditate, not in competition with Johnson's admirable account of him and his works, but as a supplement to it. He had these anecdotes, but he did not take half so much out of them as he might have done. So here is another 'remora' to Shakespeare, for the making these extracts will take some time; but then they will furnish several elucidations for an edition of Pope, which I meditate some time or other; and also some editorial matter to Aubrey's lives of the poets, which I transcribed at Oxford three years ago, and which I will print when I have time."[15] In a note on his manuscript of "extracts" Malone described his method as follows: "In these extracts I have not followed the author's order, having put together, in the first place, all that related to Pope himself and his writings, which I have entitled *Popiana;* in the second all that related to Shakespeare, Dryden, and the other English Poets; and lastly miscellaneous articles. I have, however, in the first Part, preserved the order of time in which the several minutes were made."[16] Malone's selection, of course, was not published at this time.

In addition to these authorized riflings,[17] there crept abroad from time to time "some imperfect transcripts or capricious selections," whether from the Newcastle manuscript or from another source.[18] Nevertheless, the contents of the main body of the anecdotes remained a mystery to all but a very few persons; and as the suppression which Spence's executors had decided upon continued far beyond the limits justified by reasons of policy, the interest in Newcastle's supposedly unique manuscript increased rapidly. The anecdotes developed into a literary tradition.[19] William Lisle Bowles wrote in 1806: "I tremble for every character, when I hear anything of '*Spence's Anecdotes!*' "[20] By that date, as a matter of fact, nearly every anecdote of interest to English readers had been made available by Warburton, Johnson, Warton, or Malone; but, with an understandable dislike of accepting anything at second hand when the original was in existence, the literary public continued to clamor for the publication of the entire collection.

It is not certain that Malone ever intended to publish his manuscript, but if such was his design, death overtook him (1812) before he could carry it to completion. His papers came into the hands of the Rev. William Beloe—possibly by gift prior to Malone's death.[21] Beloe announced the work for publication and promised an edition in "two large volumes,"[22] evidently intending to supply copious notes.[23] Either he changed his mind, however, or his death in 1817 frustrated his plans, and Malone's manuscript came into the possession of John Murray.[24] But to the vexation of expectant readers, Murray, after announcing the work as in press, persisted in its suppression. Probably motives of delicacy induced him to refrain from publishing material which had been obtained from its owner in so irregular a fashion, especially as the Newcastle family quite naturally refused to sanction the publication.[25] In the meantime a disturbing rumor arose that the original (and supposedly unique) manuscript had been mislaid or stolen.[26] In this state the matter was permitted to rest, and Murray gave no intimation that a change of policy on his part was to be expected.

At this point revelations from a new quarter brought matters to a head. To understand the situation one must return to Lowth and his fellow-executors, faced with the problem of what to do with Spence's papers other than the vellum-bound copy of the *Anecdotes* which they had deposited with Newcastle. The most important of the remaining manuscripts was a second copy of the *Anecdotes*, a folio divided into ten centuries. This was much fuller than the copy deposited with Newcastle, a fact indicated by Spence's own note on the title-page: "Left in this Drawer; because so many things in them that were not enter'd into the Vellum Mss."[27] There was also a bound octavo volume containing the first half of still another version,[28] as well as numerous loose papers containing earlier drafts. Finally, there were numerous documents, letters, and miscellaneous notes not concerned with the *Anecdotes*.

Though the executors had told the Duke that they proposed to commit to his custody any additional papers which they thought it "right to preserve," they followed another course. According to Singer,[29] all of Spence's manuscripts except the one given to the Duke were "consigned to a chest" and left in the care of Lowth, "by whom, at a period long subsequent, they were given to a gentleman of the name of Forster, who held some confidential post under the Bishop." At Forster's death they became the property of his nephew, who sold them to William H. Carpenter, the bookseller.[30] Carpenter decided to publish an edition of the *Anecdotes* and turned the papers over to Singer for editing and publication—apparently with the agreement that they should thereafter become Singer's property. Accordingly, Singer set about his task, and Carpenter announced that the work would soon make its appearance.

The advertisement of a forthcoming edition from manuscripts not generally known to exist came as a surprise to almost everyone—Murray included. The effect of the intelligence upon that publisher may be imagined. Since one edition of Spence's collection was about to appear whether Murray willed it or not, he felt that the bonds which had hitherto restrained him were now removed, and consequently he hurried the work through the press with all possible dispatch. Carpenter and Singer, too, lost no time.[31] The result was that in January, 1820, after decades of suppression and secrecy, after tedious retention by one possessor and careful concealment by another, the anecdotes of Joseph Spence appeared in two editions from separate manuscripts—and, according to D'Israeli, on the same day![32]

There can be no question that the edition published by Carpenter is the better and the more valuable of the two. Its editor, Singer, enjoyed several important advantages over the editor of the Murray volume. The manuscript from which he chiefly printed was fuller than that from which Malone had copied his extracts. Moreover, he had the opportunity to refer constantly to Spence's original papers, whereas Malone and his successors, the transcript having been made and the original restored to its owner, had to take for granted thereafter that no errors had been made in copying. Furthermore, Singer had at hand a wealth of additional manuscripts invaluable for purposes of corroboration and explanation—part of another redaction of the anecdotes, many of the original memorandum papers on which various entries had been jotted down, correspondence, account-books, and a considerable body of material collected subsequent to the death of Pope in 1744, with which the Newcastle manuscript stopped. Finally, the biography of the anecdotist which he prefixed to his edition and the letters which he added would alone have made his volume more useful than the bare copy published by Murray.[33]

The long-delayed appearance of Spence's already famous collection attracted widespread notice. After the first wave of interest had passed, however, the general feeling seems to have been one of disappointment: readers discovered that the bulk of the choicest anecdotes were already known to them in one form or another and hence had the effect of twice-told tales. But more penetrating critics were quick to perceive the tremendous value of Spence's work as a literary sourcebook—not solely because of the humbler but still interesting material which it made available for the first time but because it gave definite form to traditions which, though common property, could never have obtained absolute credence so long as they had to be accepted at second or third hand. The writers who reviewed the two editions for the critical journals did, for the most part, only a mediocre piece of work. The article in the *Quarterly Review*[34] is by far the best of the numerous criticisms which appeared, but it is notable chiefly for its use of the *Anecdotes* as a *point de départ* for an attack upon Bowles, the editor and maligner of Pope. Indeed, the article was partly responsible for a renewal of the bitter controversy over the character and merits of Pope which had raged at intervals ever since the appearance of Bowles's edition in 1806, and in the dust raised by that futile contest Spence and his *Anecdotes* were well-nigh lost sight of.[35] The writer in the *Edinburgh Review*[36] confined himself chiefly to presenting choice extracts from the *Anecdotes*, though he digressed to attack Spence for not being Boswell and to score Bolingbroke. The critic who reviewed the work for the *Monthly Review*[37] also contrasted Spence unfavorably with Boswell and expressed annoyance at Singer for superfluously providing an elaborate biography of "this amiable gentleman" as well as for printing the letters which were included in an appendix.[38]

Practically all the materials used by both Singer and Malone are still available. The vellum-bound manuscript from which Malone had made his transcript remained in the possession of the Dukes of Newcastle until 1938. On the death of Singer his manuscripts were sold through Sotheby and Wilkinson, August 3, 1858.[39] Most of Singer's Spence papers were acquired by the fifth Duke of Newcastle and, along with the vellum-bound manuscript, were purchased at the sale of the Clumber Library on February 16, 1938, at Sotheby's, by Mr. James M. Osborn.[40]

The document which served as Singer's chief source and which he described as "five paper books in folio"[41] was bound in morocco for the fifth Duke of Newcastle. It shows that at one time Spence planned to have ten sections, or "centuries," each containing exactly a hundred entries. A note which he made, however, indicates that he later contemplated the abandonment of this division and considered putting the entries from each year under a single head —partly in order "To rejoin sev^1 Articles that have been divided only in complaisance to ye Centuries." Another note shows that on other grounds also he was not satisfied with the arrangement: "To omit many of the Critical articles; & the most trite, & known. To avoid Repetitions.[42] Indexes to be added under different Heads. Hist?—Poet^1 History—Criticism—Arts—Gen^1." Still another note indicates his intention to supply an "Index of the Persons; where each begins & leaves off speaking." Of next importance to Singer was what he described as a "bound volume, in octavo, in which the anecdotes had been copied fair from the first loose memorandum papers."[43] Of this document, however, he had only the first part, covering the years 1728–37. Oddly, this manuscript was not listed in Singer's sale in 1858, and one cannot say where it is now; but what is obviously the second half of the same redaction, which Singer did *not* have, is now in the Huntington Library.[44] Other materials which Singer drew upon included loose papers containing early versions of various anecdotes as well as stories not appearing in the "complete" transcripts, letters to and from Spence, the four journals or memorandum books for 1755–58, the papers of Spence's executors, and numerous private documents. Most of these materials are now in the Spence Papers. All but one of the original letters which Singer printed in an appendix, however, as well as the biographical sketch which he used in preparing Spence's biography, were bound into an extra-illustrated copy of Singer's edition,[45] now in the Huntington Library.

Two other editions of the *Anecdotes* have appeared since the original dual publication of 1820. In 1858, shortly before Singer's death, John Russell Smith put out a cheap reprint of the Singer volume in his "Library of Old Authors" series. The only bit of fresh material in the entire volume was Singer's curt explanation of the means whereby he had obtained possession of the Spence manuscripts. Then in 1890 John Underhill, using Singer's text as a basis, edited a selection of the anecdotes for the "Camelot Series" published by Walter Scott.[46] Underhill adopted a modification of Malone's system of classification, ranging his selections under four heads: "General Literary Anecdotes," "Miscellaneous Anecdotes," "Biographical Anecdotes Relating to Pope," and "Critical Opinions, Table Talk, etc." He supplied a pleasant little introduction and a few notes of a type to cause regret that they are not more copious.

With Underhill's edition the bibliographical history of the *Anecdotes* comes to a close. That there is need for a new, authentic, and thoroughly annotated edition is evident. Such a work would be based upon the earliest available form of each entry included, and the editor would attempt to supply as exactly as possible the original words of each speaker. A wealth of manuscript material exists for this purpose. For the collections made between 1728 and 1744 there are the vellum-bound manuscript from which Malone made his transcript, the folio copy which was Singer's chief source, the partial redaction in the Huntington Library, and the many sheets containing early versions. For the later entries there are most of the original papers from which Singer compiled them. An edition based on these materials and supplied with copious historical and critical notes would be an important contribution to literary scholarship.[47]

Though Spence enjoyed in his own century a considerable reputation as critic, scholar, and connoisseur, he is of interest and importance to modern times chiefly as the compiler of the *Anecdotes*. One guesses that he himself had more than an inkling that such would be the case. Proud though he was of the reception accorded to *An Essay on Pope's Odyssey* and to *Polymetis*, he was still more proud of his intimacy with Pope; and the anxious care which he took with his notes of conversation, their existence in several different manuscripts in his own hand, his agreement with Dodsley for posthumous publication—all point to his belief that future generations would be interested in his records.

Spence's collections as printed by Singer consist of over

a thousand separate anecdotes or observations. Most of the entries are brief—many of them occupying only a few lines, and none extending for as much as two pages. To each entry is appended the name of the person on whose authority it is recorded, and Spence lets it appear that he has endeavored to preserve the exact words of the speaker. His original plan was to include only the materials from the years 1728–44, but Singer printed fifty-four pages of "supplemental anecdotes" culled from Spence's papers. Though Singer took certain liberties with the text and deleted entire entries which he deemed irrelevant or unworthy, his edition is a fairly complete and, in general, reliable reproduction of the manuscripts upon which he depended.

Through the greater part of Spence's work Pope occupies the center of the stage, and it is for the light which the *Anecdotes* cast upon his biography, his character, and his mind that they are chiefly valuable. When in the company of others, Spence was eager to turn the conversation upon the god of his idolatry, and the shadow of Pope falls continually across the page. A reasonably full autobiography of the poet can be compiled from Spence's records, and Pope's opinions of literary celebrities, his mannerisms, his mental and spiritual characteristics, his methods of composition, his likes and dislikes—all these appear in gratifying and realistic detail. But though Pope remains the central figure, the *Anecdotes* throw light also upon a throng of noted persons of only slightly less interest. From Pope we hear stories of Addison, Swift, Wycherley, Dryden, Buckingham, Rochester, Congreve, Gay, Prior, Parnell, Steele, and Arbuthnot—intimate details about a galaxy of brilliant personages whose history is that of late seventeenth- and early eighteenth-century literature. Furthermore, many important literary and political figures themselves speak from the pages—Bolingbroke, Young, Warburton, Cibber, Lady Mary Montagu, Dennis, Mallet, Thomson, Lord Peterborough, Hooke, and Martha Blount. The array is astonishing.

The importance of Spence's *Anecdotes* to the literary his-

torian is very great. Without them, biographers of Pope
would cut a sorry figure, and the world would be without
many a useful bit of information concerning other English
writers. A pursuit of Spence's items down through the biographical and critical literature of the past two centuries
would involve one in a hopelessly complex maze of quotations and borrowings. A mere list of the books which have
drawn upon the *Anecdotes* would fill a volume. Students of
literature, indeed, have come to take Spence for granted;
but if his manuscripts had lain forgotten for a century and
a half, if neither Warburton nor Johnson nor anyone else
had been granted a look at them, if not one of the anecdotes had ever found its way into print, and if a twentieth-
century discoverer should then have published his find—
then only would the sensation produced and the knowledge contributed have brought a realization of the true
importance of Spence's labors and the extent of the debt
which the world has been none too ready to pay him.

In view of the importance of the *Anecdotes* not only in
the biography of Pope but in the study of seventeenth- and
eighteenth-century literary history, the question of how far
one may rely upon Spence's authority becomes of great
importance. Of course, even if Spence's reports are proved
to be authentic, one can never be sure that the person
quoted was speaking truth; but it would be useful to be
able to feel confident that when Spence says Pope made a
certain remark, Pope did make it. In the past the *Anecdotes* have been variously regarded. Most scholars tend to
accept them without cavil. John Dennis, for example, says:
"There is every indication that he [Spence] strove to give
the sayings of the poet, as far as possible, in his own
words,"[48] and Robert Carruthers insists that "Spence was
incapable of wilful misrepresentation."[49] Others take a different view, as in the case of William Stebbing, who refers
contemptuously to "Spence's amusing but untrustworthy
colloquies of Pope and his friends."[50] Most writers, however, quote freely from Spence on the assumption that he
is trustworthy—and do not discuss the question at all.

189

The first move in an investigation of Spence's reliability should be the establishment of the text of each anecdote in its earliest form. In most instances Spence's entries underwent no more than certain inevitable alterations in style as they were transformed from rough notes into material for the press. Time after time the substance of an anecdote remains unchanged in its progress from loose paper to the full transcripts from which Singer and Murray printed. Sometimes the phrasing and arrangement are identical; sometimes there are alterations in phrasing and order which do not affect the content materially.

If Spence ever doctored his materials, one would expect him to soften anything which reflected discredit upon Pope. Yet more than once he preserved criticisms of Pope almost exactly as they had been first recorded. For instance, at Rome he had written thus Lady Mary Wortley Montagu's version of the warning which Addison had given her against Pope: "Leave him as soon as you can (says M^r A to L^y M) he'll certainly play you some Devlish Trick else. He has appetite to satire."[51] And the entry appears in Singer as follows: " 'Leave him as soon as you can, (said Addison to me, speaking of Pope), he will certainly play you some devilish trick else: he has an appetite to satire!'—*Lady M.*"[52] Certainly, there is no softening here, though in another remark by Lady Mary which followed immediately, Spence altered the phrasing slightly, perhaps with the intention of sparing Pope. Whereas Lady Mary, in admitting that Pope did indeed write verses well, had apparently quipped that he wrote them so well that he would "make Good Verse Scandalous,"[53] she is made by Spence to say that Pope was "in danger of bringing even good verse into disrepute!"[54]

One matter which mystifies the student is Spence's handling of the famous anecdotes related by a Mr. Rawlinson about the poet Young, to the effect that Young had received a gift of £2,000 from the Duke of Wharton for writing the *Universal Passion* and that the Duke had sent the poet a lamp formed by a candle set in a human skull.[55] These stories, along with other records, Spence read to

Young when he visited the poet in 1759,[56] and Young apparently denied them; for in the manuscript which he used on that occasion the penciled words "Not true" appear opposite the first anecdote, and opposite the other, "No such thing. D^r Y^g."[57] Yet both stories were retained in the full transcripts of the *Anecdotes* and hence were printed by Singer and Murray—and written into the history of English literature. The best that can be said for Spence is that after hearing this categorical denial, possibly he forgot to delete the stories from his finished copies.

In general, the manuscripts from which Singer and Murray printed suffer from Spence's fear of being too personal and informal. The scholar would prefer the original notes, with their omissions and abbreviations, to the polite versions prepared for the printer. It is especially unfortunate that Spence decided to suppress exact dates, throwing his collections into "centuries" or sections, each covering a period of several years. But a careful examination of his papers leads to the conclusion that he made an honest effort to preserve as it came to him the information which he received.

External evidence to support the statements recorded may be found in abundance. Such evidence is of two kinds: that which indicates that Spence's subject actually said what is recorded (whether the remark was true or not) and that which indicates that the facts alleged by Spence's subject were true. The chief means of corroboration, listed in the order of their value, are the correspondence and published works of the men quoted by Spence, such scattered records of their conversation as exist outside his pages, and the testimony of other persons. In the case of Pope, direct confirmation is possible in a surprising number of instances, and the notes of the Elwin-Courthope edition abound in references to Spence in illustration of passages in Pope's works and correspondence. For example, Spence writes: "It was a general opinion that Ben Johnson [*sic*] & Shakespear livd in enmity: Betterton has assurd M^r P that there was nothing in it, & that it was founded only on the two parties which in their life time listed under one & endeavoured to lessen ye character of ye other mutually. Dryden usd to think y^t ye Verses J^n made on ye others death had something of Satire at ye bottom; M^r P says he cant discover anything like it in them."[58]

A few years earlier Pope had written: "I am inclined to think this opinion proceeded originally from the zeal of the partizans of our author and Ben Jonson, as they endeavoured to exalt the one at the expense of the other. It is ever the nature of parties to be in extremes. . . . But however this contention might be carried on by the partisans on either side, I cannot help thinking these two great poets were good friends, and lived on amicable terms, and in offices of society with each other. It is an acknowledged fact, that Ben Jonson was introduced upon the stage, and his first works encouraged, by Shakespear. And after his death, that author writes *To the memory of his beloved Mr. William Shakespear*, which shows as if the friendship had continued through life. I cannot for my own part find anything *invidious* or *sparing* in those verses, but wonder Mr. Dryden was of that opinion."[59] Again, Pope told Spence that "Racine's character is justness and correctness; Corneille's, passion and life,"[60] and later in his *Epistle to Augustus* he was to write of "Exact Racine, and Corneille's noble fire."[61] And in the poet's boast to Spence, "As L'Esprit, La Rouchefoucault, and that sort of people, prove that all virtues are disguised vices; I would engage to prove all vices to be disguised virtues . . ."[62] is found the germ of these lines from the *Essay on Man:*

> The surest virtues thus from passions shoot,
> Wild nature's vigour working at the root.
> What crops of wit and honesty appear
> From spleen, from obstinacy, hate or fear!
> See anger, zeal and fortitude supply;
> Ev'n av'rice, prudence; sloth, philosophy;
> Lust, through some certain strainers well refined,
> Is gentle love, and charms all womankind;
> Envy, to which th'ignoble mind's a slave,
> Is emulation in the learn'd or brave;
> Nor virtue, male or female, can we name,
> But what will grow on pride, or grow on shame.[63]

Such instances may be multiplied, nor need they be confined to the remarks of Pope. Spence quotes Bolingbroke, for example, as saying, "Lord Bacon in his *Novum Organum* has laid down the whole method that Descartes afterwards followed."[64] And in Bolingbroke's *Letters or Essays addressed to Alexander Pope, Esq.* (published in 1754), he wrote: "Whilst the fame of this great man [Bacon] was fresh, and his works were in every learned hand both at home and abroad, Des Cartes arose . . . and I could easily suspect that my Lord Bacon's writings were not unknown to him."[65] Again, Ramsay said to Spence concerning Fénelon: "He was above the little distinctions of country or religion, and used to say, 'that he loved his family better than himself; his country better than his family; and mankind better than his country; for I am more a Frenchman, (added he) than a Fenelon; and more a man than a Frenchman.' "[66] And Dr. William King quoted Ramsay as reporting that Fénelon said on a certain occasion: "I am a true French-man, and love my country; but I love mankind better than my country."[67] All these instances of external corroboration are drawn from only a few pages of the *Anecdotes*.

But in an estimate of the accuracy and trustworthiness of such collections as those of Spence, the character of the recorder is perhaps the most important item to be considered. The evidence indicates that Spence, though partisan on the subject of Pope, was honest, conscientious, and painstaking. A scrupulous examination of his manuscripts and a study of his career and his published works lead to the conclusion that the invaluable information contained in the records loosely termed the *Anecdotes* is generally reliable.[68]

CHAPTER IX

"*The Amiable Mr. Spence*"

WHEN death came for Spence on that last melancholy walk in the garden at Byfleet, it found him prepared for the summons. Life had little left to offer him, and he faced the unknown with the confidence of a life well spent. Eleven years earlier he had written: "A Finishing Stroke of the palsy, should be lookd upon, (by a good man,) as a Coup de Grace; that reprieves him from the wearisomness & Tortures of a long death-bed Sickness."[1] The news of his death was received with sorrow. "Spence, thou art gone," cried an impulsive contributor to the *Oxford Magazine*,[2] " 'Oxonia's greatest pride!' " And a few years after his death it was said of him, as Charles II had said of Cowley, "He has not left a better man in England behind him."[3]

In stature Spence was small and spare, and by his own testimony and that of many friends, he was perennially in delicate health. If one may judge by his portrait, his eye was bright and inquiring, his face not unhandsome though not particularly strong, his expression alert, confident, intelligent. At the age of forty he had the appearance of one whom the years had touched but lightly, who had never suffered poverty, who had neither known despair nor soared to uncommon heights. An anonymous writer who had apparently been a friend of Spence said of him: "He was of a spare and feeble constitution, very temperate in his hours and way of life, cheerful and entertaining in con-

versation. His features bore some resemblance to the celebrated Mr. Locke, but had more sweetness and benignity
of countenance."[4]

Among his contemporaries and through the years following his death, Spence had one adjective applied to him so
often that it is almost monotonously associated with his
name. It is the word "amiable," and it indicates the
strength and weakness of Spence's temperament better
perhaps than any other adjective. In the wide circle of his
acquaintances there was none to question the "amiability"
of his character, and his intimate friends were always warm
in his praise. An early tribute—all the more significant because it was made in private—came from his devoted
friend Pitt at a time (1728) when Spence was just coming
into prominence as a man of letters. He was, said Pitt, "the
completest scholar, either in solid or polite learning, for his
years, that I ever knew," and at the same time "the
sweetest-tempered gentleman breathing."[5] And in verses
entitled "To Mr. Spence, on his Essay on Mr. Pope's
Odyssey," printed in the second edition of the *Essay* in
1737, Pitt paid a public and equally laudatory tribute to
the character of his friend:

> To point our Faults, yet never to offend;
> To play the *Critic*, yet preserve the *Friend;*
> A Life well spent, that never lost a Day;
> An easy Spirit, innocently Gay;
> A strict Integrity, devoid of Art;
> The sweetest Manners, and sincerest Heart;
> A Soul, where Depth of *Sense*, and *Fancy* meet;
> A *Judgment* brighten'd by the Beams of *Wit*,
> Were ever *Yours;*—Be what *You* were before,
> Be still Yourself; the World can ask no more.

Joseph Warton, Shenstone, Lowth, Rolle, Alexander Dick,
and others have written of Spence's benevolence, loyalty,
piety, and sweetness of temper. But perhaps the most
glowing tribute to his moral qualities was that written by
James Ridley: "Nay, but said *Mirglip*, to speak before our
Friend, is not to give our Voice to publick Fame, though
Phesoj Ecneps Virtues well deserve its loudest Blast; but

195

shall not this generous Stranger hear, how much the Dervise of these Groves exemplifies the Virtues which he teaches, when, with a fond generous Affection, he made the Life of his dear honored Mother smile in Age, and happy in Affliction; when the chief Glories of his youthful Soul, were to please her that gave him Birth; when, like the Stork, he made the Nest of Comfort for his Parent, and bore her into Light and Life on his industrious Wings; then, pleased alone with all Mankind, when they were pleased with her. Or view him in his Friendship unreserved, and blessing all around him, the virtuous Smile light up where'er he stepped, and Peace and Joy attending at his Side. Or see him condescending to the meanest [*sic*] of Mankind, diffusing Comfort, and enlightening Ignorance, pleased at each reflected Ray of Knowledge which he shed, and healing what the Rage of Poverty or Vice had maimed. Or view him in a stronger and a pious Light, his Soul in Transports rising to the Throne of Grace, his Body humble, prostrate, and submissive; no Thought of his own Merit intervening, to damp Religion with the Cloak of Sin ... to nothing but his own Perfections is *Phesoj Ecneps* blind, and rather had his Modesty concele the brightest Pattern of Humanity, than that the World in Whispers should declare from whence they caught the Virtues of their Heart."[6]

The impression of Spence's character derived from his writings tallies with that given by his friends. One of the first qualities to strike a reader is his great and at times excessive modesty. The prefaces to *An Essay on Pope's Odyssey* and to *Polymetis* best exemplify this quality in him. Again, he is a stickler for politeness and good manners, whether in conversation or in books. A breach of good nature "is certainly one of the most unpardonable faults that a writer can commit, in any age and in all countries."[7] And "That Education, or Politeness, is good for nothing, which does not make people more knowing or more pleasing."[8] In spite of his modesty, he seems to have felt a quiet satisfaction in the extent of his learning, though he condemns all manner of pedantry and the ostentatious display of knowledge. He seems never to have sunk far into the slough of despond, but serious thought was by no means unknown to him. Interested as he was in the trivia of the world, he found time for meditation on life, death, and the destiny of man. He was something of a sentimentalist. "The Happiness of Life," he wrote, "is so nice a thing, that (like the Sensitive Plant) it shrinks away, even upon thinking of it."[9]

Among Spence's qualities which paved the way to his social success, next to his amiability should probably be ranked his sense of humor. His friends call attention to this trait, and it is revealed even more clearly in his writings. Master as he was of an "infinite fund of subjects for conversation,"[10] he seasoned his talk with wit, while instances of his humor—not invariably successful—abound in his books. It was his avowed purpose to give "an agreeable turn"[11] to all that he wrote, even though it were a "lesson of morality." His sallies are sometimes not without a sting. After quoting the Dean of Winchester as saying, "Each step higher in the world brings more dependence and more trouble upon a man. I have heard the Bishop of Winchester often say the same," Spence adds: "Both the dean and the bishop, however, still endeavour to rise as much as any man."[12] Upon another occasion he observes: "As Mercury was the god of rogues and pickpockets, so was he also the god of shopkeepers and tradesmen; whom I will allow to be very angry with me for mentioning them in so bad company, as soon as ever they have left off the using secret marks for the prices of their goods."[13]

In regard to Spence's intellectual powers there was a wide difference of opinion among his contemporaries. To the ordinary observer who did not give much thought to the matter, he appeared to be a "learned and ingenious man." By his friends he was regarded still more highly, but some of his acquaintances who can hardly be termed friends held him in varying degrees of disrespect. Pitt's "completest scholar, either in solid or polite learning,"[14] was to Horace Walpole, who spoke with contempt of his learning, "more like a silver penny than a genius."[15] Warburton, with exasperating complacency, referred to him more than once as a "poor creature,"[16] and Johnson thought meanly of his powers.[17] Richard Owen Cambridge in his old age told Malone that Spence had been a *"poor creature* though a very worthy man."[18] Joseph Warton, on the other hand, declared that Spence, "notwithstanding Dr. Johnson's invidious assertion, was an excellent scholar."[19]

Such contradictory estimates seem at first hopelessly confusing, but, as Austin Dobson has said,[20] to strike a medium among them is not too difficult, especially when one considers Spence's intellect in the light of his writings. Bearing in mind that his interests were scattered throughout many fields and that his energies were therefore somewhat dissipated, one may justly term him a man of learning.[21] But as for intellectual depth, his mind was unquestionably not a powerful one: it was talented rather than masterful, ingenious rather than creative. He was incapable of producing a work of genius, but in analysis and criticism of other men's writings, in diligent and constructive research, in the application of theories to facts, he was far more than the "poor creature" that Warburton and Cambridge considered him.

Finally, Spence was something of a philosopher. The stream of life flowed smoothly for him, undisturbed by swift currents or whirlpools. He was fortunate in his worldly affairs, and though he never knew wealth, he was possessed throughout life of an adequate income. No extravagant ambitions or hopeless yearnings racked his heart. He was sincere when he wrote to his mother: "And indeed after 40, tis high time to think of a Settlement; & to get a steddy certain Income, some where or another, to prevent one's old age being uneasy to one. I guess you are already a laughing to hear a Son of yours talk of being an old man;

but that will begin to be a very serious truth, perhaps in a few years more. Whenever it happens, I dont expect it as a very disagreable thing; a good easy Chair, good company, & the being able to look back upon ones life without anything to frighten one in it, make that Season at least not so terrible: & I dont see why one may not enter upon it as agreably, as one goes into a Bed after one's tir'd with the labour of the Day. . . ."[22]

Notes

In the interest of economy, three works very frequently cited are referred to in abbreviated form: by "Singer" is meant Spence's *Anecdotes, Observations, and Characters, of Books and Men. Collected from the Conversation of Mr. Pope, and Other Eminent Persons of His Time*, edited by Samuel Weller Singer (1820); by "Elwin-Court-hope" is meant *The Works of Alexander Pope*, edited by Whitwell Elwin and William John Courthope (10 vols.; 1871–89); and by "Walpole's *Letters*, ed. Toynbee" is meant *The Letters of Horace Walpole, Fourth Earl of Orford*, edited by Mrs. Paget Toynbee (16 vols.; Oxford, 1903–5), with three supplementary volumes edited by Paget Toynbee (Oxford, 1918–25).

In general, the place of publication of a work is noted only if it was published elsewhere than in London.

CHAPTER I

Family and Early Life

1. John and J. A. Venn, *Alumni Cantabrigienses*, Part I, IV (Cambridge, 1927), 131. Other facts concerning the career of the elder Spence at Cambridge come from the same source and from *Admissions to the College of St. John the Evangelist in the University of Cambridge*, Part II (1893), p. 65.

2. He seems to have been a cook. The anecdotist's father is listed in the records of St. John's as the son of "Joseph Spence, coqui."

3. At the time of his admission to St. John's on July 14, 1677, he is said in both *Alumni Cantabrigienses* and *Admissions to the College of St. John* to have been sixteen years old.

4. Thomas Baker, *History of the College of St. John the Evangelist, Cambridge* (Cambridge, 1869), I, 300.

5. Public Records Office. Exchequer. First Fruits and Tenths Office. Institution Books, Ser. B, Vol. VI, fol. 214v.

6. *Chapter Book 1660–95*, p. 413. Facts concerning the career of the elder Spence at Winchester and references to the cathedral records have been kindly supplied by Canon A. W. Goodman, librarian of Winchester Cathedral.

7. *Ibid.*, p. 439.

8. Baker, *op. cit.*, I, 301.

9. *Cathedral Register*, Vol. XXII, fol. 52.

10. Public Records Office. Exchequer. First Fruits and Tenths

Office. Institution Books, Ser. C, Vol. II, fol. 247r. Information confirming this date has been kindly supplied from the records at Alverstoke by Canon Guy Landon, rector.

11. *Chapter Book 1696–1739*, fol. 81.
12. From the records at Alverstoke.
13. *Cathedral Register*, Vol. XXIII, fol. 90v.
14. Vaughan Richardson was one of the witnesses.
15. The will is in the Winchester District Probate Registry. On a certified copy among the Spence Papers (see Preface) a record of the probate refers to the testator as "late Rector of Alverstoke."

Among Singer's papers sold on August 3, 1858, at Sotheby's were several bundles of sermons "by Mr. Spence's father" (Sale Catalogue, Lots 202–3). British Museum Additional MS 25899 is a historical paper on which the younger Joseph Spence once wrote a signed note as follows: "Dr. Fulham, Prebendary of Winchester & Arch-Deacon of Southamton, one of the Fellows excluded from Magdalen College in Oxford, was a particular friend of my Father, and on his Death, left all his books & Manuscripts to him. This was found among the latter." Among the Spence Papers are copies of a short love song "By Mr J Spence Sr." John Wright, the editor of Bentley's edition of Walpole's letters, says that Mrs. Betty Spence, companion to the Duchess of Newcastle, was related to Joseph Spence (*The Letters of Horace Walpole* [1840], III, 40 n.). If this is correct, she may have been the means of introducing him to the Pelham family, to whom he owed much of his advancement in life. The anecdotist's brother Richard speaks of their "Great Grandmother Gregory," who lived "in Cursitors Alley next door to Rose Tavern by Chancery Lane" (Spence Papers); she must have been the grandmother of the elder Spence, for the name of Gregory does not appear in the ancestry of Spence's mother.

16. See n. 2.
17. *Collectanea topographica et genealogica*, IV (1837), 142.
18. He was the grandson of Thomas Fludd, Queen Elizabeth's treasurer of war (*DNB*, s.v. "Lunsford").
19. *Collectanea topographica et genealogica*, loc. cit.
20. *DNB*, s.v. "Lunsford, Neville."
21. *DNB*, s.v. "Lunsford." In his journal for 1755 (Spence Papers) Spence recorded some information derived from his mother concerning Lunsford's three daughters. Their maternal grandmother, Lady Thorowgood, evidently sheltered them against the will of her (second) husband, Sir John. The youngest, Mary or Maria, Spence's grandmother, appeared as "Charity in one of My Ld Mayor's Pageants; very pretty."
22. Spence was much interested in the Nevilles, and particularly in his great-great-uncle, the Colonel. In his papers there are frequent references to the merry "Harry Neville."

23. On December 19, 1755, Spence stated in a letter to his friend William Burrell Massingberd that his mother was then in her eighty-sixth year. There survive sixty-five letters from Spence to Massingberd, dated between 1738 and 1766. Extracts were published by P. C. D. Mundy in *Notes and Queries*, CLXXXVIII (1945), 252-55 and 271-73. These letters, together with sixty-three from Edward Rolle to Massingberd, are now in my possession. Massingberd (1719-1802) was a New College man who lived at South Ormesby in Lincolnshire. He was high sheriff of the county in 1745. Spence in his later years visited Massingberd frequently and played host to him occasionally at Byfleet.

That Mrs. Spence was born in or about the year 1670 is confirmed by an entry in one of the manuscript copies of the *Anecdotes*. Spence observed to Pope in February, 1744: "When I read two or three Canto's of Spenser to my Mother, a day or two ago, she said; 'That I had been showing her a Collection of Pictures.' " To the word "Mother" Spence appended this note: "Aet: 74." The manuscript quoted is now in the Huntington Library (HM 1271, fol. 84r). With regard to it see also p. 250, n. 28. This particular entry was considerably altered in the "fair copies" which were used by Singer and Malone. Not only is the lady's identity concealed and her age indicated merely as "between seventy and eighty years," but Spence's remark and Pope's reply are so handled (apparently inadvertently) that the reader assumes the whole entry to come from Pope. Singer (p. 296) and Malone (p. 86) were apparently under the same impression (for an account of the editions of the *Anecdotes* by Singer and Malone see pp. 181-86).

24. Walpole wrote to Mann on September 20, 1750: "As I am in town, and not within the circle of Pope's walks, I may tell you a story without fearing he should haunt me with the ghost of a satire. I went the other day to see little Spence, who fondles an old mother in imitation of Pope. The good old woman was mighty civil to me, and, among other chat, said she supposed I had a good neighbour in Mr. Pope. 'Lord! Madam, he has been dead these seven years!'—'Alas! aye, Sir, I had forgot.' When the poor old soul dies, how Pope will set his mother's spectre upon her for daring to be ignorant 'if Dennis be alive or dead'!" (Walpole's *Letters*, ed. Toynbee, III, 18).

25. Egerton MS 2234, fol. 171v. The letter is dated at Turin, March 30, 1740.

26. Egerton MS 2234, fol. 198r. The letter is dated at Turin, July 27, 1740.

27. James Ridley, writing as "Sir Charles Morell" in *Tales of the Genii* (2d ed., 1764), II, 329-30.

28. See n. 23.

28a. Journal for 1756, Spence Papers.

29. From the Baptismal Register. For this and other information I am indebted to the Rev. Reginald P. Rowan, vicar of Kingsclere.

29a. Egerton MS 2234, fol. 17r.

30. She is mentioned occasionally in letters to and from Spence between 1731 and 1737.

31. See p. 175. A Mrs. Collier, to whom Spence refers occasionally as his "cosin," was a member of his household for some years. She died at Byfleet in June, 1753, after a long illness (letter from Spence to Massingberd, June 28).

32. In a letter of July 27, 1751, to Massingberd and also in the draft (Spence Papers) of a letter dated April 28, 1751, at which time Spence stated that he was that day entering upon his fifty-third year.

33. This account, written on two folio leaves, is tipped into an extra-illustrated copy of Singer's edition of the *Anecdotes* now in the Huntington Library (see later, p. 212, n. 80). Singer used it (without acknowledgment) in the preparation of his biographical sketch of Spence. Comparison of the handwriting with that of Rolle makes Rolle's authorship, in my opinion, almost a certainty—a view shared by a number of scholars. The phrasing and the personal nature of the details given in this account are such as to make one suspect that Spence himself somehow had a hand in it! The explanation may be that Rolle (if he is indeed the author) based his sketch in part upon material in Spence's papers. For convenience I shall henceforth refer (with some misgiving) to the author as Rolle. For an account of Rolle see W. P. Courtney, *Dodsley's Collection of Poetry: Its Contents & Contributors* (1910), pp. 125–27.

Robert Lowth, another close friend of Spence and one of his executors, told John Nichols in 1780 that he was preparing an account of Spence for a new edition of the *Biographia Britannica* (Nichols, *Literary Anecdotes*, I, 642 n.), but the volume expected to contain it was never published. What happened to Lowth's account is not known, but the Huntington MS is at least not in his hand.

34. Singer, p. xxii.

35. *Ibid.*, p. 412.

36. See n. 24.

37. Though Spence considerably outlived his own expectation, he is found at the age of fifty-two prophesying that he was "not very likely to see many more" years (Spence Papers).

38. From a list of his chief places of residence drawn up by Spence in his journal for 1756 (Spence Papers).

39. Singer says (p. xvii n.), "There is some reason to think that he may have been disgusted with the severity of the school discipline at that time, when Dr. George was master, and Dr. Cooke (afterwards provost,) propositor." He then refers to the antiquary Cole's story of the vignette at the end of the seventeenth dialogue of Spence's *Polymetis* (1747), supposed to contain a caricature of Cooke. Cole, writing to Walpole in 1780, transcribed the following passage from a letter from Spence to Christopher Pitt: "I am glad some of the schoolmasters of your acquaintance are pleased with the grave animal at the end of the

17 Dialogue. There are others, who have been angry at it, though it could not be meant for any man of good sense, and is indeed the representative only of one real blockhead: a gowned ass who, when I offered him some of my receipts, from an old acquaintance with him, said that he could have nothing to do with them, because the book and subject was such as could not be of any use to him in his way. He was master in one of the greatest schools, and had I dedicated my plates, that print should have been consecrated to his name. As it is, it may as well be concealed. What I like most in it is that simple wisdom in the air of the face, which does not at all disagree with the gentleman who sat for it." Cole himself commented: "That it was meant for Cooke there can be no [doubt,] both from the likeness of the figure to him, and the subject of that chapter being on langu[age and gram]mar and a criticism on the Eton method of teaching boys to make Latin verses and get [by rote 600] verses of Homer and Virgil even when they have no taste for them. . . . Now to speak the truth, the case to me seems to be this: Mr. Spence, a refined and lively coxcomb, offered to get off some of his copies to this formal, solemn, insolent and proud coxcomb, who refused to oblige him. The elegant writer knew no better way to revenge himself than to make the pedant ridiculous among a few friends, for it would not have been decorous to have spoken out . . ." (*Horace Walpole's Correspondence with the Rev. William Cole*, ed. Lewis and Wallace [New Haven, 1937], II, 214–15; the words in brackets are supplied from Cole's copy of the letter). Singer, however, is wrong in suggesting that Spence's own experience under Cooke at Eton was responsible for the attack, for Cooke (1711–97) did not even become a student at Eton until 1721. The vignette in question, taken from a gem showing "An Ass, in the Greek Pallium, teaching," was deleted in the second edition of *Polymetis* (1755).

40. R. A. Austen-Leigh, *The Eton College Register 1698–1752* (Eton, 1927), p. vii.

41. My information about Spence at Winchester College comes from the school records, chiefly through the kindness of Mr. Herbert Chitty, keeper of the College Archives. Some of the facts given here appear also in C. W. Holgate, *Winchester Long Rolls 1653–1721* (Winchester, 1899), pp. 130–36, and T. F. Kirby, *Winchester Scholars* (1888), p. 225.

42. Joseph Foster, *Alumni Oxonienses 1715–1886* (1888), IV, 1333.

43. His age was listed as sixteen on May 29, 1717.

44. The election was held on or about September 11, and Spence was listed as sixteen years old on May 29, 1718.

45. Held later than August 8. Spence's age was listed as seventeen on May 29, 1719.

46. Admission records at New College.

47. *Ibid.* Richard Rawlinson, Oxford antiquary and Jacobite, asserts that at one time Spence "stood for a fellowship" at Winchester.

Rawlinson then adds the puzzling remark that Spence "left that and his old principles together" (see Bodleian Library, Rawlinson MS J.4°6, fol. 199).

48. *Alumni Oxonienses 1715–1886*, IV, 1333 .

49. From the *Registrum eorum qui juxta statuta declamandi vicibus perfuncti fuerunt*, in the Bodleian Library.

50. P. xviii n.

51. John Wilford's *Monthly Catalogue* lists the work as published in June, 1725. On the title-page of the British Museum copy the letter which is "answered" is said to have been written by Thomas Bott.

52. Spence Papers.

53. *An Essay on Pope's Odyssev*, Part II (1727), p. 154.

54. Nichols says that Spence took orders in 1724 (*Literary Anecdotes*, II, 373 n.), and Rolle names the same year. But the certificate of Spence's ordination, dated June 5, 1726, is among the Spence Papers.

55. It has been asserted that prior to 1726 Spence had made two trips abroad as a traveling tutor; but, though he may well have done so, in neither case can the assertion be accepted without cavil.

The only evidence of the first tour is a letter containing a fascinating account of an interview with James Edward Stuart at Rome, said by two authorities to have been written by Spence to his father. It was printed in part by Mrs. Katharine Byerley Thomson in 1846 in *Memoirs of the Jacobites of 1715 and 1745*, III, 515–20, where it is ascribed to Spence and said to be undated. It was again printed in part by Mrs. Catherine Hutton Beale in *Catherine Hutton and Her Friends* (Birmingham, 1895), pp. 30–37. Mrs. Beale not only ascribed it to Spence but added that he had written it "while he was travelling as tutor to the son of the Duke of Devonshire" (p. 29). She assigned it (wrongly, I think) to 1724. In Mrs. Thomson's version the writer refers to his traveling companion as "Mr. ——," but in Mrs. Beale's version he becomes "Mr. Cavendish." Though Mrs. Beale asserted that the letter had appeared in print before only in Mrs. Thomson's work, actually it is the same as *A Letter from an English Traveller at Rome to his Father, of the 6th of May 1721. O.S.*, which had been published as an eight-page pamphlet presumably in 1721 or soon thereafter. Furthermore, it had been reprinted in full at least twice in the nineteenth century—in 1844 in *The Spottiswoode Miscellany* (Edinburgh), I, 415–24, and in 1884 as a reprint issued by the Clarendon Historical Society (Edinburgh). Strangely, the editor of the Clarendon reprint, Edmund Goldsmid, stated that the letter had never been printed before. Only Mrs. Thomson and Mrs. Beale attribute it to Spence, and only Mrs. Beale uses the name "Cavendish" and mentions the Devonshire connection. There are differences in spelling, punctuation, and phrasing among some of the various printed versions. It is almost impossible to accept this letter as having been written by Spence, and one is reassured to find it ascribed in the British Museum Catalogue to William Godolphin, Marquis of Blandford (though this ascription, too, might be challenged). The chief cause for skepticism with regard to Spence's authorship is the intimate knowledge which the Pretender is said in the letter to have showed of the writer's father and grandfather. As for the Devonshire connection: Spence seems to have had no subsequent relations with the Cavendish family, whereas with the families of his later pupils he remained on terms of intimacy. It is true that young Goldophin's sister was the wife of Thomas Pelham-Holles, Duke of Newcastle, who was to become a patron of Spence. But unless further evidence is uncovered, one must describe the basis for belief in this tour of 1721 as very flimsy.

Information as to the other tour is supplied by a contributor to the *Gentleman's Magazine* in 1819 (LXXXIX, Part II, 412), who asserts that Spence attended Edward Rudge, Esq., of Wheatfield, Oxfordshire, "as a travelling tutor on a continental tour, about the year 1725." The writer is apparently correct in saying that Spence "long lived in habits of intimacy" with Rudge, but he lessens one's confidence in his reliability by asserting that Spence was drowned in the garden of the property owned by Rudge's widow at Weybridge: there is every reason to believe that Spence was drowned in his own garden (see p. 174).

CHAPTER II

FRIEND OF POPE AND PROFESSOR OF POETRY

1. The *Monthly Catalogue* lists the work as published in June. Pope mentions it in a letter of June 4 (Elwin-Courthope, VIII, 119).

2. A writer in the *London Journal* for July 17, 1726, observed: "I have a great admiration for this admired poet, and also for his ingenious bookseller, but I hope they will not always hope to impose extravagant prices upon us for bad paper, old types, and journey work poetry" (*ibid.*, V, 202).

3. For the best account of the public reception of the work see George Sherburn, *The Early Career of Alexander Pope* (Oxford, 1934), pp. 262–65.

4. Elwin-Courthope, VIII, 119.

5. *Ibid.*, p. 120.

6. *Lives of the Poets*, ed. Hill (Oxford, 1905), III, 143.

7. *Works of Pope* (1797), I, xxxv.

8. In the MS the word *misapply'd* has been crossed out and replaced by *made too free with*.

9. Egerton MS 1960. This MS was first properly identified as Spence's by Professor A. E. Case in *Modern Philology*, XXXIII (1935–36), 187–93.

10. At his death it came into the hands of Robert Lowth, one of his

executors, who allowed Joseph Warton to examine it (see Warton, *An Essay on the Genius and Writings of Pope*, II [1782], 239). Along with most of Spence's papers, it was for some years the property of S. W. Singer, who in 1850 contributed a detailed description of it to *Notes and Queries*, 1st ser., I, 396–97. At Singer's death it was sold through Sotheby and Wilkinson (August 3, 1858, Lot 191) to Peter Cunningham, later passed into the possession of the Dukes of Newcastle, and is now among the Spence Papers (see Preface).

11. P. 7. However much Pope had to do with its final form, the second part of the *Essay* is beyond question more lavish of praise and more sparing of condemnation than the first had been.

12. The *Monthly Catalogue* for August, 1727, lists Part II as published in that month. My references are to the first edition of each part.

13. See p. 10.

14. See pp. 33–34.

15. A phrase in Part II of the *Essay* suggests that at the time it was written Spence felt qualified to speak of Pope's eminence in friendship as well as in poetry: "A virtuous generous Soul is certainly as necessary to constitute a Great Poet as a Great Orator: and in Sentiments like these, we may discover that temper of Mind, which I dare say has contributed much towards making that Gentleman so good a Poet, as well as so good a Friend" (p. 105).

16. Underhill's edition of Spence's *Anecdotes* [1890], p. x.

17. Bowles's edition of Pope (1806), VII, 414–15. As early as the preceding August 2, Pope knew that Spence and Pitt were acquainted, for on that date he added a postscript to a letter which Spence wrote to Pitt from Twickenham (Bowles, *loc. cit.*); but no doubt in the letter of November 12 Spence was referring to a conversation which had taken place prior to August 2—possibly during that same visit at Twickenham.

18. For a fuller account of the evidence concerning the date of Spence's first meeting with Pope see my article in *Modern Language Notes*, LIV (1939), 359–61.

19. *Epistle to Jervas*, ll. 21–22.

20. P. 101 (Part I).

21. *Polymetis* (1747), p. iv.

22. Spence later deceived himself as to his good fortune in having largely spared Pope's portion of the translation. He told Warburton (Egerton MS 1960), "Mr. P has himself ~~often~~ [*sic*] told me, that there are very few lines of his, in proportion to those of the other Translators; which I have happend to find fault with: & Capt: Cleland, has assurd me; that he took the pains to compare [*consult* crossed out] all ye places, found fault w^th; (by M^rP^s Mss:) & that there were but four, of M^r P^s own verses, among them." And Malone observed: "It is remarkable that of twelve passages objected to in Spencer's [*sic*] *Essay on the English*

Odyssey, two only are found in those books which were translated by Pope.—(This comes from Mr. Langton, who had his information from Mr. Spence)" (Prior, *Life of Malone* [1860], pp. 429–30; almost the identical information is given in a note in Malone's hand in his copy of the 1747 edition of the *Essay*, cited by Bolton Corney in *Notes and Queries*, 1st ser., I [1849–50], 363; perhaps Prior derived his material from the same source).

Spence's statements are puzzling, and careful investigation would have convinced him (and Malone) that he was in error. In Part I of the *Essay*, for example, he cites 101 passages to justify his strictures (a few passages are criticized for more than one fault), 42 of which are in the books translated by Pope. Since Pope translated half of the 14 books criticized, Spence does not seem to have been extraordinarily fortunate in the proportion of his blows which fell upon Broome and Fenton. Book iv, translated by Fenton, received the most censure, but Pope's Book v was not far behind.

23. Pp. 2–3 (Part I).

24. A. F. B. Clark, in *Boileau and the French Classical Critics in England* (Paris, 1925), pp. 268–69 n., contends, with some reason, that Spence is probably indebted to Bouhours's *Manière de bien penser* for the contrasting mentalities of his two speakers.

25. P. 3 (Part I).

26. P. 28 (Part I).

27. *Lives of the Poets*, ed. Hill, III, 143.

28. This passage was omitted from the title-page of the second edition.

29. P. 10 (Part I).

30. P. 18 (Part I).

31. P. 42 (Part I). The last sentence was omitted in the second edition.

32. He had been aided in part of the book by Henry Layng, who later tried to help him discover the authorship of the *Essay* (see p. 10). See Austin Warren in *Review of English Studies*, VIII (1932), 77–82.

33. P. 98 (Part I).

34. P. 105 (Part I).

35. *Ibid.*

36. *Ibid.*

37. P. 109 (Part I).

38. The remarks are of course always put into the mouth of one or the other of the two speakers.

39. P. 118 (Part I).

40. P. 123 (Part I).

41. P. 135 (Part I). Evidently suggested by the concluding lines of Roscommon's *Essay on Translated Verse* (1684), from which Spence quotes on the same page.

42. Pp. 155–56 (Part I).

43. A favorite topic with Spence. Compare his chapter in *Polymetis* on "The Defects of Our Modern Poets, in their Allegories: instanced from Spenser's Fairy Queen" (Dialogue XIX).

44. Spence commends Pope especially (p. 90, Part II) for avoiding Homer's awkwardness in inserting eighty lines of narrative between Eurycleia's discovery of the scar of Ulysses and her joy at recognizing him.

45. P. 99 (Part II).

46. P. 108 (Part II).

47. P. 206 (Part II).

48. He uses it in his discussion of rhyme in "Evening the Third." See also Singer, p. 9.

49. Clark (*op. cit.*, p. 267) notes that the arrangement of Spence's *Essay* in five "Evenings" does, indeed, recall the division of Fontenelle's *Entretiens sur la pluralité des mondes* into six "Soirs."

50. By Clark (*ibid.*, pp. 267–68).

51. It was listed in the *Gentleman's Magazine* for August (VII, 518).

52. The first two editions had been published by Samuel Wilmot, of Oxford, who sold the copyright to Dodsley on September 1, 1744, for fifteen guineas. The record of the transaction, together with the agreement between Spence and Dodsley for the publication of the third edition, is in the British Museum, Egerton MS 738.

53. This was printed anonymously in the second edition of the *Essay*. Pitt's MS copy is in the British Museum, Additional MS 30370, beginning on fol. 19v.

54. *Remarks and Collections of Thomas Hearne*, ed. Salter ("Oxford Historical Society") (Oxford, 1915), X, 31.

55. Chalmers, *English Poets* (1810), XI, 200. Ramsay's second volume appeared in 1728, and Somerville's poem is usually dated 1729.

56. James Hervey (1714–58) was "delighted by the *Essay on Pope's Odyssey* . . . to which elegant and judicious discourse Mr. Hervey often acknowledged that he owed more of his improvement in style and composition, than to any other which he had ever read" (*Works* [Edinburgh, 1792], I, vi).

57. Warton's edition of Pope's *Works*, I, xxxvi. Warton's assertion that he speaks "from experience" may mean that he used the *Essay* with his students at Winchester College, of which he was long (1766–92) Master.

58. From the preface to *The Preceptor*, in Johnson's *Works*, ed. Murphy (1796), II, 247.

59. This is an error on Johnson's part, for Spence was not appointed to the professorship until 1728.

60. *Lives of the Poets*, ed. Hill, III, 142–43.

61. From *Essays Moral and Literary* in Knox's *Works* (1824), II, 250. Knox, primarily an educator, may, like Warton, be speaking from experience when he testifies to the value of Spence's criticism in forming the taste of young men.

62. Prior, *Life of Malone*, p. 430.

63. *Miscellaneous Works*, ed. Sheffield (1814), V, 583.

64. Margaret Evans, *Letters of Richard Radcliffe and John James, of Queen's College, Oxford, 1755–1783* ("Oxford Historical Society") (Oxford, 1888), pp. 81–82.

65. George Saintsbury, *History of Criticism and Literary Taste in Europe* (1900–1904), II, 454 n.

66. Thomas R. Lounsbury, *The Text of Shakespeare* (New York, 1906), p. 194.

67. A more recent and more temperate critic than Lounsbury says that Spence's dialogues, "with all their excessive praise, still embody the most incisive and just criticism of Pope's *Odyssey*" (see Sherburn, *op. cit.*, p. 269). George Finsler, in *Homer in der Neuzeit von Dante bis Goethe* (Leipzig and Berlin, 1912), pp. 330–32, gives a summary of Spence's "bemerkenswerte Beobachtungen über epische Kunst."

68. Some notes dated in that year are in the Spence Papers.

69. See pp. 72–75.

70. For a full description of the MSS of the *Anecdotes* see chap. viii.

71. So Professor Sherburn calls it (*op. cit.*, p. 265). He concludes: "In view of Spence's later collection of anecdotes about Pope, one may surely say that if Pope had never received a guinea for the *Odyssey*, he would yet have 'found his account' in it through gaining Spence as a friend" (p. 269).

72. *A Catalogue of All Graduats . . . in the University of Oxford, 1659–1770* (Oxford, 1772), p. 331.

73. *Portland MSS—Historical Manuscripts Commission*, VII (1901), 452.

74. *Ibid.*

75. *Post Boy*, No. 6084, Saturday, July 13—Tuesday, July 16, 1728; Nichols, *Select Collection of Poems*, VIII (1782), 1 n.; *Gentleman's Magazine*, LXXVI, Part I (1806), 329. Hearne, writing on July 20, 1728, observed that "about a Fortnight since" Spence had been "elected without opposition" (Hearne, *op. cit.*, X, 31).

76. John Duncombe, *Letters by Several Eminent Persons Deceased* (1773), II, 13 n.

77. *Ibid.*, II, 12–13.

78. See p. 28.

79. Stratford had been active in Spence's interest. He wrote to Oxford on December 19, 1727: "I hear Mr. Spence and his competitor, one Jones of Balliol, are very busy already, though the election will not be till the next Act. I have not yet seen Mr. Spence, but I believe

I shall secure him a pretty good interest in this College" (*Portlana MSS—Historical Manuscripts Commission*, VII [1901], 454).

80. *Historical Register of the University of Oxford* (Oxford, 1888), p. 59. See also Rolle's letter to Spence in Singer, p. 442. The originals of this and all but one of the other letters printed by Singer are preserved in a four-volume, extra-illustrated copy of Singer's edition of the *Anecdotes* in the Huntington Library (call number RB 131213). This copy also contains Rolle's manuscript biographical account of Spence (see earlier, p. 204, n. 33).

81. George Saintsbury, *A History of English Criticism* (1911), p. 526.

82. Original letter in the Huntington Library (see Singer, p. 388).

83. So described in the Sotheby and Wilkinson catalogue, August 3, 1858 (Lot 197).

84. Pope later confirmed Spence's opinion that the *Aeneid* was "evidently a party piece" (see Singer, p. 217).

85. These two lectures, now in Additional MS 17281, were presented in 1848 by W. H. Carpenter, publisher of Singer's edition of the *Anecdotes*.

86. Egerton MS 2234, fol. 8r.

87. *Ibid.*, fols. 22v and 23r. Both letters are quoted by Underhill in his edition of the *Anecdotes* [1890], p. xxi n.

88. H. Rashdall and R. S. Roit in *New College* (1901), p. 205, and A. O. Prickard, in *New College, Oxford* (1906), p. 55, point to Spence as a specimen of the better sort of college Fellow in the eighteenth century.

89. From the records at New College.

90. From the Register Book at Birchanger.

91. Spence Papers.

92. That is, Spence, his mother, and his sister.

93. Egerton MS 2234, fols 114v–115r.

94. Warton's *Works of Pope*, I, 236 n.

95. Léon Morel, *James Thomson: Sa vie et ses œuvres* (Paris, 1895), pp. 48, 62, 68.

96. *Ibid.*, p. 70.

97. *Winter:* by Mr. Thompson [Spence's note].

98. *An Essay on Pope's Odyssey* (Part II), p. 15.

99. Original letter in the Huntington Library (see Singer, p. 389).

100. Warton's *Works of Pope*, I, 236 n.

101. Morel, *op. cit.*, p. 87, n. 2.

102. See Spence's letter to his mother dated July 13, Egerton MS 2234, fol. 24r.

103. Egerton MS 2235. Spence kept a list of persons whom he met in different cities.

104. Singer, p. 327. Spence recorded that on this occasion Thomson "laughed very heartily."

105. *Ibid.*, pp. 327–28.

106. From a sheet in the Spence Papers.

107. Proof of this association is found in the *Anecdotes*, many entries in which exist in an earlier form in the Spence Papers.

108. Singer, p. 316.

109. *Ibid.*, p. 144.

110. *Ibid.*, p. 338 and n.

111. See p. 33.

112. In the Spence Papers are notes on conversations with Ramsay dated June 6–11, 1729, and with Lockier dated September 1–6, 1730. Spence's intimacy with Ramsay, an ardent Freemason, makes one wonder whether Spence had ties with Freemasonry (see also n. 4, below).

113. See Singer, p. 310, and *Polymetis* (1747), p. 82.

114. *Polymetis* (1747), p. 82.

115. Warton's *Works of Pope*, I, xxxvi.

CHAPTER III
YEARS OF TRAVEL

1. Middlesex' letter to Spence and two from A. Smyth on the same subject are printed in Singer, pp. 391–97 (originals in the Huntington Library extra-illustrated copy). The Earl and his companions were accused by a mob of insulting the memory of Charles I on the anniversary of that monarch's execution.

2. That this nickname persisted and was not frowned upon by Spence (at least, not when it was used by nobility!) is proved by an undated note from the Duke of Manchester and Spence's reply, preserved in the Huntington Library extra-illustrated copy of Singer. Spence is there addressed as "Friend Spanco" and uses the name in his reply.

3. The society was formed probably in 1733, but the first meeting noted in the minute books was that of May 2, 1736, when Spence's name appears on the roll of members (see *Historical Notices of the Society of Dilettanti* [1855], p. 116).

4. Walpole's *Letters*, ed. Toynbee, I, 339–40. Humphrey Johnson credits Middlesex (and, by implication, Spence) with introducing Freemasonry into Italy during this tour (see "Freemasonry in Italy," *Dublin Review*, No. 445 [Spring, 1949], p. 94).

5. Most of the originals are in Egerton MS 2234. Three are in the Huntington Library extra-illustrated copy of Singer.

6. In Egerton MS 2235 and the Spence Papers.

7. Egerton MS 2234, fol. 229r.

8. *Ibid.*, fol. 3v.

9. *Ibid.*, fol. 9r.

10. See Spence's edition of Holdsworth's *Remarks and Dissertations on Virgil* (1768), p. iv.

11. Egerton MS 2234, fol. 70v.

12. See letter dated March 19, 1732, in *Gentleman's Magazine*, LXXXIII (1813, Part I), 539.

13. After his return to England, Spence wrote to Colonel Henry Rolle four letters (dated from Oxford in 1734) describing the Duke's Gallery at Florence (Egerton MS 2234, fols. 297 ff.). Colonel Rolle was the cousin and patron of Edward Rolle.

14. Walpole's *Letters*, ed. Toynbee, I, 88.

15. This was in 1754. See Walpole's *Letters*, ed. Cunningham (1877), I, 104, n. 2.

16. During the last two days of the trip to Paris they covered the remarkable distance of 246 miles (Egerton MS 2234, fol. 84r).

17. To this period would seem to belong a little manuscript "History of English Poetry" found among the Spence Papers. It has been printed for the first time and discussed in detail by Mr. James M. Osborn in an article entitled "The First History of English Poetry," in *Pope and His Contemporaries: Essays Presented to George Sherburn*, ed. Clifford and Landa (Oxford, 1949), pp. 230-50. Osborn believes that the essay, written in "wretched anglicized French," was a product of Spence's leisure hours on the tour with Middlesex. He praises it for its style and its just evaluations and says that in its pages Spence shows himself to be far ahead of his time as a critic and historian of English poetry. Osborn also calls attention to numerous notes indicating that Spence had made progress in the compilation of a "Poetical Dictionary; in 12 Sections."

18. The *Gentleman's Magazine*, I (1731), 136, lists *Memoirs of the life of that celebrated Wiltshire Poet, Mr. Steph. Duck, pr. 6d.*

19. Egerton MS 2234, fols. 20v and 21r.

20. Rose Mary Davis, *Stephen Duck, the Thresher-Poet* ("University of Maine Studies," 2d ser., No. 8 [Orono, Maine, January, 1927]), p. 185. The article was also published in an abridged form in the *Gentleman's Magazine* in 1736 (VI, 317 ff.).

21. P. xiv.

22. Nichols, *Literary Anecdotes* (1812), I, 643 n. In the account of Spence in *Literary Anecdotes*, II, 373 n., based in part upon information derived from this letter of Lowth's, Nichols states that Spence left his account of Duck "in the hands of his friend Mr. Lowth." As can be seen from what Lowth actually wrote, this statement, though possibly correct, is unjustified unless Nichols had additional information.

23. The "rascal bookseller" who published the pamphlet was J. Knapton, one of the distributors of Spence's *Essay on Pope's Odyssey* a few years before. It may or may not be significant that Knapton published nothing for Spence after 1731.

24. P. 5.

25. The original notes are in the Spence Papers.

26. After a few days' acquaintance with Lord Sandwich in Turin,

Spence wrote his mother that he knew that nobleman better than he knew Duck "the three first days he was at Winchester" (Egerton MS 2234, fol. 159r).

27. Mrs. [K. B.] Thomson, *Memoirs of Viscountess Sundon* (1847), I, 197–98.

28. See p. 46.

29. *Account of Duck*, p. 24.

30. *Ibid.*, p. 15.

31. *Ibid.*, p. 5.

32. *Ibid.*, p. 26.

33. The appointment is listed in the *Gentleman's Magazine*, XXII (1752), 45. The annual stipend is there said to have been £130.

34. *Caesar's Camp: or, St. George's Hill. A Poem* (1755). Joseph Warton attributes Duck's preferment directly to Spence: "By the interest of Mr. Spence, who had a sincere regard for Stephen Duck, whose life he wrote, and published his poems, he obtained the living of Byfleet in Surrey" (Warton's *Works of Pope* [1797], IV, 226 n.).

35. From evidence found in Spence's journals for 1755–56, in the Spence Papers.

36. See J. M. Attenborough in the *Cornhill Magazine*, new ser., XIV (1903), 806.

37. If the identification is correct, Spence seems to have advised Duck early in his career to cease writing while his fame was at its height and before inspiration failed—"To quit the Muse before her Spirits sink" (see the poem *Every Man in his Own Way: An Epistle to a Friend* [1741], l. 3).

38. Elwin-Courthope, X, 131. On the note is said to appear in an unknown hand the date 1733.

39. The original letter is tipped into the extra-illustrated copy of Singer in the Huntington Library. Singer prints it on pp. xxii–xxiii.

40. Most of the anecdotes printed by Singer on pp. 151–57.

41. Original letter in the Huntington Library extra-illustrated copy of Singer (see Singer, pp. 383–84).

42. *The Tragedy of Gorboduc: Written by Thomas Sackville Lord Buckhurst, afterwards Lord Treasurer to Queen Elizabeth, and Earl of Dorset* (1736), p. i.

43. From Mr. Langton [Malone's note].

44. Prior, *Life of Malone* (1860), p. 430. According to Bolton Corney (*Notes and Queries*, 1st ser., I [1849–50], 363–64), almost the same comment appears in a note signed "E. M." in Malone's copy of the 1747 edition of Spence's *Essay on Pope's Odyssey* (see pp. 208–9, n. 22).

45. They formed part of Lot 200, which brought 10s. 6d. Extracts from them were announced for publication in *Notes and Queries*, 2d ser., XI (1861), 1, but only an account of Swift (now in the Spence Papers) and an article on Pope's letters made an appearance.

46. Dodsley's *Select Collection of Old Plays* (including *Gorboduc*) was published in twelve volumes in 1744–45. Coxeter's slur and Spence's intimacy with Dodsley suggest that the anecdotist may have had a hand in the selection and publication of the collection.

47. Nichols, *Literary Anecdotes*, II, 512 n.

48. Singer, pp. 179–80. Singer printed (pp. 475–78) specimens of Dobson's version which he found among Spence's papers.

49. No incumbent was permitted to occupy the chair for more than two five-year terms.

50. Part of this letter is quoted on p. 36.

51. Spence Papers. To this letter was added the following postscript concerning a "Mr Littleton" who may have been George, later first Baron Lyttleton, whom Spence must certainly have known at Oxford and whom he was later to visit at Hagley Park:

"I have recd yours. I dont promise myself any great things with Mr Littleton; for to tell you the truth (& I believe I hinted it at first) I a long time avoided any acquaintance with him, because I took him to be a Coxcomb. If my Acquaintance sd grow with him, (& I shall encourage it all I can, on Mr Morecrofts account) I sd be very glad to be of service there: but I think that is not a thing at all to be depended upon. . . ."

52. *DNB*, *s.v.* "Lowth."

53. Walpole's *Letters*, ed. Toynbee, I, 197. His father, also named John Morley Trevor, had married Lucy Montagu, a first cousin of Thomas Pelham, Duke of Newcastle, and Henry Pelham. The younger Trevor, who died in 1745, was a first cousin of George Montagu, Walpole's correspondent (*ibid.*, XVI, xiv–xv).

54. This identification is established beyond reasonable doubt by several pieces of evidence: John Morley Trevor was elected M.P. for the Pelham-controlled Sussex borough of Lewes in 1738, and Spence's Trevor hurried back to England in January of that year at the request of Newcastle and Sir Robert Walpole to stand for Parliament; John Morley Trevor was one of three persons each of whom subscribed for the unusually large number of twelve copies of Spence's *Polymetis*, the others being, significantly, Spence's other pupil-companions, Lords Middlesex and Lincoln; Spence was on friendly terms with the Pelhams, as is proved by his appointment to accompany their favorite nephew, Lincoln, on the grand tour two years later. For Trevor see Walpole's *Letters*, ed. Toynbee, I, 197, and Foster, *Alumni Oxonienses 1715–1886*.

55. Writing from New College, December 3, 1738, Spence tried to interest Massingberd, then in Paris, in purchasing Trevor's Italian chaise, which had been left at Calais.

56. Since the first edition of Part I of the *Essay* had appeared prior to the inception of the friendship between Pope and Spence, it is of interest to note what changes in that portion of the work were made

in the second edition. It is to Spence's credit that little was done to soften the adverse criticism, though he did withdraw two brief passages of censure. In the more severe of these he had found fault with the poet for employing certain forced and unnatural metaphors, going so far as to say that they reminded him of the work of Nahum Tate (Part I [1st. ed.], p. 36)! In the other he had good-naturedly pointed out that in a footnote on an unpoetically translated line the poet had given a prose translation more poetic than that in verse (*ibid.*, p. 108).

57. Rolle wrote to Massingberd on February 16, 1738/9, that Spence was then "with his Old Landlord Jonquiere in Suffolk Street," and Spence dated several letters from Suffolk Street in 1739. He and Rolle had visited Bath together in the early summer of 1738 (letter from Rolle to Massingberd, July 2, 1738).

58. July 31, 1739.

59. July 31, 1739.

60. *Letters and Works of Lady Mary Wortley Montagu*, ed. Thomas (rev., 1898), II, 91. Sir Charles Hanbury Williams, however, later celebrated Lincoln's prowess with the ladies in an indecent ode, and Horace Walpole intimated that his relations with Lady Mary herself were irregular (*Works of Sir Charles Hanbury Williams* [1822], II, 33–35 and note). See also for testimony by Walpole to Lincoln's "vanity and amorous propensities" *Horace Walpole's Correspondence with Gray, West, and Ashton*, ed. Lewis, Lam, and Bennett (New Haven, 1948), I, 10, n. 61.

61. Walpole's *Letters*, ed. Toynbee, I, 129.

62. Additional MS 33065, fol. 340v.

63. Thus Walpole in a letter to West, November 11, 1739 (Walpole's *Letters*, ed. Toynbee, I, 40).

64. Original in Huntington Library extra-illustrated copy of Singer (see Singer, pp. 399–400). Walpole describes the same production briefly to West on November 11, 1739 (Walpole's *Letters*, ed. Toynbee, I, 42).

65. Singer, misled by the phrasing of one of Spence's letters, supposed that the sprain had occurred when Lincoln was dancing (Singer, p. xxv).

66. Singer, pp. 400–403 (original in Huntington Library). The incident of the sprain is also described by both Lincoln and Spence in letters in Additional MS 33065, fols. 374–78.

67. Her correspondence with the Countess of Hertford (later Duchess of Somerset) was published in 1805.

68. Walpole's *Letters*, ed. Toynbee, I, 75–76.

69. From Rome on April 8, 1741, Lincoln himself, in fulfilment of a promise to Spence, wrote a distracted six-page letter to the Duke about the affair (Additional MS 33065, fols. 405–7). Of his "dearest

Mr Spence" he says: "I am sure my L^d I shou'd be very ungrateful & very undeserving ye infinite obligations I owe him, if I did not let you know ye truely friendly part he has profess'd for me throughout ye whole affair; yes my L^d he has done everything y^r Grace cou'd possibly expect, or ev'n more y^n I am afraid I have deserv'd f^m his hands, he has in ye most friendly manner imaginable pointed out to me my fault, in encouraging a passion, wch alas I do but too well see myself, ye little prospect I have of ever being happy in, he has constantly repeated to me w^t I owe to my self, y^r Grace & all my friends, & in such a manner, y^t tho' I had not resolution enough to follow in every thing his excellent advice, I cou'd not but help approving, & heartily wishing y^t I deserv'd ye fondness & friendship he has wth so much sincerity shown he had for me."

70. Walpole's *Letters*, ed. Toynbee, Supplement (1918), I, 40.

71. *Letters*, ed. Toynbee, I, 129.

72. *Ibid.*, II, 42.

73. Years later Spence, apparently callous to the tragedy of Lady Sophia, wrote to Lincoln that the prevention of this match was an effort which "I thank God, (tho' with much pain both to y^r L^p & myself) I succeeded in" (from a draft of a letter in the Spence Papers, dated April 28, 1751).

74. Egerton MS 2234, fol. 222v.

75. See Singer, pp. 222–25, where they are described as those of "Lady O" (Lady Walpole's husband succeeded his father, the former Sir Robert Walpole, as Earl of Orford in 1745. Singer incorrectly assigns Lady Orford's remarks to "Lady Oxford").

76. Walpole's *Letters*, ed. Toynbee, I, 81–82.

77. *Letters and Works*, II, 217.

78. Walpole's *Letters*, ed. Toynbee, I, 104 n.

79. *Correspondence of Thomas Gray*, ed. Toynbee and Whibley (Oxford, 1935), I, 172.

80. Additional MS 33065, fol. 392.

81. Egerton MS 2234, fols. 247–52.

82. Spence Papers.

83. *Ibid.* In the version from which Singer printed (p. 224), "Lady Mary's" has been altered to "that lady's." Lady Mary makes a spirited defense of her tastes in literature in a letter of 1750: "I thank God my taste still continues for the gay part of reading. Wiser people may think it trifling, but it serves to sweeten life to me, and is at worst better than the generality of conversation" (*Letters and Works*, II, 211–12).

84. Thus recorded in the Spence Papers (see Singer, p. 237).

85. Spence tells the story of Walpole's illness in a letter dated at Bologna, May 29, 1741 (Egerton MS 2234, fols. 263–64). That Spence did not magnify the severity of the illness is indicated by Walpole's own statement in his "Short Notes of My Life": "I fell ill at Reggio of

a kind of quinsy, and was given over for five hours, escaping with great difficulty" (Walpole's *Letters*, ed. Toynbee, I, xxxvi).

86. Original in Huntington Library extra-illustrated copy of Singer (see Singer, p. 406). At Florence in the preceding autumn Spence had dined with Walpole "almost every day" (see *Horace Walpole's Correspondence with Gray, West, and Ashton*, ed. Lewis, Lam, and Bennett, I, 10, n. 64).

87. See a letter from Spence to Walpole, dated October 27, 1757, in Walpole's *Letters*, ed. Toynbee, Supplement (1918), II, 103–4. Walpole passed on Spence's information, without acknowledgment, to Mann on November 20 (*Letters*, ed. Toynbee, IV, 111–12).

88. See pp. 162–65.

89. Walpole's *Letters*, ed. Toynbee, III, 18.

90. See *ibid.*, V, 336, and Supplement, II, 126.

91. Walpole's *Letters*, ed. Toynbee, XI, 175.

92. Walpole also came to think less highly of Lincoln than he had done in 1741.

93. Walpole's *Letters*, ed. Toynbee, Supplement, I, 40.

94. Spence Papers (see Singer, pp. 249–51).

95. Egerton MS 2234, fol. 283v.

96. On July 27, 1740, he had written to her: "I want to be setting out; for that's doing something: & looks, at least, like being nearer coming home. As much as I long to see Rome, I long more to be with you; & to be settling our little affairs, in order to live together in a comfortable ma[nner?] the rest of our time, that we have to be [in?] this wicked world. Whether that is to be long or short, I think does not signify a great deal; but one w^d make the time, whatever it is, as agreable as one can. Thank Heaven, we are likely at present (ev'n in the very worst view, of three or four, that I cou'd reckon up to you) to have enough to live comfortably, & to do some little good round about one; & that I always reckon among the highest diversions both for You and Me" (*ibid.*, fol. 198r).

97. "The large work I have on my hands will take up near four Year after I come home, before it is all publisht: & after that, I have some other little things which I think at present of publishing; & which, in the leisurely way I shall go about it, merely for my amusement, will take up six year more" (*ibid.*, fol. 171r, March 30, 1740).

98. Additional MS 33065, fol. 405r.

99. *Ibid.*, fol. 463v.

CHAPTER IV

RESIDENCE IN LONDON

1. A copy of the contract, indorsed by Spence "Ld Lincoln's Grant of 100 G's a year," is in the Spence Papers. The contract was witnessed by Horace Walpole and Thomas Ashton.

2. The salary was £400, reduced by fees of office to £371 (*Historical Register of the University of Oxford* [Oxford, 1888], p. 60). Spence succeeded Dr. William Holmes, who resigned to become Dean of Exeter. The appointment is listed in the *Gentleman's Magazine*, XII (1742), 331. Spence's professorship was renewed by George III on September 28, 1761, and on the following February 3 he took the oaths required before Lord Mansfield at the King's Bench in Westminster Hall (certificates in the Spence Papers).

3. From the records at New College. A copy of the "Instrument of Institution," dated July 19, 1742, is in the Spence Papers.

4. In 1928 the emoluments at Great Horwood were approximately £590, the outgoings approximately £85. From the records at New College.

5. See p. 204, n. 38.

6. During that period a number of extant letters were addressed to him at Stratton Street—near Piccadilly and Horace Walpole's house in Arlington Street—and in Stratton Street he may have found the house "near the parks" concerning which he had written to his mother from Paris (see p. 66). If we may believe Rolle, Spence at this period cherished a love for London and a distaste for the country which were the reverse of the feelings he was to develop not much later. Writing to Massingberd from Oxford on October 30, 1741, in anticipation of Spence's return, Rolle observed: "You know what an infinite aversion he hath for Rooks & the Solitude of a country Town, that if we have him here at all I suppose it will be but for a moment, & then with as sad a countenance as Mr Pope's young Lady leaving the town after a coronation, in short he hath that invincible attachment to a certain great town, which most of us good country People abuse most heartily, & yet are seldom easy if we do not once a year visit it, that I am very much afraid we are like to have but little of him, all of whom is yet so very little, here."

7. In the Spence Papers and in the Huntington Library MS of the *Anecdotes* (HM 1271), entries are usually dated by months and sometimes even by days.

8. Spence's notes on the events of May are headed, at intervals, "Twitnam, May 1–4," "Chelsea, May 10–17," and "Twitnam, May 19–29." This dating, which is preserved also in the Huntington MS, seems to mean that he was at Pope's side on twenty-three of the last thirty days of the poet's life. These notes are preserved in an extra-illustrated copy of Singer's edition owned formerly by Peter Cunningham and now by Mrs. A. H. Cleaver, of Hoylake, Cheshire, who has kindly allowed me to make use of them. Wherever possible, my quotations are from these apparently early notes, but a few are from the Huntington MS (see Singer, pp. 318–22).

9. This remark appears in the original notes as "quoted by Chis,"

and it is attributed to Chiselden in HM 1271 also. In the manuscripts from which the Singer and Malone editions were printed it is given (wrongly, I think) to Bolingbroke (Singer, p. 320; Malone, p. 76).

10. In 1755 Spence set down (in his journal) some remarks by Warburton about Pope's last days (see Singer, p. 367).

11. But in his journal for 1757 (p. 12) Spence wrote the following curious note: "*M^r W^n of Newark, is said to have got into Orders, by Spitt^g in a Nobleman's Face. Q? (Ab^t 30 y^r Ago: in Election time. A Man of such Resol^n worth hav^g for a Friend" (Spence Papers). Singer (p. x) paraphrases the first part of this remark and assumes that it proves Spence's contempt for Warburton.

12. Spence's journal for 1755, p. 17 (Spence Papers). Quoted imperfectly by Singer, p. 365.

13. *Letters from a Late Eminent Prelate to One of His Friends* (Kidderminster, [1808]), p. 82.

14. *Ibid.*, p. 209.

15. Spence Papers, notes dated "Apr: 5:7, 1744." Quoted by Singer, p. viii.

16. Warton's *Works of Pope*, IV, 19 n.

17. Egerton MS 1960 (see pp. 10 and 207, n. 9).

18. [Thomas Tyers], *An Historical Rhapsody on Mr. Pope* (2d ed., 1782), p. 96.

19. See, for example: Bolingbroke to Mallet, July 25, 1745, in Carruthers' *Life of Pope* (2d ed., 1857), p. 397; Lyttelton to Warburton, September 2, 1745, in *A Selection from Unpublished Papers of the Right Reverend William Warburton*, ed. Kilvert (1841), p. 208; and Warburton to Hurd (1750?), in *Letters from a Late Eminent Prelate to One of His Friends*, p. 33.

20. [Tyers], *op. cit.*, p. 96.

21. Singer, p. x.

22. Spence, like Walpole, attended the trial of the Scottish peers. On March 23, 1746-47, he sent Massingberd the following account of Lord Lovat's behavior: ". . . all the world here has been taken up with my Ld Lovat's Tryal. There is a print of him, from a drawing of Hogarth, which is not unlike him; & a friend of mine has the design of a Satir's head, by Rubens, which is a good deal more like him: but, to say the truth, they are both likenesses of the caricatura-kind; for there is something of the Gentleman mixt in his appearance, wch is quite sunk in the other. Secretary Murray's Evidence was very strong & full against him; & that with his own letters, & two or three other witnesses, was so irrefragable, that when it was his Turn to make his defence, he forbore to call any witnesses; & begd leave to read a paper, which he had prepard, to the Court. This was to invalidate the testimony that had been offer'd against him; to blacken the witnesses, & to whiten himself as much as he cou'd. In the whole course of the Tryal he seem'd

steddy; not cast down; & rather too much inclin'd to a low kind of merriment, that c^d scarce become a Peer in his condition. One of the witnesses against him happend to have ye name of *Charles Stuart;* & at the close of his evidence, his L^p was askt 'w^r he had anything to say against Charles Stuart?' On wch he sayd, 'No my L^ds, *not a word,* I'le assure you': with an air & tone, that shew'd he did not mean the witness.—Sr Everard Falkener was a witness too against him: & the like question being askd him, at ye close of his Evidence; he said, 'No; only that he was Sr Everard Falkener's most humble servant; & heartily wishd him joy of his *young* wife.' On the Attorney General's having said something, pretty warmly, against him; he stood up & said; 'That he had often troubled their Lordships with complaints of his infirmities; that what he lamented the most of them, was his loss of Memory; that that indeed might be expected at his great age: but what surprized him most extreamly was—that the great man at the head of the Law, who spoke last; had forgot what was said, but half an hour before:' & then instanc'd in w^t the Attorney General had forgot himself. Even when Sentence [was given], he desir'd the L^ds wou'd recommend him to the King for Mercy; & turning to the Managers of the House of Commons, he said; 'he hop'd that they, as they were *stout,* w^d also be *merciful.*' I was not there the last day; but they say, he behav'd as indifferent, even w^n the Sentence was giv'n. Upon ye whole, there is a sort of odd Resolution about him, wch makes me suspect, (what has been already said of him,) that he does not design to stay for the Ceremony of the Scaffold."

23. *Literary Anecdotes,* II, 375 n.

24. *Ibid.,* I, 643 n.

25. Journal for 1755 (Spence Papers), p. 25.

26. Spence is evidently the author of a letter which appeared in the *General Advertiser,* No. 4017 (September, 1747), signed "Philocepus." It calls attention to the skill of an artist named Vetter, who had constructed a model of a rock in the garden of a London coffee-house. A clipping containing the letter is found in the Spence Papers, with proof corrections in Spence's hand. He took this opportunity to sing the praises of the English style of gardening: "It seems to be in our own Country, that People have hit on the true and general Principle in the Art of Gardening; that the chief Aim of it should be, 'To assist, and not to oppress Nature;' And it is in the Gardens of Stow, Chiswick, Clermont and Esher, that the Practice of this Great Rule, has been brought gradually to its greatest Perfection."

27. Most of Spence's identifiable contributions to the *Museum* were reprinted in his *Moralities* (1753), discussed later, pp. 140–44.

28. Ralph Straus, *Robert Dodsley* (1910), p. 103. W. P. Courtney says: "Many poems were inserted in the third and the later volumes from members of New College, Oxford, who had passed through their

school education at Winchester College, and these were probably supplied through Spence, Dodsley's warm friend for many years, and a member of both these establishments" (*Dodsley's Collection of Poetry* [1910], p. 2).

29. *Museum*, II, 259–61; *Collection of Poems* (1770 ed.), III, 58–61.

30. Nichols, *Literary Anecdotes*, I, 643 n.

31. III, 160–62. Oddly, Bell reverses the original title and makes it *To a Swiss Officer, From his Friend at Rome.*

32. Bell said of it: "Though not without merit of its own, its principal value appears to arise from the circumstance, of having suggested to Goldsmith the idea of his Traveler" (*Fugitive Poetry*, III, 184). Bell seems to have felt that he was stating a well-known fact, and a comparison of the poems reveals surprising similarities.

33. I, 57.

34. It is printed as Spence's in Nichols' *Select Collection of Poems* (1782), VIII, 24.

35. "These first stanzas of the 24th canto of the Inferno, printed in Dodsley's Museum, No. 2, p. 57, is by Mr. Spence" (Warton's *Works of Pope*, IV, 283 n.). Warton was in a position to know the facts, since he was Spence's intimate friend and was himself the author of the poem immediately preceding the verses in question in the *Museum*.

36. See pp. 22–24.

37. *Epithalamia Oxoniensia, sive Gratulationes in Augustissimi Regis Georgii III. et Illustrissimae Principissae Sophiae Charlottae Nuptias Auspicatissimas* (Oxford, 1761).

38. In Vol. VIII. The poem *On the happy Nuptials of the Prince and Princess of Wales* (1736) was reprinted in the *Gentleman's Magazine*, IX (1739), 39, and that *On the Marriage of King George III. and Princess Charlotte* (1761) in the *Annual Register*, IV (1761), Part II, 225–26. Lowth informed Nichols of an amusing incident in connection with the printing of Spence's poem on the birth of the Prince of Wales (1762): "If you have any design of adding here Mr. Spence's poem on the birth of the Prince of Wales, I must desire you carefully to consider of that matter. That Poem was published in the Oxford Verses very imperfectly; and, I may add, unwarrantably. Mr. Spence had introduced, by way of episode, the *Russian Tragedy*, which was then first in every one's mouth, and was received with universal horror and detestation. The Oxford Critics very rightly, and prudently, thought it not fit to be published by the University; they ought therefore to have sent it to the Author to be re-formed, or to have suppressed it entirely. Instead of this, they cut out the whole episode, about one-third of the Poem, and which was the principal part in the Author's view, and for the introduction of which the whole plan of the Poem was formed; and printed the beginning and end, without any connexion or meaning, to the total destruction of the Poem. If you print it from the

NOTES TO PAGES 81-86

Oxford copy, you must put asterisks in the middle, to shew that it is a mere fragment. But this will raise curiosity, and enquiries will be made after the middle part, of which I believe some copies may be found; and the publication of that avowedly by you, will, I think, even now be improper. Pray let me know what you intend to do as to this matter; and I beg you to do nothing in it without consulting me" (Nichols, *Literary Anecdotes*, I, 644 n.). Nichols, presumably with Lowth's concurrence, printed the poem with asterisks and with the following note: "The Editor has been informed that some lines which followed this in the original MS. were omitted by the publishers of the Oxford Collection" (*Collection of Poems*, VIII, 23).

Lowth also called Nichols' attention to an error in the poem on the death of George II (1761) whereby "History" had been printed as "Hist'ry," to the "utter ruin of the verse, and to set the reader's teeth on edge" (*Literary Anecdotes*, loc. cit.).

39. *Dodsley's Collection of Poetry*, p. 127.

40. John Wooll, *Biographical Memoirs of the Late Revd Joseph Warton, D.D.* (1806), p. 279.

41. In the library of the University of Chicago, PR 3699. S4 1722.

42. Though it appears in the University of Chicago manuscript, a much fuller version, on which I base my remarks, is found in the British Museum Additional MS 25897.

43. John Underhill, *Spence's "Anecdotes, Observations, and Characters of Books and Men"* [1890], p. xxx.

44. *The Dunciad* [Spence's note].

45. A fuller account of *The Charliad* appears in my article, "*The Charliad*, an Unpublished Mock-Epic by Joseph Spence," *PMLA*, XLVII (1932), 554-58.

CHAPTER V

"POLYMETIS"

1. Part I, p. 86.

2. Part II, pp. 17-18. Other passages which show that the germ of *Polymetis* was lodged in Spence's mind at this time are found on pp. 75-76 and 83-84 (Part I) and 30 and 173 (Part II).

3. *Polymetis*, pp. v and 82. Among the Spence Papers is a notebook in which Spence has copied a host of pertinent passages from the Latin poets.

4. *Polymetis*, p. 321.

5. *Ibid.*, p. 68.

6. Bernard de Montfaucon, *L'Antiquité Expliquée et Représentée en Figures* (15 vols.; Paris, 1719-24).

7. Pietro Santi Bartoli, *Admiranda Romanorum antiquitatum ac veteris sculpturae vestigia . . .* (Rome, 1693).

8. Domenico de' Rossi, *Gemme antiche figurate date in luce da Dome-*

nico de' Rossi, colle sposizioni di Paolo Alessandro Maffei . . . (Rome, 1707–9).

9. *Polymetis*, p. 256.

10 *Ibid.*, p. 320. Spence wrote to Massingberd about *Polymetis* on December 15, 1747: "For my own part I am extreamly glad that I have got that vast burthen off my hands." To add to his impatience, the a tist's slowness in executing the plates caused a vexatious delay (see p. 88).

11. *Correspondence of Thomas Gray*, ed. Toynbee and Whibley (Oxford, 1935), I, 265, 268.

12. Walpole's *Letters*, ed. Toynbee, Supplement, I (1918), 53.

13. From a clipping in Bodleian MS Rawl. J.4°6, fol. 200.

14. Some of the subscribers, notably Pope and Trevor, died before publication of the work.

15. *Museum*, I, 99.

16. Spence Papers.

17. *Museum*, I, 99.

18. Ralph Straus, *Robert Dodsley* (1910), p. 333. The work is listed in the *Gentleman's Magazine* (XVII, 108) among publications for February. With regard to the success of *Polymetis*, Rolle wrote to Massingberd on April 24, 1747, as follows: "Tis indeed so well receiv'd by the Public, that the price of it to non-Subscribers is already pretty much advanc'd, wch I think is a substantial proof of its being approv'd of: I believe Besides the credit [it is like] to give its author, it will yield him in the long run a pretty considerable Sum of money, w^{ch}, as the times go, is a consideration likewise, not altogether to be despised." Spence wrote Massingberd on April 21 that the book had already enabled him to "give away 300 £, to put 5 in the Stocks; & I believe will enable me to make the latter 10."

19. The date is uncertain, but the portrait is assigned to 1739 by a writer in the *Gentleman's Magazine* (LXXXIX, Part II [1819], 412) and by Herbert H. Raphael in *Horace Walpole: A Descriptive Catalogue*, etc. (Bristol, 1909), p. 550.

20. The present location of the original is not known. Spence and his friends felt that Vertue had done a poor piece of work. Spence wrote to Massingberd on April 21: "Every body blames the picture before the Book; all which blame aforesaid is due to Mr Vertue. I left it wholy to him; he chose what original to follow, & in w^t manner to do it: & has done it indeed very badly. One comfort to myself is, that tis the only picture in the book which I s^d not have been concernd to see very ill done; & as to my own face I may safely say, that I have not any manner of concern for it at all."

21. *Polymetis*, pp. 3–4.

22. From the *Oratio pro Archia* i. 2.

23. See pp. 106–110.

24. P. iii.

25. *Polymetis*, p. 285.

26. Addison professed to employ the Greek poets as well as those of Rome, but not a single passage among his illustrative texts is derived from the Greek.

27. *Polymetis*, Dialogues XVIII–XX.

28. Singer, p. 93.

29. Joannes Georgius Graevius, *Thesaurus Antiquitatum Romanarum* . . . (12 vols.; Utrecht, 1694–99).

30. Jacobus Gronovius, *Thesaurus Antiquitatum Graecarum* . . . (13 vols.; Leyden, 1697–1702).

31. See esp. *Polymetis*, p. 4 and n. 4.

32. In ll. 45–46:
    "The Verse and Sculpture bore an equal part;
    And Art reflected images to Art."

33. Line 16:
    "Each from each contract new strength and light."

34. Singer, p. 217.

35. *Polymetis*, pp. 20–21.

36. Compare Singer, p. 217, and *Polymetis*, p. 295.

37. The poem *De arte graphica* by Charles Alphonse Dufresnoy was published in 1668 (Paris), after the death of the author, with a translation into French prose and with notes by Roger de Piles. De Piles also wrote a *Cours de Peinture par Principes* (Paris, 1708), which Spence knew.

38. Numbers 411–21, beginning June 21, 1712.

39. André Félibien, author of *Conférences de l'Academie Royale de Peinture* ... (Paris, 1669); *Des Principes de l'Architecture, de la Sculpture, de la Peinture, et des autres Arts qui en dépendent* ... (3 vols.; Paris, 1676–90); and *Entretiens sur les Vies et sur les Ouvrages des plus excellents Peintres, Anciens et Modernes* ... (5 vols.; Paris, 1666–88).

40. Jean Baptiste du Bos, *Réflexions critiques sur la Poésie et sur la Peinture* (Paris, 1719).

41. *Three Treatises. The first concerning art. The second concerning music, painting, and poetry. The third concerning happiness* (1744).

42. W. G. Howard has presented a study of "that long-lived esthetic theory founded upon the proposition *Ut pictura poesis*" in an article in *PMLA*, XXIV (1909), 40–123. Some of the writers cited by Howard may well have influenced the development of Spence's theories.

43. *Polymetis*, Preface, p. iv.

44. In this respect *Polymetis* may be considered a belated blast of the trumpet in the quarrel of the ancients and moderns, with Spence siding definitely with the ancients.

45. Addison's speakers are also three in number, the leader being named Philander.

46. Spence criticizes Bartoli for inserting in his *Admiranda* the copy of an inferior relievo, when there existed a far better relievo on the same

subject, simply because the baser of the two was more easy of access to the engraver. He adds that he had his own designer erect a special scaffold so that he might procure a copy of the better work (*Polymetis*, p. 80).

47. There is a brief account of Boitard in *Bryan's Dictionary of Painters and Engravers*, where his engravings for *Polymetis* are mentioned as one of his principal works.

48. Gray, however, thought the illustrations "better done than one could expect," and said that their neatness was partly responsible for his liking the finished work better than he had liked it in manuscript (*Correspondence of Thomas Gray*, ed. Toynbee and Whibley, I, 268.)

49. Dialogue X, pp. 155–62.

50. See p. 88.

51. *Polymetis*, p. 290.

52. For example: "A very learned comment, is like a very learned man; it is rather troublesome, than useful to you. When you consult them, their answers are for the most part as dark, and as equivocal, as those of oracles. There never can be but one meaning wanting; and they are so over-good as to furnish you with half a dozen. Or else they play at cross-purposes with you. As for example; I should be glad, to learn, what colour the Romans meant by the word Glaucus? Glaucus, answers the commentator, signifies blue; brown; green; red; and iron-grey.—How far was Alba from Rome? O, says the commentator, Alba is the place where Æneas met with the white sow and her thirty pigs; and there was a very fine flitch of bacon, of this very sow, kept in the chief temple there; even to Augustus's time: as I find it recorded in that excellent historian, Dionysius Halicarnassæus.—If you ask what Niobe is doing, in such a part of Ovid's description of her, they will tell you who was her father: or if you enquire for the situation of one of the Grecian cities, they will bestow half an hour in proving, that it was first inhabited by a colony from Assyria; and perhaps add all the adventures and distresses that the poor people met with, both by sea and land, in coming to it" (*Polymetis*, p. 286).

53. Cesare Ripa, *Iconologia, overo Descrittione di diverse imagini cavate dall' antichita, & di propria inventione* (Rome, 1603).

54. Otto van Veen [always called "Vaenius" by Spence], *Q. Horatii Flacci Emblemata* (Antwerp, 1607).

55. Spence says that he reread the *Faerie Queene* for the purposes of his argument (*Polymetis*, p. 301).

56. In an article in *Blackwood's Magazine*, XXXVI (1834), 415 ff., "Mr Polymetis Spence" is attacked for his criticism of Spenser.

57. *Polymetis*, p. 321.

58. Bolton Corney in *Notes and Queries*, 1st ser., I (1849–50), 363.

59. Both editions were published by Dodsley—that in 1755 by Robert and that in 1774 by James. Spence assigned his "right in the Copy and Plates" to Robert Dodsley on February 1, 1755, "in con-

sideration of a Note" for £200, but a later receipt (March 26, 1756) seems to indicate that the amount finally paid was only £150. Both papers were formerly in the Grosvenor Library collected by the late R. B. Adam and are now owned by Mr. and Mrs. Donald F. Hyde, of Somerville, New Jersey, who kindly provided me with copies.

60. Singer, p. xxxvii.

61. *A Guide to Classical Learning; or Polymetis Abridged . . . Being a Work, necessary, not only for Classical Instruction, But for all those who wish to have a True Taste For the Beauties of Poetry, Sculpture and Painting.*

62. *Von der Übereinstimmung der Werke der Dichter mit den Werken der Künstler, nach dem Englischen des Herrn Spence, von J. Burkard* (*Zweiter Theil, von F. F. Hofstäter*) (2 vols.; Wien, 1773–76).

63. XII (1807), 57–69.

64. By a graduate of Cambridge [P. W. Buckham] (Cambridge, 1825).

65. *The Rise, Progress and Decline of Poetry and the Fine Arts in Ancient Rome. Being the first five dialogues of Mr. Spence's Polymetis* (Winchester: J. Robbins, 1823).

66. *Elegant Extracts, or Useful and Entertaining Passages, from the Best English Authors and Translations* (1783).

67. II, 359 ff., 403 ff., 429 ff. It should, of course, be remembered that Dodsley was the publisher!

68. II, 437.

69. His acquaintance with Spence did not begin until later.

70. Shenstone's *Letters*, ed. Mallam (Minneapolis, 1939), p. 93, letter to Jago, February 14, 1747–48.

71. *Correspondence of Thomas Gray*, ed. Toynbee and Whibley, I, 268–70.

72. See p. 87.

73. *Correspondence of Thomas Gray*, I, 268.

74. *Ibid.*, p. 269.

75. A contributor to the *Gentleman's Magazine* (XLV, 523) for 1775, commenting upon Mason's edition of Gray's poems and letters, wrote: "The conceited animadversions on Mr. *Spence's* 'Polymetis,' a work of established merit, reflect no honor on the judgement or candor either of Mr. *Gray* or Mr. *Mason*. Happily for Dr. *Hurd*, he had his education at *Cambridge;* so that his 'Dialogues' are commended, while Mr. *Spence* is ridiculed. . . ."

76. *Literary Anecdotes*, I, 643 n.

77. *De sacra poesi Hebraeorum praelectiones Academicae Oxonii habitae*, etc., ed. J. D. Michaelis (Göttingen, 1758), p. 232. Quoted in *Literary Anecdotes*, II, 377 n.

78. Original letter in the Huntington Library (see Singer, p. 434). The work in question was an account of the antiquities at Herculaneum.

79. See Warton's *The Works of Virgil, in Latin and English* (1753) I, xvii ff.

80. See p. 30.

81. *The Miscellaneous Works of Edward Gibbon, Esq.* (1814), IV, 6.

82. *A Guide to Classical Learning* (1764), Introduction.

83. Lionel Cust, *History of the Society of Dilettanti* (1898), p. 119.

84. *Lessings Laokoon*, ed. Hugo Blümner (2d ed.; Berlin, 1880), Book VII, p. 201.

85. *Ibid.*, VII, 201–2.

86. *Ibid.*, p. 202.

87. Tibullus *Elegies* iii. 4; *Polymetis*, p. 84; *Laokoon*, Book VII, p. 209.

88. Statius *Sylvae* iii. 1. 131–33; *Polymetis*, p. 81; *Laokoon*, Book VII, p. 209.

89. *Aeneid* viii. 725; *Polymetis*, p. 230; *Laokoon*, Book VII, p. 210.

90. *Laokoon*, Book X, p. 224.

91. *Ibid.*, VIII, 211.

92. *The New Laokoon* (Boston and New York, 1910), pp. 32–33.

93. *Laokoon*, Book X, p. 224.

94. See p. 108.

95. See W. G. Howard, *Laokoon: Lessing, Herder, Goethe* (New York, 1910), Introduction, p. lxxxv.

96. *Polymetis*, pp. 67–68.

97. *Ibid.*, p. 311.

98. *Laokoon*, Book VII, p. 201.

99. From a letter by the Rev. E. Clarke in Nichols' *Literary Anecdotes*, II, 374–75 n.

100. Charles and Mary Cowden Clarke, *Recollections of Writers* (New York, 1878), p. 124.

101. Roberta D. Cornelius, "Diana's Scarf," *Modern Language Quarterly*, V (1944), 449. See n. 3 on the same page for a succinct bibliography of the subject.

102. William Goodhugh, *The English Gentleman's Library Manual*, pp. 155–56.

103. Knox wrote: "Mr. Spence was a truly classical writer. That he chiefly wrote in dialogue is to be lamented; for that form, where the persons are fictitious, has seldom been approved in England, though it has often succeeded in France. His Polymetis would have been much more read than it has been, if it had not been written in dialogue" (*Works of Vicesimus Knox* [1824], II, 250–51).

104. Ludwig von Urlichs.

105. Ivan von Müller, *Handbuch der klassischen Altertums-Wissenschaft* (2d ed.; Munich 1892), I, 91.

106. See pp. 108–9.

107. "Reiz ist Schönheit in Bewegung," *PMLA*, XXIV (1909), 286 ff.

108. George Saintsbury, *A History of Criticism and Literary Taste in Europe* (1902), II, 454 n.

109. Thomas Seccombe, *The Age of Johnson* (1926), p. 34.

CHAPTER VI

AT BYFLEET

1. Time never hung heavy on his hands. For example, he wrote to Massingberd from Stratton Street on December 15, 1747: "Indeed, this Autumn has been so fine, that I have been much out of town in it; engaged in several country Visits; in visiting my parishioners; & in preaching Visitation Sermons."

2. Spence Papers.

3. Original in Huntington Library extra-illustrated copy of Singer (see Singer, p. 426).

4. Once in his journal for 1756 and again in a letter to a Mr. Wheeler, dated at Byfleet, September 9, 1751, in which he says that he is no, "quite three Years Old in this place" (Spence Papers).

5. On the basis of references by Spence, Leonard R. Stevens, Esq., eminent Byfleet antiquary, believes that the house stood on the site of the present "Clock House" in Byfleet.

6. In a letter of September 9, 1751, described later, p. 119.

7. But later (January 16, 1754) Spence wrote to Massingberd: "I have taken another little bargain, of 12 or 13 Acres, near the bridge."

8. He wrote to Massingberd on November 2, 1749: "I have near twenty men this day at work, & shall have every day this fortnight."

9. Mrs. C. H. Beale, *Catherine Hutton and Her Friends* (Birmingham, 1895), p. 25. Though the letter from which the quotation is taken is undated, the visit which it describes occurred almost certainly in 1766.

10. A list preserved among the Spence Papers calls for memorials of some kind for more than thirty relatives and friends, many of them identified only by initials. Among those honored are Dodsley, Lowth, Pitt, Pope, Richardson, Ridley, Rolle, and Thomson.

11. Rolle's phrase.

12. Beale, *op. cit.*, p. 39.

13. *Ibid.*, p. 25.

14. See earlier references to this letter, nn. 4 and 6 above. There are several drafts of it among Spence's papers, and the final copy is in a neat hand not Spence's. The document was probably intended for publication.

Wheeler was probably the "Rev. Mr. Robert Wheeler, Canon of Wells," who was one of the subscribers to Blacklock's *Poems* in 1756. He was also no doubt the "Mr. Wheeler" who wrote the letter of February 25, 1748, to Spence, printed by Singer on pp. 423–26.

15. *Moral Essays*, IV, 55–56.

16. From such remarks and from such passages in the *Anecdotes* as that in Singer, p. 260, where Pope himself calls Spence's attention to the couplet just quoted, it is clear that Spence's taste in gardening was largely formed at Twickenham. Another person who influenced his ideas was his neighbor Philip Southcote. Writing to Massingberd on March 16, 1750, he said: "I was yesterday at Mr Southcote's, & walkd all round his Paradise with him; & had so much pleasure in seeing it, & hearing his explanations & reasonings in every step he had taken, that it actually turn'd two hours into one to me; the time stole with so much pleasure, & imperceptibleness, away. He had favour'd me with a Visit, about ten days before: & was so kind, as to tell me some of my faults; & so polite, as to Compliment the rest of my Flat-works, in Miniature." In another letter, undated but apparently written about the same time, he said of Southcote's garden: "I am absolutely in love with [it]; &, like a Mistress, every visit I pay it, am more & more charm'd with it. He was here with two of his brothers last week; & I there again, last Munday. Where the old place of Paradise was I know not; but where the present is, I know full well."

17. Spence's relations with many of these men are discussed later. The names of most of them occur repeatedly in his journals for 1755–58.

18. John Wooll, *Biographical Memoirs of Dr. Joseph Warton* (1806), pp. 226–27. The letter is dated November 2.

19. Five such letters are in Additional MS 32736. The first (fol. 83) is dated July 24; the last (fol. 312), August 19.

20. *Account of Blacklock* (1754), p. 4.

21. See p. 123.

22. This was probably Edward Moore, whose first comedy, *The Foundling*, was produced at Drury Lane on February 13, 1748. For Moore see pp. 138–39.

23. The letter is reproduced in the Sotheby sale catalogue of March 8, 1939 (p. 97), and in No. 79 (1939) of *The Ingatherer*, a catalogue of manuscripts offered for sale by Colbeck Radford & Co., Ltd., of London (p. 10).

24. Journals for 1756–58, Spence Papers.

25. These letters, dated March 31 and May 3, 1758, and July 24, 1759, are among the Spence Papers. Young Lawman, it appears, was something of a scapegrace, who was later to forfeit Spence's favor entirely by continued misbehavior (see p. 247, n. 131). In his letter to Richardson of July 24, 1759, Spence transcribes the following passage from a letter received from Lawman: "I had the happiness last Thursday to be a long while with that best of Men, dear Mr Richardson; who sure is dearer to me, than a Father! For his study, is, my Welfare. Had you but seen what Goodness over-spread his face, when he told me what pleasure it gave him to find I had continu'd so long, & behav'd so well at M^r

Whitworth's; sure your heart wou'd have overflow'd with Joy, & the Tears stood in your eyes, as mine did." One seems to detect here the accents of Joseph Surface, but the passage moved Spence to the following outburst: "I wou'd rather copy such an honest, feeling, passage as this; than any of the most flowing eloquence of Cicero, or the most forcible Stroke of Demosthenes."

26. Two volumes of *Clarissa* had appeared in the preceding November. Two more followed in April, 1748, and the remaining three in December of the same year.

27. The entire letter is printed in Mrs. A. L. Barbauld, *The Correspondence of Samuel Richardson* (1804), II, 319–27. Rough drafts of this letter, which was obviously composed with great care, are in the Spence Papers.

28. The remainder of the letter is occupied with the account of a dream which visited Spence when he dozed off after reading from *Clarissa*—a dream involving two "allegorical ladies" who turn out to be Nature and Art. Spence concludes with an invitation to Richardson to share a vegetable dinner with him the following Saturday.

29. Original in Huntington Library extra-illustrated copy of Singer (see Singer, p. 455). There is no evidence that Spence ever met Henry Fielding, but the following passage on *Tom Jones* in a letter of April 15, 1749, to Massingberd is of interest: "Tom Jones is my old acquaintance, now; for I read it, before it was publisht: & read it with such rapidity, that I began & ended within the compass of four days; tho' I took a Journey to St Albans, in ye same time. He is to me extreamly entertaining; & will be so, I believe, to you. A set of 2500 Copies was sold, before it was publisht; which is perhaps an unheard-of case. That I may not seem to write Riddles, you must know that the way here generally is, to send in their number of Books to each of the Booksellers they deal with, four or five days before the Publication; that they may oblige people, who are eager for a new thing. In y^s case, the 10th of Febr^y was fixt for ye Publication; & by the 10th, all the books were disposd of. The author sold ye Copy for 100^L each Volume; & might probably have got 5 times as much by it, had he kept the right in his own hands: but authors at first dont know, whether their works are good or bad; much less, whether they will sell or not."

30. See p. 121.

31. Spence's notes on the conversation are in the Spence Papers. They were printed, with minor alterations, by Singer, pp. 348–49.

32. The remarks of Miss Blount in Singer, pp. 212–13 (dated 1737–39) and p. 260 (dated 1742–43), were really made in 1749 (Spence Papers).

33. From the records of the conversation in the Spence Papers. Singer printed Spence's notes on pp. 356–60.

34. The second half of this manuscript is now HM 1271 in the Huntington Library (see p. 250, n. 28).

35. Published in May, 1749, prior to the seventeenth, when Walpole discussed it in a letter to Mann (Walpole's *Letters*, ed. Toynbee, II, 378–81.)

36. In the second number, advertised several times in the *General Evening Post* beginning with the issue for May 18–20.

37. Advertised in the *General Evening Post* for May 25–27.

38. Walpole's *Letters*, ed. Toynbee, II, 380.

39. In the later (expanded) version from which Singer printed, the remark which I attribute to Spence is assigned to Miss Blount (Singer, p. 212); but in the Huntington Library manuscript from which Spence read to Miss Blount, it is placed within parentheses (Spence's usual procedure with remarks of his own) and Miss Blount seems simply to have confirmed it with "Ay, those were the ways" (HM 1271, fol. 17v).

40. Compare Pope's cryptic remark to Spence concerning Bolingbroke's ability: "The proofs are ready, and the world *will* see them" (Singer, p. 301).

41. Singer, p. 358. Spence's notes on this conversation are in the Spence Papers.

42. For a fuller discussion of the evidence see my article in *Modern Philology*, XXXVI (1938–39), 139–44.

43. Spence, writing to Massingberd on January 31, was expecting *Crito* "every day," and Ralph Straus, in *Robert Dodsley* (1910), p. 343, says that the date of publication was February 23. Yet the Duchess of Somerset is found writing to Lady Luxborough as early as December 31, 1751: "There are some Particulars in Archbishop Tillotson's Life, that may amuse you, and a Dialogue upon Beauty, by Sir Harry Beaumont; these are the only new Things I have seen" (Hull, *Select Letters* [1778], I, 169).

44. Of *Crito*, Spence wrote to Massingberd on January 31, 1752: "It will come out under the borrowd name of Sr Harry Beaumont. You must know there are several of us, (no less than 7,) that have little things to publish; & dont care to publish any more under our own names: we have therefore pitcht upon that name in common between us; & call ourselves the Beaumont-Club. So that if you see anything for the future come out under that name, you will know from what quarter at least it comes." As things turned out, Spence was apparently the only one to make use of the pseudonym.

45. Straus, *op. cit.*, p. 345.

46. A second edition of *Fugitive Pieces* was published in 1765, a third in 1771.

47. W. G. Howard, "Reiz ist Schönheit in Bewegung," *PMLA*, XXIV (1909), 288.

48. P. 6.

49. Pp. 6–7.

50. The germ of this classification—and perhaps of the entire dia-

logue—is to be found in Spence's notes on his conversation with Lady Mary Wortley Montagu at Rome in 1741. The lady observed: "Ld Bacon makes Beauty to consist in Grace & Motion," and Spence in his notes added: "Mr Locke, in Figure & Colour. The two Definitions together w^d perhaps make one much better than either of them" (Spence Papers; see Singer, pp. 231–32).

51. P. 9.

52. P. 8.

53. For the material in this and the following paragraph I am largely under obligation to W. G. Howard's article "Reiz ist Schönheit in Bewegung," pp. 286 ff.

54. Henry Home, Lord Kames, published his *Elements of Criticism* in 1762.

55. *Laokoon*, ed. Blümner (2d. ed.; Berlin, 1880), Book XXI, p. 293.

56. For example, F. T. Vischer (*Aesthetik* [Reutlingen and Leipzig, 1846], I, 184) asserts: "Lessing hatte zuerst die Anmuth ... als Schönheit in Bewegung definirt."

57. G. E. Guhrauer, *Gotthold Ephraim Lessing, sein Leben und seine Werke* (2d ed.; Leipzig, [1856]), II, 47.

58. Kames says: "[Grace] is undoubtedly connected with motion; for when the most graceful person is at rest, neither moving nor speaking, we lose sight of that quality as much as of colour in the dark. Grace then is an agreeable attribute, inseparable from motion as opposed to rest, and as comprehending speech, looks, gestures, and loco-motion" (*Elements of Criticism* [3d ed.; Edinburgh, 1765], I, 347).

59. *Laokoon*, pp. 640–41.

60. Daniel Webb published his *Inquiry into the Beauties of Painting* in 1760 and dedicated it to Spence.

61. C. L. von Hagedorn, *Betrachtungen über die Mahlerey* (Leipzig, 1762).

62. *Die Bedeutung Homes für die Ästhetik und sein Einfluss auf die deutschen Ästhetiker* (Halle, 1894), p. 121. Neumann quotes and paraphrases brief passages from *Crito*. It is obvious that he made an error of ten years in the date of the work, and he was apparently ignorant that Spence was the author.

63. Franz Pomezny, supported by W. G. Howard (*op. cit.*), says that the history of the conception in English aesthetics must go back to Shaftesbury (*Grazie und Grazien in der deutschen Litteratur des 18. Jahrhunderts* [Hamburg and Leipzig, 1900], pp. 42 ff.). Shaftesbury, however, merely touches upon the subject, and Spence cannot have been indebted to him for more than a suggestion. Pomezny traces the conception back as far as Lomazzo's *Trattato dell'arte della pittura, scultura ed architettura* (Milan, 1585).

64. Pp. 35–36.

65. Lessing, *Laokoon*, ed Blümner, Book XXI, p. 293.

66. See p. 109.

67. P. 36.

68. P. 38.

69. Spence refers the reader to De Piles's *Lives of the Painters*, but it is in *Cours de Peinture par Principes* that the "Dissertation sur la balance des peintres" appears. In this borrowing from De Piles, Spence was influenced by "The Ballance of Poets" which, also modeled on De Piles, had appeared in the *Museum* in 1746 (II, 165–69).

70. P. 44.

71. Pp. 57–58 and 59–60.

72. Letter to Massingberd, October 19, 1751.

73. Letter to Massingberd, January 31, 1752.

74. In a note he quotes Bacon's "In Beauty, that of Favour is more than that of Colour; and that of gracious and decent Motion, more than that of Favour" (*Crito*, p. 35).

75. Pp. 15 ff.

76. See p. 233, n. 43.

77. *Letters Written by the late Right Honourable Lady Luxborough, to William Shenstone, Esq.* (1775), p. 338.

78. XXI, 141.

79. *Académie des Grâces par Mr L. Le M ...* (Paris, 1755).

80. *Criton, ou de la grâce et de la beauté. Extrait d'un dialogue traduit librement de l'anglois* (in *Les Grâces*, ed. A. G. Meusnier *a* [Paris, 1769]).

81. There is an interesting reference to Kames and his *Elements of Criticism* in a letter from Alexander Dick to Spence, June 15, [1762]: ". . . have you lookd into the *criticism by Lord Kaims:* his Lordship wrote a great part of it in your chapel, when he was my guest, so that you are so far concernd; and he and I would be glad of your opinion of these three volumes. If you have not read them you shall read them here: and you shall see my Lord either in your going or coming from Durham . . ." (original in Huntington Library extra-illustrated copy of Singer; see Singer, pp. 464–65).

82. For example, Spence had written that Virgil "makes the Motion of *Venus* the principal thing, by which *Aeneas* discovers her under all her Disguise" (*Crito*, pp. 35–36); Webb says: "Venus was but guessed at by her beauty; she was known by her motions" (*Inquiry into the Beauties of Painting* [2d ed., 1761], p. 56).

83. *Inquiry into the Beauties of Painting*, p. 107.

84. *The Life and Opinions of Tristram Shandy, Gentleman*, Book I, chap. ix.

85. For my references to this pamphlet I am indebted to W. L. Cross, *The Life and Times of Laurence Sterne* (3d ed.; New Haven, 1929), p. 229.

86. *Crito* was reprinted in 1885 by Edmund Goldsmid ("Bibliotheca Curiosa" [Edinburgh]).

87. Straus, *op. cit.*, p. 345. A criticism appeared in the *Monthly Review* for December (VII [1752], 421–26). Spence's translation was reprinted in Dodsley's *Fugitive Pieces* (1761, 1765, 1771).

88. See Georges Gazier, *Un Artiste Comtois à la cour de Chine au xviiie siècle* (Besançon, 1912).

89. One authority goes so far as to refer to Spence's translation of Attiret's letter as a spark which "kindled a flame of enthusiasm throughout Europe" (A. F. Sieveking, *Gardens Ancient and Modern* [1899], p. 390).

90. "Essay on Modern Gardening," in *The Works of Horace Walpole, Earl of Orford* (1798), II, 533. Walpole's essay was originally printed at Strawberry Hill in 1785.

91. *Fugitive Pieces* (1761), I, 69. A contemporary drawing of the Yuen-ming-yuen is reproduced in Sieveking, *op. cit.*, p. 391.

92. Marie Luise Gothein, *A History of Garden Art*, ed. W. P. Wright, trans. Mrs. Archer-Hind [1928], II, 283.

93. Whately's *Observations on Modern Gardening* were published in 1770.

94. See p. 117. Miss Cartwright was writing in 1766.

95. Add. MS 35339, fol. 2.

96. Arthur Murphy, *The Life of David Garrick, Esq.* (1801), I, 231–32.

97. Charles Dibdin, *A Complete History of the English Stage* [1800], V, 180. See also *The Dramatic Souvenir* (1883), p. 120. Spence was a warm admirer of *The Gamester*. Writing to Massingberd some months later (June 28, 1753), he said: "The Gamester was so moving in the very beginning of it, that when I first began to read it in Manuscript, I was very much afraid for the Author; I thought, he had drawn such a Bill upon himself, as was impossible to be paid by him: or in plain English, that the Compassion was toucht so strongly in the first Act, that it c^d not be affected more & more strongly, in each Act on to the End. However, as I read on, I found the Distress allways encreasing; & that my fears for the Author had been groundless. Garrick was so mov'd in the Rehearsal, that he was forced to make several interruptions, for his Tears; & some times said, 'he was so much affected with it, that he shou'd never be able to get thorough the acting of it; if it was very succesful.' "

98. Straus, *op. cit.*, p. 144. Spence wrote Massingberd on January 17, 1758: "I had the pleasure of seeing the Langton Family at their own house; & afterwards of dining with Bennet, Garrick, & a Mob of Poets, at Dodsly's."

99. See pp. 153–54.

100. In his *Journal of a Tour to the Hebrides* Boswell reported: "At Captain McLean's, I mentioned Pope's friend, Spence. JOHNSON. 'He was a weak conceited man.' BOSWELL. "A good scholar, Sir?' JOHNSON. 'Why, no, Sir.' BOSWELL. 'He was a pretty scholar.' JOHNSON.

'You have about reached him.' " At "weak conceited man" Boswell added a note: "Mr. Langton thinks this must have been the hasty expression of a splenetic moment, as he has heard Dr. Johnson speak of Mr. Spence's judgment in criticism with so high a degree of respect as to shew that this was not his settled opinion of him. Let me add that, in the preface to the *Preceptor*, he recommends Spence's *Essay on Pope's Odyssey*, and that his admirable Lives of the English Poets are much enriched by Spence's Anecdotes of Pope" (Boswell's *Journal*, ed. Pottle and Bennett [New York, 1936], p. 308).

101. *Lives of the English Poets*, ed. Hill (Oxford, 1905), III, 78.

102. James Boswell, Jr., wrote: "Mr. Langton informed me that he once related to Johnson (on the authority of Spence), that Pope himself admired those lines [the conclusion of the *Dunciad*] so much that when he repeated them his voice faltered: 'and well it might, Sir,' said Johnson, 'for they are noble lines' " (Boswell's *Life of Johnson*, ed. Hill [New York, 1891], II, 96 n.).

103. "On being asked if Mr. Spence had not paid him a visit? 'Yes,' says he [Johnson], and he probably may think he visited a bear' " (*Johnsonian Miscellanies*, ed. Hill [Oxford, 1897], II, 3).

104. See p. 180.

105. It was advertised on April 5 (Straus, *op. cit.*, p. 348).

106. See p. 133.

107. Notes in the Spence Papers show that the story of Florio and the letter to Sir Charles Easy were originally designed by Spence "for the use of a young nobleman whom I equally love & respect." The nobleman referred to was probably Lord Lincoln. There is also evidence to indicate that the letter to Sir Charles Easy was to have been the first of a series which was never completed.

108. Among the Spence Papers are notes for what was apparently to be called "Byfleet Letters," also to be exchanged between a mother and her daughter. "Robin" was to be "yᵉ Kattle-lover; Ralph, yᵉ sly one; & Thˢ, yᵉ Honest." At the sale of Singer's papers in 1858, one lot was catalogued thus: "Letters from a Maid-Servant lately come to Town to her Relations in Hamshire. This appears to have been a Jeu d'Esprit intended for publication by Mr. Spence."

109. III, 357–73.

110. P. 91.

111. P. 92.

112. I, 379–86.

113. Among the Spence Papers is the draft of Spence's version, which he apparently wrote in two days in June, 1748.

114. P. 167.

115. See pp. 148–49 and 195–96.

116. See p. 167.

117. Some of the papers, however, had been written earlier. Spence

refers to the history of Florio in a letter dated August 25, 1740 (Singer, p. 403), and in the Spence Papers is the draft of "Pericles" (*Moralities*, pp. 1-10) dated February 26, 1741.

118. Spence Papers.

119. Singer, pp. 446-47. Hooke sent the lines to Spence in a letter dated October 27, 1753.

120. Among the Spence Papers are a fair copy and a rough draft of an unfinished "Life of Mr. Charles Magot," which Spence apparently toyed with over a period of many years and perhaps intended to publish. British Museum Additional MS 25898 contains rough notes and plans for the same work. The project is obviously an imitation of the Scriblerus papers, and many of the objects of satire are the same in both cases. The fair copy comprises the first seven chapters of Book I. This portion of the story covers the early history of the Magot family, the studies and experiences of Dr. Thomas Magot (father of the prospective hero, Charles), and the birth of Charles himself and the death of Mrs. Magot. Throughout these apparently completed chapters Dr. Magot is ridiculed continually, and good-natured scorn is heaped upon faulty education, bad taste, and false learning, with passing shots at such diverse targets as the practice of vivisection and the Stuart doctrine of the divine right of kings.

121. *The Works of Virgil, in Latin and English. The original Text correctly printed from the most authentic Editions, collated for this Purpose. The Æneid Translated By the Rev. Mr. Christopher Pitt, The Eclogues and Georgics, with Notes on the Whole, By the Rev. Mr. Joseph Warton. With several New Observations By Mr. Holdsworth, Mr. Spence, and Others....* The work was published by Dodsley in four volumes. Straus (*op. cit.*, p. 346) gives the date of publication as January 25, 1753.

122. *Letters from a Late Eminent Prelate to One of His Friends*, (Kidderminster [1808]), p. 82 (see earlier, p. 73).

123. I, xxviii-xxix. A great many remarks on Virgil by Holdsworth were incorporated by Spence into the manuscript *Anecdotes*, and Warton may have copied what he considered useful from Spence's manuscript.

124. I, xvii-xviii.

125. *The Works of Alexander Pope, Esq.* (1797), I, xxxvi. If Warton is correct about the date of this visit, he could not have obtained on this occasion Spence's Holdsworth material for the 1753 edition of Virgil. Warton's gracious acknowledgment is in direct contrast to Warburton's silence concerning much greater obligations (see earlier, pp. 73-75).

126. *Biographical Memoirs of Dr. Joseph Warton* (1806), p. 30.

127. On at least two occasions Spence sought information from Warton upon points involving examination of the College registers (see Warton's letter of January 15, 1764, and Spence's letter of January 19,

1765, printed in Singer, pp. 471–74; originals in Huntington Library).

128. *Remarks and Dissertations on Virgil* . . . (1768), p. v. See pp. 172–73.

129. On December 7, 1753, Spence addressed from Byfleet to Dr. Richard Mead a letter which was read before the Royal Society on January 10, 1754, and was printed in part in the *Philosophical Transactions* for that year (XLVIII, Part II, 486). It begins: "I have lately received a letter from Signor Paderni at Portici; in which, speaking of the publication of the antiquities found at Herculaneum, he says, *Spero che il primo tomo non tarderà molto tempo ad uscire;* and then mentions some particular things, that had been lately discovered among the ruins." Spence then gives a brief account of the discoveries.

CHAPTER VII
DURHAM AND THE CLOSING YEARS

1. [Thomas Tyers], *An Historical Rhapsody on Mr. Pope* (2d ed., 1782), p. 58.

2. Left vacant by the death of Thomas Eden on March 3 (William Hutchinson, *The History and Antiquities of the County Palatine, of Durham* [Newcastle, 1785–94], II, 199).

3. A certificate to this effect is among the Spence Papers.

4. Hutchinson, *op. cit.*, II, 200.

5. Nichols, *A Select Collection of Poems* (1782), VIII, 5 n.; Hutchinson, *op. cit.*, II, 324.

6. Hull, *Select Letters* (1778), I, 242.

7. Hutchinson, *op. cit.*, II, 324.

8. (2d ed., 1764), II, 328.

9. Spence Papers.

10. Journal for 1755, p. 30.

11. Journal for 1756, p. 7.

12. Journal for 1758, p. 3.

13. *Ibid.*, p. 4.

14. Journal for 1755, p. 5 (printed by Singer, p. 362). In the draft of a letter to Lord Lincoln, written April 28, 1751, Spence urged his former pupil to "dispose of the Overflow of your income each year, In doing Good, to honest & deserving persons, round about you," adding that such a course would "contribute more than anything, toward making you Happy" (Spence Papers). Thomas Hooke's verse tribute to Spence (see p. 144) suggests that Spence made it a practice to urge "the Great" to "win true Glory by Munificence."

15. A. S. Collins says: "A man like Joseph Spence, the friend of a wide aristocratic and literary circle, with a genuine love of literature and active desire to bring forward deserving but neglected writers, could do much in those days by canvassing in their behalf among his

acquaintance. They are little figures, viewed against a Halifax or a Bedford, but not the less patrons in their small way, because they exercised their influence, not their money, to help writers who had no claim on them but merit" (*Authorship in the Days of Johnson* [1927], p. 188).

16. It was published on November 13 (Ralph Straus, *Robert Dodsley* [1910], p. 352). An article on Blacklock based largely on Spence's account appeared in the *Gentleman's Magazine* for November, 1754 (XXIV, 499 ff.), and a criticism appeared in the *Monthly Review*, Appendix for 1754 (XI, 481–86). Spence told Massingberd (letter of September 4, 1754) that he wrote the account during his summer visit of that year to Cheltenham with Lord Lincoln (see p. 120).

17. As Rolle states, this and other works of the sort by Spence were "intended meerly to raise little Sums" for the beneficiaries, and "to place in a more comfortable State, the Persons he hoped to benefit by them."

18. John Hill Burton, *Life and Correspondence of David Hume* (Edinburgh, 1846), I, 398.

19. Original letter in Huntington Library extra-illustrated copy of Singer (see Singer, pp. 448–53). This letter, dated October 15, 1754, clearly arrived too late to be of service to Spence in the preparation of his *Account of Blacklock*. It was sent to Dodsley with the request that it be forwarded to Spence (see E. C. Mossner, *The Forgotten Hume* [New York, 1943], p. 24).

20. So Professor Mossner considers it (*op. cit.*, p. 236).

21. See *Account of Blacklock*, p. 4, n. 2. The letter was dated March 12, 1754, and probably accompanied the copies of Blacklock's poems which Hume had sent to Dodsley (see p. 150).

22. Burton, *op. cit.*, I, 435–36.

23. The lines quoted by Hume appear thus in the subscription volume:

> "The wise in ev'ry age conclude
> Thy fairest prospects, rightly view'd,
> The Paradise of Fools" (p. 64).

The line containing the reference to Shaftesbury—

> "Would Ashley's Genius dart a ray"—

is altered to

> "Would Truth's bright source emit one ray" (p. 67).

It was not altogether fair, however, for Hume to charge that in the biographical sketch Spence mentioned "some people to whom he had been obliged" but deliberately avoided reference to Hume, for the fact is that Spence, apparently feeling that the information derived from Blacklock himself was better authority than the sources he had had to rely upon in composing the original sketch, omitted *all* references to source materials other than statements or poems of Blacklock. But

Professor Mossner, who is severe with Spence for his treatment of Hume (*op. cit.*, pp. 22–27), is justified in believing that Spence took from Hume's letter of October 15, 1754, at least one statement used in the revised account.

24. It would seem that relations between Spence and Hume were not permanently strained. Alexander Dick wrote to Spence on March 6, 1762: "I agree with you extremly in thinking Mr. Hume's last performance a Masterpiece: *He passd* two days with me here *lately, & rememberd* you most sincerely with all good wishes" (original in Huntington Library extra-illustrated copy of Singer; see Singer, p. 461). And on another occasion Dick wrote to Spence: "David Hume is well, as is Dr Robinson [*sic*]; and will be both glad to see you when you come" (original in Huntington Library; see Singer, p. 464). It is also to be noted that a coolness developed in later life between Hume and Blacklock (Mossner, *op. cit.*, pp. 32 ff.), whereas Spence remained throughout life a staunch friend of the poet.

25. Boswell's *Life of Johnson*, ed. Hill (New York, 1891), I, 539.

26. *The Works of the Right Honorable Edmund Burke* (Boston, 1894), I, 252–53. Hume, too, would apparently have sided with Spence against Johnson on this point (see Singer, pp. 449–50).

27. *Account of Blacklock*, p. 61.

28. The letter is in the Autograph Collection of Simon Gratz, now in possession of the Historical Society of Pennsylvania, in Philadelphia.

29. See p. 151. Without mentioning Hume's name, Spence also confirms Hume's story (p. 150) that it was he who first brought Blacklock to Dodsley's notice.

30. Apparently 232 large-paper and 264 small-paper copies were taken by subscribers. This total of 496 subscription copies, bringing in nearly £400, seems reasonably high.

31. According to the journal for 1755 (Spence Papers), Blacklock was apparently with Spence at Durham for several weeks in July.

32. It was advertised on February 26 (Straus, *op. cit.*, p. 358).

33. *Ibid.*, p. 359.

34. *Ibid.*, p. 360.

35. Journal for 1758, Spence Papers.

36. Original in Huntington Library extra-illustrated copy of Singer (see Singer, p. 469).

37. *Poems by the late Reverend Dr. Thomas Blacklock* (Edinburgh, 1793), p. 189.

38. Earlier in the year of publication (Edinburgh, 1767) Blacklock had received the honorary degree of Doctor of Divinity from the Marischal College of Aberdeen University.

39. In the Spence Papers is the draft of a letter, dated July 7, to the Earl of Darlington concerning his seat at Raby, a few miles from Durham. Spence begins: "As Y^r L^p was so good as to desire me to take

a view of Raby; I beg leave to write down the thoughts that naturally rose in my mind, in seeing that delicious place." He then goes on to make suggestions concerning possible alterations in the grounds.

40. See p. 5.

41. Straus, *op. cit.*, p. 43.

42. *Literary Anecdotes*, II (1812), 374 n. Dodsley had published Richard Glover's *Leonidas* in April, 1737.

43. See pp. 53–54.

44. Straus, *op. cit.*, p. 64.

45. *Ibid.*, p. 103.

46. Dodsley mentions in it a "*Pope's Works* (which came from Mr. Warburton)." Warburton's edition of Pope appeared in 1751.

47. Singer, pp. 426–29 (originals in Huntington Library).

48. Some of my information concerning this tour comes from Dodsley's letters to Shenstone in Add. MS 28959.

49. After the travelers' departure Shenstone wrote to Richard Graves: "I have seen few whom I liked so much, upon so little acquaintance, as Mr. Spence" (*Letters of William Shenstone*, ed. Duncan Mallam [Minneapolis, 1939], p. 352).

50. Graves tells the story as follows in his *Recollections of Some Particulars In the Life of the late William Shenstone, Esq.* (1788), pp. 85–87: "Another circumstance, which has, with as little reason, been supposed to imply a jealousy of a similar kind, is in relation to Mr. Spence, who, in consequence of Mr. R. Dodsley's having greatly extolled Mr. Shenstone's place, and his amiable character, had commissioned him to inform Mr. Shenstone, that, by his leave, he would spend a week with him that summer at the Leasowes. This having, by some means, come to Lord Lyttelton's knowledge, his Lordship wrote to Mr. Spence (whom he had met at Mr. Pope's), and insisted on his making Hagley his home, if he came into that country. This invitation Mr. Spence accepted of; staid near a fortnight at Hagley, but was not once taken to the Leasowes.

"This Mr. Shenstone mentioned to me with some surprize; yet this also, I believe, was entirely without any other meaning, than that my Lord and Mr. Spence, having so many literary subjects to converse upon, were too happy in each other's company to look abroad for further amusement; and, as Mr. Spence found himself much at his ease at Hagley, and still determined to spend a week at the Leasowes the first opportunity, he might be indifferent, or, perhaps, too indolent, to wish to be carried thither for a few hours. And this, I believe, was the apology afterwards made to Mr. Shenstone by Mr. Spence on this occasion."

The apology, though apparently satisfactory to Shenstone, seems hardly sufficient to us. But Spence's conduct as described by Graves seems so entirely out of character that one is justified in suspecting that there was another side to the story.

51. *Letters of Shenstone*, p. 352, letter of July 22.

52. *Ibid.*, p. 356, letter of November 25.

53. See Hull, *op. cit.*, I, 240. This is probably the document entitled "The Round of Mr. Shenstone's Paradise," tipped into the extra-illustrated copy of Singer's edition of the *Anecdotes* in the Huntington Library.

54. *Letters of Shenstone*, p. 356, letter to Graves, November 25, 1758. Shenstone also copied the inscription into a letter to Percy (received December 1, 1758), where the first word is "peramabili" instead of "eximio" (*ibid.*, p. 360).

55. During the visit they saw something of Shenstone's friend and neighbor John Baskerville, the Birmingham printer (see Hull, *op. cit.*, I, 242). Dodsley had known Baskerville for some years, but this may have been the first occasion on which Spence met him.

56. *Letters of Shenstone*, p. 356, letter to Graves, November 25, 1758. Spence's "handsome letter," dated August 19, 1758, is printed in Hull's *Select Letters*, I, 238–43.

57. *Letters of Shenstone*, p. 352, letter of July 22, 1758.

58. Spence wrote him from Durham on August 19: "Secondly, I hope you won't forget your Promise of a Visit to me at B— next May" (Hull, *op. cit.*, I, 242).

59. *Ibid.*, p. 240.

60. Dodsley to Shenstone, August 22, [1758], Add. MS 28959, fol. 101r.

61. When Dodsley's tragedy *Cleone* was produced in the succeeding December, Spence was among its supporters. Warburton wrote to Garrick on January 18, 1759: "I think the applause given to it by Spence, Lowth and Melmoth was very sincere" (Straus, *op. cit.*, p. 240).

62. Hull, *op. cit.*, I, 238.

63. *Letters of Shenstone*, p. 356, letter of November 25, 1758.

64. *Ibid.*, p. 366.

65. Shenstone to Jago, January 6, 1759 (*ibid.*, p. 362).

66. See p. 166 and p. 244, n. 85.

67. Letter of December 1, 1759 (Hull, *op. cit.*, I, 274).

68. Letter of January 4, 1760 (*ibid.*, p. 278).

69. The British Museum copy—the only one I have seen—has no title-page, but the letter itself is dated December 10, 1753.

70. Hill wrote to Spence on April 6, 1757, that he and his family would have starved "if It was not for your goodness and the Rest of my worthy Benefactors" (original letter in Huntington Library extra-illustrated copy of Singer; see Singer, p. 454).

71. "It was but last April that he was with me," Spence wrote in *A Parallel* (p. 78), and in his journal for 1758 (Spence Papers) he mentions Hill under April 12 and 26. Hill made the journey of "near sixty miles" on foot (*A Parallel*, p. 74).

72. Spence Papers. Spence uses almost the same words about the

books in *A Parallel* (p. 78) and adds that Hill "declared that I had now furnished him with reading at his leisure hours from work, for these seven years." One assumes that Hill did not have to carry the books to Buckingham on foot!

73. Hill is mentioned under June 17, 19, and 20 in the journal for 1758 (Spence Papers).

74. Paget Toynbee, *Journal of the Printing-Office at Strawberry Hill* (1923), pp. 7–8, and Walpole's *Letters*, ed. Toynbee, IV, 236. The title-page, however, is dated 1758. On January 6, 1759, Shenstone wrote to Jago: "Spence, I see, has advertised his 'Parallel betwixt Malliabecqui and his Taylor.' It is merely a charitable design: and such are now all Spence's views" (*Letters of Shenstone*, p. 363).

75. Walpole's *Letters*, ed. Toynbee, I, xliii. A review of the work, possibly contributed by Spence himself, appeared in the *London Chronicle* (V, 129–30) for February 6–8, and a summary was published in the *Annual Register* for 1759 (II, 293 ff.).

76. Straus (*op. cit.*, p. 367) gives February 22 as the date of publication.

77. This collection was reprinted in 1765 and 1771. In *Fugitive Pieces* the statement is made on the title-page of *A Parallel* that the work was first printed in 1757!

78. *A Parallel*, pp. 103–4.

79. From a Signor Buonamici, to whom Spence attributes his information in Huntington Library HM 1271, fol. 41r.

80. Walpole's *Letters*, ed. Toynbee, IV, 236.

81. See p. 38.

82. Most of these are printed in Singer, pp. 350–56.

83. Strangely, two famous stories about Young which Spence is responsible for preserving were flatly denied by the poet. See pp. 190–91.

84. Original letter in Huntington Library extra-illustrated copy of Singer (see Singer, p. 455).

85. The irresolute Shenstone had hoped to be in Bath at the same time, but on October 3 he wrote to Graves: "The mischief is, that, with as violent a propensity as ever person felt, I shall not be able to reach your hemisphere while Mr. Spence, Mr. Dodsley, and Mr. Whitehead, give it such peculiar lustre in my eyes. . . . I wish to God he [Dodsley] may have brought you acquainted with Mr. Spence; to whom you are, in my estimation, the most *like* of any one I know" (*Letters of Shenstone*, pp. 373, 375).

86. Straus, *op. cit.*, p. 283.

87. Preface to *Select Fables of Aesop and Other Fabulists . . . A New Edition*, [1761?].

88. *Letters of Shenstone*, p. 411.

89. Dick to Spence, March 6, 1752. Original letter in Huntington Library extra-illustrated copy of Singer (see Singer, p. 459).

90. See p. 241, n. 24.

91. So Dick asserts in a letter to Spence, March 6, 1762 (original in Huntington Library; see Singer, p. 459).

92. Spence Papers.

93. Notes on the journey, dated August 8–16, are in the Spence Papers. One reads: "At East-Stower, 5 Miles beyond Shaftesbury, pasd by the House where Fielding farm'd & kept his Chariot, with his Amelia." Another reports of an Exeter hostelry: "The Oxford Inn, is— the Devil!"

94. So Spence says in a letter to Dr. Thomas Birch, dated February 9, 1762 (Add. MS 4318, fol. 229r). Spence offered to present to the British Museum an alphabetical catalogue of the allegorical figures of the Greeks and Romans which he had begun while writing *Polymetis* and had extended since; also a collection of medals relating to the same subject, in a case. The Museum authorities state that their records contain no mention of such a gift from Spence.

95. Straus, *op. cit.*, pp. 297, 382.

96. *Ibid.*, p. 296. Dodsley called her "cousin."

97. A song written by her (about 1760) appeared in the *Lady's Magazine* (see Mrs. C. H. Beale, *Catherine Hutton and Her Friends* [Birmingham, 1895], p. 6).

98. Letter of December 15, 1763 (*ibid.*, p. 19).

99. The omission was Miss Cartwright's failure to pay Spence a visit when she was in London with the Dodsleys.

100. A. Stapleton, *New Notes about Robert Dodsley and the Dodsley Family* (Mansfield, 1909), p. 64. Stapleton says that in a part of the letter which he does not quote Spence expressed obligations to Miss Cartwright for a visit which she had already made to Byfleet.

101. *Ibid.*, pp. 63–64.

102. The Hon. Judith Noel, later to become mother-in-law of Byron, was then a girl of thirteen, living at Kirkby. She was the daughter of Viscount Wentworth.

103. Beale, *op. cit.*, p. 21. One of the visits had been from Lowth, who wrote to Dodsley from Byfleet on May 5 (Add. MS 35339, fol. 35).

104. This letter is printed by both Beale (pp. 22–23) and Stapleton (p. 65). There are some omissions in each version, and I have tried to reconstruct the entire letter.

105. A photograph of the stone appears in Straus, *op. cit.*, facing p. 302.

106. See pp. 148–49 and 195–96.

107. Alexander Dick, at Spence's request, interested himself in Ridley's proposals to print by subscription. See his letter of June 15, [1762?], in Singer, pp. 462–65 (original in Huntington Library).

108. John Duncombe, *Letters, by Several Eminent Persons Deceased* (2d ed., 1773), III, 141. Spence's letter is dated June, 1764.

109. Alexander Dick speaks of the visit in a letter to Spence dated August 25 (Singer, p. 468; original in Huntington Library).

110. In an undated letter Miss Cartwright tells her fiancé that she has just spent "the pleasantest fortnight, I think, of my life" at Byfleet, and in another undated letter she thanks Spence for his hospitality and writes flatteringly of his "sprightly and instructive converse" and the beauty of his garden (Beale, *op. cit.*, pp. 24–26).

111. *Ibid.*, p. 27.

112. A copy is in the Spence Papers.

113. Beale, *op. cit.*, p. 61.

114. See p. 145.

115. Nichols, *Literary Anecdotes*, I, 643 n. Spence had been at work on the book at least since October, 1763, when he discussed it in a letter to Massingberd.

116. P. 286.

117. One of the dissertations—"On the Fountain of Egeria, and her Grotto"—is in the shape of a "Letter to Mr. Spence."

118. A review and criticism appeared in the *Monthly Review* in two instalments: XXXVIII (June), 417–26, and XXXIX (September), 169–76. The writer concluded thus: "In short, we look upon this work to be an excellent acquisition to the republic of letters; and we are equally obliged to Mr. Spence for the part he has taken in the publication of it, and for what he has performed in the work itself."

119. For example, William Melmoth named him among the editors and commentators on Virgil whom he had consulted in preparing his edition of *The Whole Genuine Works of Virgil* [1790?].

120. From the way in which Dick speaks of Armstrong in letters to Spence, one guesses that Armstrong and Spence were already acquainted (Singer, pp. 464, 468).

121. C. B. Tinker, *Letters of James Boswell* (Oxford, 1924), I, 152, 157.

122. *Ibid.*, I, 157.

123. *Ibid.*, p. 165.

124. Beale, *op. cit.*, p. 28. Spence's offer was declined "on account of Mr. and Mrs. Coltman's different views as Dissenters" (p. 65). The Coltmans were Quakers.

125. A contributor to the *Gentleman's Magazine*, LXXXIX, Part II, 412, in 1819 asserted that Spence died not in his own garden but in that of an old friend, Mrs. Edward Rudge, at Weybridge, near Byfleet. He added the detail that Spence's hat was found "on the bank, and his dog sitting by it." But there is convincing contemporary evidence—including that of Ridley and of Lowth—to prove that the event occurred at Byfleet.

126. So says Lowth (Nichols, *Literary Anecdotes*, I, 643 n.).

127. Rolle sent the following account to Massingberd on October

24,1768: "I was at Byfleet a few days after, & f^m ye account I heard f^m all; as his Health had been better than usual, & himself at least as cheerfull tho rather more feeble than ordinary, on visiting ye Spot where he was found & wch seem'd hardly capable of such an accident, make no doubt but that his feebleness hinder'd him f^m extricating himself when slipping in, or, wch seems most likely, that he was just at the time seiz'd wth one of his Fits; as he was found within half an Hour, & the same methods tried immediately for recovering him, wch he used to mention before his Servants & every one f^m Mr Herbert, who had recover'd many persons after a much longer time; as if he had presag'd that this way of going out of the world was like to be his own."

128. Nichols, *Literary Anecdotes*, I, 643 n.

129. Among the Spence Papers are preserved "Dr Ridley's Memoranda respecting Spence's affairs," a journal covering the period from August 20 to October 11. Also preserved are accounts and letters having to do with the settlement of the estate. From these sources comes most of my information concerning the procedure of the executors.

130. Apparently suicide was not suggested at the inquest, for Ridley, who had been present, had not heard the rumor when he talked to Lincoln on September 18.

131. A passage in a letter from Rolle to Ridley (November 30, 1769) suggests that Spence had once intended to choose as executor and partial heir his cousin Hall Lawman (presumably Mary Lawman's son), in whose welfare he had long been interested and concerning whom he had sought the advice and aid of Richardson (see p. 121). Rolle apparently believed that the "worthy young spark" had lost favor and an inheritance through misbehavior.

132. Lord Lincoln expressed to Ridley the hope that Mrs. Coltman would allow him to purchase a picture of his three sons which Spence had owned. In a letter of February 20, 1769, acknowledging receipt of her inheritance, she promised Ridley to send the picture to Lincoln.

133. This is apparently the wife or widow of Spence's friend Thomas Hooke, son of Nathaniel Hooke.

134. Among the people to benefit by Spence's benevolence in his closing years was a young man named E. Hercules, who is described as a mercantile agent and who wrote a series of letters to Spence from India in 1763–67 (Add. MS 22559. Included were drawings, in India ink, of Persepolis). Apparently he was in some trouble in the summer of 1768, for on July 11 Spence wrote that he was extremely distressed at Hercules' situation and was trying to get him a free merchant's indenture (letter to Granville Sharp, Add. MS 6468). Spence had been paying a pension of £6 a year to his mother, and on September 17, 1768, Lowth wrote to Ridley: "If there sh^d come any Letter to Mr Spence from Mr Hercules, pray send it to me, that I may give it to his Mother, who lives at Durham. And, I think, all his letters to M^r

Spence sh^d be delivered to her. She has a notion, that her Son may have returned money to Mr Spence for her use: pray examine his acc^{t}s as to y^s matter, that I may give her some satisfaction about it" (executors' papers, Spence Papers).

135. Lowth wrote to Ridley on October 24, 1768, that Spence's effects would "not have run so short, if he had lived till Mich: mass; he w^d then have rec^d f^m his Prebend perhaps £230 more; & as much more still, if he had lived till the middle of Nov^r" (executors' papers, Spence Papers).

136. Ridley was permitted to keep a cane, "with a Pebble Head" and bearing the name of Pope, which had been presented to Spence by the poet.

137. The tablet is now on the west wall of the nave. The total cost, including installation, was £33.

CHAPTER VIII

THE "ANECDOTES"

1. Letter to Massingberd, July 29, 1769.
2. A copy of the contract is among the Spence Papers.
3. Unless otherwise noted, quotations in this section are made from the executors' papers in the Spence Papers.
4. The following account which Rolle wrote to Massingberd on July 29, 1769, confirms at several points the story pieced together above: "You make many natural & fond inquiries relative to our dear departed friend, & his writings. I am apt to believe that tho his papers were very voluminous, as you remember he was quite indefatigable, yet that scarce any more of em will see the Light. One of em wch was thought very entertaining & w^d have excited the curiosity of many the most of all, is w^t I dare say you have perused often y^r self, as it used to be left open & for the entertainment of his Friends; This was his collection of conversazioni or hints & stories picked up f^m the most celebrated of his acquaintance: This, his great Friend, thinking possibly it might here & there give some little offence, wish'd might be suppressed, & I believe will be so accordingly; and as our dear Friend wanted not many & those too incontestable memorials of his great Genius as a writer, f^m the Several Publications he himself had made, I conclude that hardly any thing more will be made Publick."

Fairly accurate accounts of the suppression of the *Anecdotes* are given by Thomas Tyers (*An Historical Rhapsody on Mr. Pope* [2d. ed., 1782], pp. 59–60) and Joseph Warton (*Works of Pope* [1797], IV, 180–81 n.). Malone, who derived his information from Warton, also gives a truthful description (Prior, *Life of Malone* [1860], p. 184). Warton and Malone are wrong, however, in stating that Spence's agreement had been concluded with Robert Dodsley, for it had been made with James Dodsley three years after Robert's death.

5. Singer, p. xiii. The manuscript is now among the Spence Papers, but the inscription quoted by Singer is illegible.

6. It is difficult to sympathize with Lincoln and the executors in their decision to suppress the *Anecdotes*. Spence's own desire was clear to them; and, if the materials communicated to Warburton and Warton had "partly forestalled" publication, that same fact removed the only real argument in favor of suppression. Further, an examination of the manuscript must have shown that it contained nothing to give offense.

7. He succeeded his uncle, Thomas Pelham-Holles, on November 17, 1768.

8. The materials which Spence planned to publish consisted of ten sections covering the years 1728–44 and ending with the death of Pope. These materials constitute the *Anecdotes* proper. Singer printed fifty-four pages of "supplemental anecdotes" from Spence's papers.

9. Spence Papers.

10. [Thomas Tyers], *op. cit.*, p. 60.

11. Herbert Croft, who contributed the life of Young, seems to have had access to the manuscript (see Hill's ed. of *Lives of the Poets* [Oxford, 1905], III, 372). Boswell evidently saw Spence's collection, while Johnson wrote to Mrs. Thrale on April 6, 1780: "Seward called on me one day and read Spence" (*Letters*, ed. Hill [Oxford, 1892], II, 133).

12. *Life of Johnson*, ed. Hill (New York, 1891), IV, 74.

13. *The Works of Samuel Johnson, Ll.D.*, ed. Hawkins (1787), II, 4.

14. *Quarterly Review*, XXIII (1820), 402.

15. *Historical Manuscripts Commission Reports*, XIII, Part VIII (1894), 254. Malone's edition of *The Critical and Miscellaneous Prose Works of John Dryden* was published in 1800. A biography of Dryden was included. Malone exceeded Johnson in tactlessness by making no public acknowledgment whatsoever to Newcastle!

16. Malone's manuscript is now in the Folger Shakespeare Library in Washington, D.C.

17. Malone states that the manuscript was also lent to the Dowager Duchess of Portland (Prior, *Life of Malone* [1860], p. 185).

18. There is such a collection, dating from the eighteenth century, in the Huntington Library.

19. Goldsmith seems to have had the peculiar notion that the anecdotes had been written not by Spence but by Pope himself (*Works*, ed. Gibbs [1885], IV, 169).

20. Pope's *Works*, II, 417–18 n.

21. *Quarterly Review*, XXIII (1820), 402.

22. Singer, pp. xii, xv.

23. In the Folger Shakespeare Library is a transcript of the Newcastle manuscript which was owned in 1893 by Richard Garnett. Garnett believed that the transcript had been made for Beloe's use, but this seems unlikely in view of the fact that the Malone-Beloe-Murray edition was based upon Malone's original manuscript.

24. Isaac D'Israeli, who may be presumed to have known the truth, since he was writing for Murray's own periodical, says that the manuscript was sold to Murray by Beloe himself (*Quarterly Review*, XXIII, 402).

25. That Murray had the work in preparation as early as January, 1818, is proved by some jesting verses in a letter which Byron wrote to the publisher on January 8 of that year:

"You can make any loss up
With 'Spence' and his Gossip,
A work which must surely succeed . . ."

(see Byron's *Works*, ed. Ernle, *Letters and Journals* [1922], IV, 192).

26. *Quarterly Review*, XXIII, 402.

27. Spence Papers.

28. Singer, p. xii. The second half of this manuscript is now in the Huntington Library, HM 1271. Apparently Singer never saw it, but how it became separated from the other Spence manuscripts is not known.

29. In his edition of 1820 Singer did not reveal the source of his materials. His edition of 1858, however, contained a brief "Preliminary Notice" on the subject.

30. Peter Cunningham wrote in his copy of Singer's 1820 edition (see p. 220, n. 8) the following penciled note, now partly illegible: "The story of *Spence's Anecdotes* (this edition at least) is as follows. *Lowth* gave the MS.—with some Fulham Bridge Shares [?]—& the sweepings of his study to [name illegible] his servant—This servant gave them to James Wadmore (Picture Collector) who gave them to Carpenter bookseller." But Cunningham also recorded the statement, no doubt transcribed from Singer's "Preliminary Notice" of 1858, that "Lowth . . . gave them to a Mr. Forster his sec^y—from whose nephew they were purchased for pub^n."

31. In *Bell's Weekly Messenger* for January 2, 1820, appeared several extracts from the *Anecdotes* with the explanation that the editor had availed himself of a preview of Singer's volume to give his readers a sample of the forthcoming work.

32. *Quarterly Review*, XXIII (1820), 401. The *Times* for January 20, 21, and 22 carried an advertisement of the Singer edition as being published "this day." It sold for 14*s.*, while the Murray edition sold for 8*s.* 6*d.* The title-page of the Singer edition reads, *Anecdotes, Observations, and Characters, of Books and Men. Collected from the Conversation of Mr. Pope, and Other Eminent Persons of His Time. By the Rev. Joseph Spence. Now First Published from the Original Papers, with Notes, and a Life of the Author. By Samuel Weller Singer.* The title-page of the Murray edition reads, *Observations, Anecdotes, and Characters, of Books and Men: By the Rev. Joseph Spence. Arranged with Notes by the Late Edmund Malone, Esq.*

33. As might be expected, numerous discrepancies between the two editions are found. Some of these stem from inconsistencies in the manuscripts from which the two editors respectively transcribed their materials, but others are attributable to errors on the part of editor or printer.

34. XXIII (1820), 400–434. Isaac D'Israeli received £50 for this article and wrote to Murray: "I think it extremely handsome, and *begin* to fear the article does not deserve it" (Samuel Smiles, *A Publisher and His Friends* [1891], II, 53).

35. Bowles, who believed that Octavius Gilchrist had written the *Quarterly* article, came to his own defense with *A Reply to an "Unsentimental Sort of Critic," the Reviewer of "Spence's Anecdotes" in the Quarterly Review for October 1820,* etc. This shot began a war of pamphlets which involved Bowles, Gilchrist, Byron, and even Hazlitt, and which did not subside until 1826.

36. XXXIII (1820), 302–30. This writer may have been Hazlitt.

37. XCI (1820), 245–57.

38. Additional reviews appeared in the *London Magazine,* I (1820), 191–94; the *London Literary Gazette,* vol. for 1820, pp. 20, 40, and 56 ff.; the *New Monthly Magazine,* XIII (1820), 168–73; and the Boston *Atheneum,* VII, 64–67. The article in the *London Magazine* was written by Gilchrist but does not mention Bowles.

39. Singer's Spence papers were sold for a total of £10 3*s.* 6*d.*! Peter Cunningham, who bought more than any other purchaser, may have acted as agent for the Duke. All the MSS purchased by him were then or later added to the Clumber Library, along with a few obtained by other bidders.

40. These papers, together with a few Spence items acquired at other times by Mr. Osborn, are now known as the "Spence Papers" (see Preface, p. vii).

41. Singer, p. xii.

42. Spence apparently made some excisions in accordance with these resolutions when he had the vellum-bound "fair copy" made.

43. Singer, p. xii.

44. See p. 250, n. 28.

45. Lowndes, *Bibliographer's Manual,* ed. Bohn [1857–64], III, 2475, says that fifty copies were printed in large paper in folio "for the purposes of illustration."

46. Spence's *"Anecdotes, Observations, and Characters of Books and Men." A Selection, Edited, with an Introduction and Notes, by John Underhill.*

47. Mr. James M. Osborn is currently at work upon a definitive edition of the *Anecdotes.* As early as 1859 the need for such an edition was evident. Reviewing the 1858 reprint of Singer's edition (*Athenaeum,* February 19, 1859, pp. 249–50), C. W. Dilke scored the work as un-

happily stopping the way for the "carefully revised, collated, and annotated" edition which should have been published instead.

48. *The Age of Pope* (1894), p. 206.

49. *The Life of Alexander Pope* (2d ed., 1857), p. 126.

50. *Some Verdicts of History Reviewed* (1887), p. 77.

51. Spence Papers.

52. Singer, p. 237.

53. Spence Papers.

54. Singer, p. 237.

55. Singer, p. 255. Spence's source may have been Richard Rawlinson (1690–1755), the Oxford antiquary.

56. See p. 165.

57. Huntington Library HM 1271, fol. 45v.

58. Spence Papers. The slightly polished version prepared by Spence for his "fair copy" is printed by Singer on p. 5.

59. *Preface to the Works of Shakespeare*, in Elwin-Courthope, X, 541–42.

60. Singer, p. 10 (dated 1728–30).

61. Line 274.

62. Singer, p. 11 (dated 1728–30).

63. Part II, ll. 183–94.

64. Singer, p. 14 (dated 1728–30).

65. *The Works of Lord Bolingbroke* (Philadelphia, 1841), III, 316.

66. Singer, pp. 26–27 (dated 1728–30).

67. William King, *Political and Literary Anecdotes of His Own Times* (1818), p. 21.

68. I have already printed much of the material in these pages in my article entitled "The Veracity of Spence's *Anecdotes*," *PMLA*, LXII (1947), 123–29.

CHAPTER IX

"The Amiable Mr. Spence"

1. Journal for 1757, Spence Papers (see Singer, p. 374).

2. *Oxford Magazine or University Museum* (1768), I, 115.

3. [Thomas Tyers], *An Historical Rhapsody on Mr. Pope* (2d ed., 1782), pp. 58–59.

4. *Gentleman's Magazine*, XC, Part I (1820), 29. The passage comes from an account of Spence found in a copy of Dodsley's *Fugitive Pieces* and communicated to the magazine by a Dr. Luke Booker.

5. See p. 34.

6. *Tales of the Genii* (2d ed., 1764), II, 329–30.

7. *Polymetis*, p. iv.

8. Journal for 1757, Spence Papers (see Singer, p. 373).

9. Journal for 1756, Spence Papers (see Singer, p. 371).

10. Thus Shenstone (see earlier, p. 160).

11. *Polymetis*, p. iv.
12. Singer, p. 328.
13. *Polymetis*, p. 108.
14. See p. 34.
15. See p. 65.
16. See p. 73.
17. See pp. 29–30, 153, and 236, n. 100.
18. Prior, *Life of Malone* (1860), p. 430.
19. Warton's *Works of Pope*, I, xxxv.
20. *Eighteenth Century Vignettes*, 1st ser. (1892), p. 33.
21. It should be remembered that Spence's was an age in which Pope could say of the *Essay on Criticism* that "not one gentleman in sixty, even of liberal education, could understand it" (Elwin-Courthope, II, 5).
22. Egerton MS 2234, fol. 172r (letter dated March 30, 1740).

Index

INDEX

⎡ PRINTED ⎤
⎣ IN U·S·A· ⎦